CW01647678

Effective Altruism

ENGAGING PHILOSOPHY

This series is a new forum for collective philosophical engagement with controversial issues in contemporary society.

Disability in Practice
Attitudes, Policies, and Relationships
Edited by Adam Cureton and Thomas E. Hill, Jr.

Taxation
Philosophical Perspectives
Edited by Martin O'Neill and Shepley Orr

Bad Words
Philosophical Perspectives on Slurs
Edited by David Sosa

Academic Freedom
Edited by Jennifer Lackey

Lying
Language, Knowledge, Ethics, and Politics
Edited by Eliot Michaelson and Andreas Stokke

Treatment for Crime
Philosophical Essays on Neurointerventions in Criminal Justice
Edited by David Birks and Thomas Douglas

Games, Sports, and Play
Philosophical Essays
Edited by Thomas Hurka

Effective Altruism
Philosophical Issues
Edited by Hilary Greaves and Theron Pummer

Effective Altruism

Philosophical Issues

Edited by

HILARY GREAVES AND THERON PUMMER

OXFORD
UNIVERSITY PRESS

OXFORD
UNIVERSITY PRESS

Great Clarendon Street, Oxford, OX2 6DP,
United Kingdom

Oxford University Press is a department of the University of Oxford.
It furthers the University's objective of excellence in research, scholarship,
and education by publishing worldwide. Oxford is a registered trade mark of
Oxford University Press in the UK and in certain other countries

© the several contributors 2019

The moral rights of the authors have been asserted

First Edition published in 2019

Impression: 2

All rights reserved. No part of this publication may be reproduced, stored in a retrieval system, or transmitted, in any form or by any means, without the prior permission in writing of Oxford University Press, or as expressly permitted by law, by licence or under terms agreed with the appropriate reprographics rights organization. Enquiries concerning reproduction outside the scope of the above should be sent to the Rights Department, Oxford University Press, at the address above

You must not circulate this work in any other form
and you must impose this same condition on any acquirer

Published in the United States of America by Oxford University Press
198 Madison Avenue, New York, NY 10016, United States of America

British Library Cataloguing in Publication Data
Data available

Library of Congress Control Number: 2019947210

ISBN 978-0-19-884136-4

Printed and bound in Great Britain by
Clays Ltd, Elcograf S.p.A.

Links to third party websites are provided by Oxford in good faith and for information only. Oxford disclaims any responsibility for the materials contained in any third party website referenced in this work.

Foreword

Peter Singer

The emergence of effective altruism caught me by surprise. Thirty years earlier I had argued, in "Famine, Affluence and Morality,"[1] that it is wrong to spend money on things we do not need when elsewhere people cannot get enough to eat, and we could use the money we are spending to help them meet their basic needs. The article was discussed in philosophy journals, reprinted in ethics anthologies, and assigned to thousands of students to read and discuss; but most of the professors assigning it presented it as an intellectual challenge, rather than an ethical one. "Here is an argument that proceeds from plausible premises," they would say, "and seems to use sound reasoning. Yet it concludes that we are all doing something seriously wrong, like failing to rescue a drowning child from a shallow pond. That conclusion can't be right, so where does the mistake lie?" Many professors told me that they enjoyed teaching the article because it always provoked a lively discussion, but very few students did anything to help people in extreme poverty.

I became accustomed to that disappointing response. During the first decade of the new millennium, however, there was a perceptible uptick in concern about global poverty. The Millennium Development Goals contributed to that, as did the example set by Bill and Melinda Gates putting most of their wealth into a foundation focused on eliminating the preventable diseases like malaria and diarrhea that claim the lives of so many people in extreme poverty.

So when Professor Julian Savulescu invited to give the Uehiro Lectures in Practical Ethics at Oxford University in 2007, I decided to revisit the theme of global poverty and what we ought to do about it. As I was preparing the lectures, Julian emailed me about an Oxford graduate student in philosophy named Toby Ord who wanted to meet me. Toby said that my argument for individual action on poverty had struck a chord with him, and he had founded an organization called Giving What We Can. The email quoted him as saying that Giving What We Can "aims to help people give more effectively and share ideas about making donation a central part of their lives." Toby (who explains more of his thinking in his essay in this book) asked if I would be able to take part in a discussion with students while I was in Oxford. I replied that I would be happy to do so. That was the first inkling I had of the movement that was to become effective altruism.

[1] *Philosophy & Public Affairs* 1 (1972), 229–43.

Since 2007 effective altruism has grown in many different ways including the number of people involved, the research done into the most effective ways to give, and the amount of money that has gone to those charities that the research has suggested will do the most good with every dollar they receive. (Will MacAskill gives some relevant figures in his contribution to this book, so I won't repeat them here.) Effective altruism has spread around the world, facilitated by the internet, and generated an immense amount of discussion on web forums and blogs. The scope of the movement has also broadened. It can no longer be assumed that effective altruists focus solely or even primarily on helping people in extreme poverty, because there are rival contenders for how we can do the most good. (Although I continue to think that helping people in extreme poverty compares well with the other contenders.)

With so much online discussion about effective altruism and the issues it raises, it was difficult to get an overall sense of the field, or its key issues. Nor was it easy to separate the contributions that were well argued and worth reading from more casual comments that did not stand up to scrutiny. That is why I welcome this volume. Its carefully selected set of essays will serve for a long time as a high-quality introduction to the philosophical and ethical issues raised by effective altruism.

There is often a danger that getting to know all the different views about a complex question can, by undermining our confidence that we know what we ought to do, lead to a kind of paralysis. I will therefore close this foreword with a reminder: even if there is disagreement among thoughtful effective altruists about what is the *best* thing to do, there is a consensus that several actions open to us—including helping people in extreme poverty and reducing the suffering of animals on factory farms—are far better than doing nothing at all.

Contents

List of Contributors

Amanda Askell, New York University

Christian Barry, Australian National University

Nick Beckstead, Open Philanthropy Project

Mark Budolfson, University of Vermont

Stephanie Collins, Australian Catholic University

Iason Gabriel, University of Oxford

Hilary Greaves, University of Oxford

Holly Lawford-Smith, University of Melbourne

William MacAskill, University of Oxford

Brian McElwee, University of Southampton

Andreas Mogensen, University of Oxford

Toby Ord, University of Oxford

Laurie Paul, Yale University

Theron Pummer, St Andrews University

Ben Sachs, St Andrews University

Emma Saunders-Hastings, Ohio State University

Jeff Sebo, New York University

Peter Singer, Princeton University and University of Melbourne

James Snowden, GiveWell

Dean Spears, University of Texas at Austin

Travis Timmerman, Seton Hall University

Richard Yetter Chappell, University of Miami

Introduction

Hilary Greaves and Theron Pummer

The two key ideas of *effective altruism* are represented in its name. *Altruism*: If we use a significant portion of the resources in our possession—whether money, time, or talents—with a view to helping others, we can improve the world considerably. *Effectiveness*: When we do put such resources to altruistic use, it is crucial to focus on how much good this or that intervention is reasonably expected to do per unit of resource expended (for example, how many lives are saved, in expectation, per $1,000 donated). How wisely one chooses among available interventions tends to matter far more than how large a pot of resources one is willing to assign for altruistic purposes. Even setting aside those interventions that, while well-intentioned, turn out to be useless or even counterproductive—the familiar theme of the "aid scepticism" literature—interventions routinely vary in cost-effectiveness by multiple orders of magnitude.

The effective altruism movement consists of a growing global community of people who organize significant parts of their lives around these two ideas. For some, this takes the shape of donating a proportion of their income—10 per cent is a standard figure, although many donate much more—to carefully chosen charitable organizations. Others choose their career path with an explicit and keen eye towards what will be most beneficial for the world at large. In all cases, the appeal to evidence and reason is crucial to the purpose of an impartial assessment of expected effectiveness.

Assessing expected effectiveness is, of course, no easy matter. Sometimes it requires paying attention to large and complex bodies of evidence, as well as expending time and effort in processing that evidence. In other cases, the issue is more the *paucity* of available evidence, and the potentially daunting task of determining how confident to be about the possible outcomes of interventions in such an evidentially impoverished area. Things are more complicated still, as what matters is the difference an intervention makes—what does it bring about that wouldn't have happened otherwise? For these reasons, effectiveness assessments are often centralized. For example, the non-profit organization GiveWell is entirely devoted to assessing charities that help those in extreme poverty in terms of the additional benefits delivered for each extra dollar donated; Animal Charity Evaluators has a similar mission with respect to charities focusing on animal welfare. Many people who would self-identify as members of the effective altruism movement base charitable donations very closely on the recommendations of such "meta-charities". For graduates and young professionals interested in choosing careers with the objective of maximizing their beneficial impact, the organization 80,000 Hours specializes in providing advice on choosing careers aimed at doing the most good.

A further issue follows naturally from the idea of effectiveness. While global poverty is a widely used case study in introducing and motivating effective altruism, if the aim is to *do the most good one can* per unit resource expended, it is far from obvious that global poverty alleviation is the best cause to intervene on. In addition to ranking possible poverty-alleviation interventions against one another, one can also try to rank interventions aimed at very different types of outcome against one another, again in terms of good done per unit resource expended. Here the comparisons are difficult even in the presence of full descriptive information—one is to some extent comparing apples with oranges—but it does not follow that all bets are off. It is not uncommon for mediocre interventions in one area to do much less good than the best interventions in another area, based on any credible theory of the good. This is very plausibly the case, for example, when comparing donations to support museums with donations to support the best global health interventions.[1] Indeed, it is plausible that even the best interventions in some areas do much less good than the best in others. A core part of effective altruism is thus *cause-neutrality*: choosing causes to intervene on on the basis of which afford the opportunity to do the most good with one's limited resources, rather than on the basis of (say) personal connections or passions.

None of these ideas is entirely new. The idea of keeping self-indulgences relatively low for the sake of spending more on helping others, in particular, has been around for centuries. As early as the fourth century BC, the Chinese philosopher Mozi advocated a concept of universal caring (jiān'ài, 兼爱) according to which one should not prioritize oneself or one's own family over strangers, and criticized indulgence in such things as fine food, music, and dance for consuming resources that would better be spent enhancing the prosperity and stability of society at large.[2] Christian ethics through the ages has consistently emphasized moral obligations to provide only for one's family's basic needs, and to give whatever is left over for the benefit of the poor, sometimes adding that the resources in question rightfully *belong* to the poor in any case, so that not to behave in the recommended way is theft.[3] Utilitarian moral philosophy famously holds that one ought to give resources for the benefit of others whenever doing so would benefit

[1] Singer (2015). [2] Johnston (2010).

[3] See, for example: Basil of Caesarea (372), *Homily on Luke 12:18*; Thomas Aquinas (1274), *Summa Theologica*; and Paul VI (1967), *Encyclical Letter (Populorum Progressio) of His Holiness Paul VI on Fostering the Development of Peoples*. Full references, and a useful overview, can be found in Ord (2014, section 4).

others more than it would harm oneself. More recently—but still nearly half a century ago—Peter Singer has defended a "Principle of Sacrifice", according to which "if it is in our power to prevent something very bad from happening, without thereby sacrificing anything morally significant, we ought, morally, to do it".[4] As Singer rightly emphasizes, in a world of radical economic inequality, this perhaps innocuous-sounding principle in fact requires very significant sacrifice from those at the richer end of the wealth spectrum; it suggests that keeping any degree of luxury in one's life is morally on a par with walking past a child who is drowning in a pond, refusing to incur the minimal cost and inconvenience that would be involved in saving the child's life.

The focus on effectiveness is somewhat newer. In the context of philanthropic donation, in particular, it is quite common to assess acts of donation more or less *exclusively* in terms of amount donated and cause area supported, with little or no thought given to questions of effectiveness. The prevalence of this "effectiveness-free" mode of thinking is arguably quite odd, given that we do not assess *self-interested* expenditures purely in terms of amount expended, without paying any attention to the returns thereby generated. But on the topic of effectiveness as well as that of altruism, there are clear forerunners of the effective altruism movement. Carnegie's Gospel of Wealth urges that those who have had great success in business should devote the last period of their life to carefully disposing of their fortune for the public good, as their success indicates a more general talent for identifying wise investments, which is as crucial in philanthropy as it is in business.[5] Since at least the 1990s, there has been an increasing focus on the use of randomized controlled trials (RCTs) to investigate the effectiveness of interventions that are intended to alleviate global poverty, and increasing uptake of the results of such investigations by governmental and voluntary sector aid agencies.

What, then, is new about effective altruism? Perhaps 'only' its scale, and (relatedly) community organization.[6] But these are significant. In particular, the fact that there now exists such a community is a spur to "outsiders" to reconsider whether they should follow suit, and to "insiders" to engage in careful dialogue about the best form of their activity. Questions that have perhaps long been there are thrown into new and sharper relief, and previously unnoticed questions arise.

That is the state of affairs that gives the impetus for the present volume. We have invited a group of internationally recognized philosophers, economists, and political theorists to contribute in-depth explorations of issues that arise once one takes seriously the twin ideas of altruistic commitment and effectiveness.[7]

[4] Singer (1972). [5] Carnegie (1889).

[6] It is arguably unsurprising that the explosion of scale and organization has come at this point in history, with the growth of the internet and wider availability of relevant evidence concerning opportunities for impact.

[7] For the most part, the essays are not reflections on effective altruism itself as a social movement; accordingly, most do not mention the movement by name, or do so at most in passing.

In the remainder of this introductory chapter, we briefly summarize the topic of each contribution.

The first two chapters introduce some of the basics of effective altruism. The term "effective altruism" has no official definition, meaning that different authors will inevitably understand the term in different ways. Since this harbours the potential for considerable confusion, we invited William MacAskill, one of the leaders of the effective altruism movement, to contribute a chapter aimed at forestalling some of these potential confusions. The result was this book's opening chapter: "The Definition of Effective Altruism". In this chapter, MacAskill first outlines a brief history of the effective altruism movement. He then proposes his preferred definition of "effective altruism", aiming to capture the central activities and concerns of those most deeply involved in the movement. Finally, he replies to various common misconceptions about the movement. These include the views that effective altruism is just utilitarianism, that it is purely about poverty alleviation, that it is purely about donations, and that it in principle ignores possibilities for systemic change.

"The Moral Imperative Toward Cost-Effectiveness in Global Health" by Toby Ord was written at a relatively early stage of the development of the effective altruism movement.[8] This piece focuses on the notion of cost-effectiveness that is central to effective altruists' decisions among courses of action. Using vivid examples from the context of global health, Ord illustrates the point that we have already alluded to above—that cost-effectiveness can vary by several orders of magnitude, even between alternative interventions within the same cause area. Ord argues that, because of this, considerations of cost-effectiveness deserve very high priority in the ethics of deciding among interventions.

The next three chapters concern evidence and decision-making. In "Evidence Neutrality and the Moral Value of Information", Amanda Askell takes up the question of whether there is a case for favouring interventions whose effectiveness has stronger evidential support, when expected effectiveness is equal. Of course, in practice expected effectiveness might well not be equal: as Askell notes, given a sceptical prior, it might be only in the presence of substantial positive evidence that any intervention can have an expected value significantly higher than that of "doing nothing". But is there a case for favouring evidence-backed interventions *over and above* this contribution of evidence to expected value? Via consideration of an analogy to the multi-armed bandit problem, Askell argues that in fact, the reverse is true: when expected value is equal one should prefer to invest in interventions that have *less* evidential support, on the grounds that by doing so one can

[8] This piece was originally commissioned by the Center for Global Development (CGD), and was published as "The Moral Imperative toward Cost-Effectiveness in Global Health", in the following report: A Glassman and K. Chalkidou (eds.), *Priority setting in health: building institutions for smarter public spending*, Washington DC: The Center for Global Development, 2012.

acquire evidence of their effectiveness (or ineffectiveness) that may then be valuable for future investment decisions. The tendency to behave otherwise, she suggests, is due to the widespread but irrational tendency towards ambiguity aversion.

In "Effective Altruism and Transformative Experience", Jeff Sebo and Laurie Paul investigate the phenomenon of experiences that transform the experiencer, either epistemically (having the experience is a necessary condition for knowing what it is like to have that experience), personally (having the experience causes a change in a core personal belief, value, or practice), or both. The possibility of such experiences, Sebo and Paul argue, frequently complicates the practice of rational decision-making. First, in cases in which your own experience is a relevant part of the outcome to be evaluated, in transformative cases one cannot make well-evidenced predictions of the value of the outcome at the time of decision; this creates a challenge for any attempt to base decision-making on a strong body of evidence (rather than e.g. on plausible speculation). Second, in cases in which one foresees that one's preferences would change following the decision, there are issues about whether rational decision-making should be based only on one's *ex ante* preferences, or should also incorporate some element of deference to foreseen future preferences. While these issues arise quite generally, Paul and Sebo suggest that they are especially pressing in the context of effective altruism.

In "Should We Give to More Than One Charity?", James Snowden examines whether and why a donor might have good reason to split their donations among different charities, rather than give to a single charity. Snowden argues that, in simplified decision contexts, donors maximize expected utility by giving to only one charity. He engages with recent work on risk aversion in decision theory (e.g. by Lara Buchak), arguing that there is an important difference between self-regarding and other-regarding choices. When choosing between lotteries that affect the welfare of others, we should reject risk aversion, instead maximizing expected welfare. In more complex and realistic contexts, there may be various reasons to donate to multiple charities, consistent with maximizing expected utility. However, Snowden argues that the most persuasive such reasons apply to large grant-making institutions rather than typical individual donors.

The next two chapters are on cause prioritization. In "A Brief Argument for the Overwhelming Importance of Shaping the Far Future", Nick Beckstead argues that the best available interventions gain most of their expected value via the effects that they have on the long-run future, rather than via their more immediate effects. Because of the vastness of humanity's possible future, this line of argument tends to favour actions that reduce risks of premature extinction, and actions that increase probabilities of other significantly beneficial "trajectory changes" to the course of humanity's long-run future, even where the change in probabilities that we are able to bring about is very small.

In "Effective Altruism, Global Poverty, and Systemic Change", Iason Gabriel and Brian McElwee examine the status of interventions aimed at bringing about large-scale systemic change, within effective altruism's efforts to tackle issues of poverty. Given the standard framework for assessing decisions taken under uncertainty in terms of expected value, they point out, there are in principle several different ways in which an intervention could score highly: by delivering only relatively modest benefits but doing so with high probability ("low value/high confidence"), by delivering very large benefits with low probability ("high value/low confidence"), or something in between ("medium value/medium confidence"). According to Gabriel and McElwee, in the domain of global poverty, (*i*) philanthropic interventions favoured by effective altruists tend to take the form of narrowly focused practical interventions designed to help those living in extreme poverty, which achieve fairly high expected value via the "low value/high confidence" route, but (*ii*) it is quite likely that there are *ex ante* better interventions—interventions, that is, with higher expected value per unit cost—that tackle global poverty via systemic change, achieving high expected value instead via the "medium value/medium confidence" pattern. In other contexts, however, effective altruism definitely does take seriously some very "high value/low confidence" interventions (namely, efforts to mitigate extinction risk), so there does not seem to be any simple bias towards high confidence at work here. The explanation, Gabriel and McElwee suggest, lies in a related and understandable, yet still misguided, preference for political neutrality within the effective altruism movement.

In "Benevolent Giving and the Problem of Paternalism", Emma Saunders-Hastings argues that some attempts to promote welfare through charitable giving can be objectionably paternalistic, and explores what avoiding such paternalism would require. She defends a view according to which our moral reason to avoid paternalistic behaviour is grounded in the importance of social and political relations, which in turn require respect for autonomous agents. This respect is potentially compromised when donors act as if they are entitled to maximally pursue their own conception of the good. Saunders-Hastings argues that we should at least take account of the instrumental importance of these relations, e.g. their importance to welfare. If they have intrinsic importance, then they have to be balanced against the independent importance of promoting welfare.

The next two chapters concern demandingness: the issue of how much sacrifice, relative perhaps to a life that would count as minimally decent by the standard of common-sense morality, true morality requires of us. Rather than telling people that they are *morally required* to give large amounts of money or time to the most cost-effective interventions, the effective altruism movement has usually adopted an approach of *inspiring* others to view engaging in the project as a great *opportunity*; several authors have worried, or anyway assumed, that confronting people with highly demanding moral requirements would be counterproductive, in the sense of causing people to turn away from morality, and thus actually decreasing (for instance) amounts donated. In "Demanding the Demanding", Ben Sachs notes that whether or not such behaviour would be counterproductive is a non-obvious empirical matter. After reviewing the available evidence, Sachs concludes that we should not be at all confident that "demanding the demanding" would be counterproductive. Sachs argues that more empirical studies are needed, but tentatively defends a theory of moral psychology according to which, when people are confronted with a demanding ethical theory (like act consequentialism) they will, if they accept the theory, respond by *coming close* to conforming to it.

A familiar theme in discussions of demandingness is whether there comes a point at which one is no longer morally obliged to do further good (except perhaps in "emergency" cases) even though there continue to be opportunities to do *a lot* more good at *very low* cost to the agent, on the grounds that one has already done enough. In their chapter "On Satisfying Duties to Assist", Christian Barry and Holly Lawford-Smith take up this question. More specifically, they ask: under precisely what conditions is it plausible to say that that "point" has been reached? A crude account might focus only on, say, the amount of good the agent has already done, but a moment's reflection shows that this is indeed too crude. Barry and Lawford-Smith develop and defend a nuanced account according to which considerations of three types are all relevant to whether one has satisfied one's duties to assist: "inputs" (types and quantities of sacrifice made), "characteristics" (the beliefs and intentions that informed the donor's decisions), and "success" (the extent to which the donations in question succeeded in generating value).

In attempting to do the most good, should you, at a given time, perform the act that is part of the best series of acts you can perform over the course of your life, or should you perform the act that would be best, given what you would actually do later? Possibilists say you should do the former, whereas actualists say you should do the latter. In "Effective Altruism's Underspecification Problem", Travis Timmerman explores the debate between possibilism and actualism, and its implications for effective altruism. Each of these two alternatives, he argues, is implausible in its own right as well as at odds with typical effective altruist commitments. Timmerman argues that the best way out of this dilemma is to adopt a hybrid view. Timmerman's preferred version of hybridism is possibilist at the level of criterion of right action, but actualist at the level of decision procedure.

The next two chapters concern group action and coordination. In "The Hidden Zero Problem: Effective Altruism and Barriers to Marginal Impact", Mark Budolfson and Dean Spears analyse the marginal effect of philanthropic donations. The core of their analysis is the observation that marginal good done per dollar donated is a product (in the mathematical sense) of several factors: change in good done per change in activity level of the charity in question, change in activity per change in the charity's budget size, and change in budget size per change in the individual's donation to the charity in question. They then discuss the "hidden zero problem" that some of the terms in the equation (in particular, the last term) might be "hidden zeros" that prevent donations from doing any good—or worse, imply that they do harm—even if the charity is at the top of rankings that are based on one or more of the other factors. One illustration of their worry is that while it might initially seem that one saves a life if (say) one's contribution to the Against Malaria Foundation funds the bed net that prevents a child from contracting a fatal case of malaria, there is a clear sense in which one is not, if that same bed net would otherwise simply have been funded instead by a billionaire who regularly "tops up" that charity to meet all of its fundraising goals.

In "Beyond Individualism", Stephanie Collins examines the idea that individuals can acquire "membership duties" as a result of being members of a group that itself bears duties. In particular, powerful and wealthy states are duty-bearing groups, and their citizens have derivative membership duties (for example, to contribute to putting right wrongs that have been done in the past by the group in question, and to increase the extent to which the group fulfils its duties). In addition, she argues, individuals have duties to signal their willingness to coordinate with others so as to do more good than the sum of what each could do on their own. Putting these two things together, Collins suggests, individuals' duties in (for instance) matters of global poverty might be largely driven by such group-based considerations, leaving little room for the duties that would follow from more individualistic reasoning.

Richard Yetter Chappell's contribution, "Overriding Virtue", examines the moral status of a disposition he calls "abstract benevolence", viz. the disposition to allow abstract considerations of the greater good to override one's natural inclinations towards prioritizing those whose needs are lesser but in some way more emotionally salient. Many people feel that it is callous to act in this manner, and this view seems to comport well with the traditional view of "sympathy" as an important virtue. Chappell argues to the contrary: according to him, we must recognize abstract benevolence as an important virtue for imperfectly virtuous agents living in present times.

Andreas Mogensen's chapter "The Callousness Objection" is on a related theme. It discusses the suggestion that one might be morally obligated to let the child drown in Singer's infamous "Shallow Pond" case, so that one can donate the resources saved to effective organizations, thereby saving more lives. Intuitively, there would be something morally horrendous about doing this. Yet a moral requirement to let the child drown seems to be the conclusion of reasoning very similar to that used by Singer and his allies to argue for demanding duties to donate on the basis of cases like "Shallow Pond"; what should we make of this? Mogensen considers three lines of response. The first two responses involve biting the bullet; Mogensen argues against these. The third line of response attempts to capture *both* the intuition that our obligations to donate to effective life-saving organizations are as strong as our obligations to save the child in "Shallow Pond" *and* the intuition that one should not allow the child to drown even if by doing so one could save a greater number of lives through donations. The key to doing this, Mogensen suggests, lies in a distinction, noted by Parfit, between the "cost-requiring" and the "conflict-of-duty" sense of strength of moral obligation.

References

Carnegie, Andrew. 1889/2017. *The Gospel of Wealth and Other Timely Essays*. Carnegie Corporation.

Johnston, Ian. 2010. *The Mozi: A Complete Translation*. Columbia University Press.

Ord, Toby. 2014. "Global poverty and the demands of morality". In *God, The Good, and Utilitarianism: Perspectives on Peter Singer*, John Perry, ed. Cambridge: Cambridge University Press, pp. 177–91.

Singer, Peter. 1972. "Famine, Affluence, and Morality". *Philosophy & Public Affairs* 1.

Singer, Peter. 2015. *The Most Good You Can Do: How Effective Altruism Is Changing Ideas About Living Ethically*. New Haven, CT: Yale University Press, Chapter 11.

1

The Definition of Effective Altruism

William MacAskill

There are many problems in the world today. Over 750 million people live on less than $1.90 per day (at purchasing power parity).[1] Around 6 million children die each year of easily preventable causes such as malaria, diarrhea, or pneumonia.[2] Climate change is set to wreak environmental havoc and cost the economy trillions of dollars.[3] A third of women worldwide have suffered from sexual or other physical violence in their lives.[4] More than 3,000 nuclear warheads are in high-alert ready-to-launch status around the globe.[5] Bacteria are becoming antibiotic-resistant.[6] Partisanship is increasing, and democracy may be in decline.[7]

Given that the world has so many problems, and that these problems are so severe, surely we have a responsibility to do something about them. But what? There are countless problems that we could be addressing, and many different ways of addressing each of those problems. Moreover, our resources are scarce, so as individuals and even as a globe we can't solve all these problems at once. So we must make decisions about how to allocate the resources we have. But on what basis should we make such decisions?

The effective altruism movement has pioneered one approach. Those in this movement try to figure out, of all the different uses of our resources, which uses will do the most good, impartially considered. This movement is gathering considerable steam. There are now thousands of people around the world who have chosen their careers, at least in part, on the basis of effective altruist ideas: individuals have gone into scientific research, think tanks, party politics, social entrepreneurship, finance (in order to do good through donating), and non-profit work.[8] Every year, over a thousand people in total gather at various Effective Altruism Global conferences, in locations as diverse as San Francisco, London, Hong Kong, and Nairobi.[9] Over 3,500 people have taken Giving What We Can's pledge to give at least 10 per cent of their income for the rest of their lives to

[1] World Bank Group (2016, ch. 2). [2] UNICEF (2017).
[3] Broome (2012); Nordhaus (2015).
[4] United Nations Department of Economic and Social Affairs (2015). [5] Davenport (2018).
[6] World Health Organization (2016). [7] Norris and Inglehart (2018).
[8] For more information on effective altruism as applied to career choice, see www.80000hours.org.
[9] See www.eaglobal.org.

the organizations they believe to be most cost-effective, together pledging over $1.5 billion of lifetime donations.[10] Individuals donate over $90 million per year to GiveWell's top recommended charities,[11] and GoodVentures, a foundation that currently has potential assets of $14 billion, is committed to effective altruist principles and is distributing over $200 million each year in grants, advised by the Open Philanthropy Project.[12]

As a result of this, the effective altruism community has contributed to significant achievements in the areas of global catastrophic risk reduction, farm animal welfare, and global health. In 2016 alone, the effective altruism community was responsible for protecting 6.5 million children from malaria by providing long-lasting insecticide treated bednets, sparing 360 million hens from living in caged confinement, and providing significant impetus and support in the development of technical AI safety as a mainstream area of machine learning research.[13]

This movement has also inspired significant academic discussion. Books on the topic include *The Most Good You Can Do* by Peter Singer and my own *Doing Good Better*;[14] academic articles on effective altruism, both supportive and critical, have appeared in *Philosophy and Public Affairs*, *Utilitas*, *Journal of Applied Philosophy*, *Ethical Theory and Moral Practice*, and other publications.[15] A volume of *Essays in Philosophy* is dedicated to the topic and there is discussion of effective altruism by academics in the *Boston Review*.[16]

However, if we are to have a meaningful academic debate about effective altruism, we need to agree on what we're talking about. This chapter aims to help with that aim, introducing the Centre for Effective Altruism's definition, explaining why the Centre has chosen the definition it has, and providing a precise philosophical interpretation of that definition. I believe that this understanding of effective altruism, which is widely endorsed by those within the effective altruism community, is quite different from the understanding of effective altruism possessed by many in the general public and by many critics of effective altruism. In this essay, I explain why I prefer the definition I give, and then use the opportunity to correct some prevalent misunderstandings of effective altruism.

Before we begin, it's important to note that, in defining 'effective altruism', we are not attempting to describe a fundamental aspect of morality. In empirical research fields, we can distinguish between science and engineering. Science is the attempt to discover general truths about the world we live in. Engineering is

10 'The Giving What We Can Pledge.' Available at https://www.givingwhatwecan.org/pledge
11 'GiveWell's Impact.' Available at https://www.givewell.org/about/impact.
12 'How Can We Accomplish as Much Good as Possible?' Available at https://www.openphilanthropy.org/
13 Bollard (2016); Dewy (2015).
14 Singer (2015a); MacAskill (2015a).
15 For example Berkey (2018); Pummer (2016); Gabriel (2017); MacAskill (2014); McMahan (2016).
16 Singer (2015b).

the use of our scientific understanding to design and build structures or systems that benefit society.

We can make the same distinction within moral philosophy. Typically, moral philosophy is concerned with discovering general truths about the nature of morality—the equivalent of normative science. But there is also scope for the equivalent of engineering within moral philosophy, for example by creating new moral concepts whose use, if taken up broadly by society, would improve the world.

Defining 'effective altruism' is a matter of engineering rather than of describing some fundamental aspect of morality. In this vein, I suggest two principal desiderata for the definition. The first is to match the actual practice of those who are currently described as engaging in effective altruism, and the understanding of effective altruism that the leaders of the community have. The second is to ensure that the concept has as much public value as possible. This means, for example, we want the concept to be broad enough to be endorsable by or useful to many different moral views, but still determinate enough to enable users of the concept to do more to improve the world than they otherwise would have done. This, of course, is a tricky balancing act.

1. Previous definitions of effective altruism

The term 'effective altruism' was coined through the founding of the Centre for Effective Altruism, in a democratic process among seventeen people involved in the organization, on 3 December 2011.[17] However, no official definition of the term was introduced. Over the years, effective altruism has been defined in a number of distinct ways by different people. Here are some examples:

(1) To us, "effective altruism" means trying to do as much good as possible with each dollar and each hour that we have.[18]
(2) Effective altruism is about asking, "How can I make the biggest difference I can?" and using evidence and careful reasoning to try to find an answer.[19]
(3) Effective altruism is based on a very simple idea: we should do the most good we can... Living a minimally acceptable ethical life involves using a substantial part of our spare resources to make the world a better place. Living a fully ethical life involves doing the most good we can.[20]

[17] These people were: Will MacAskill (then 'Crouch'), Toby Ord, Nick Beckstead, Michelle Hutchinson, Holly Morgan, Mark Lee, Tom Ash, Matt Wage, Ben Todd, Tom Rowlands, Niel Bowerman, Robbie Shade, Matt Gibb, Richard Batty, Sally Murray, Rob Gledhill, and Andreas Mogensen.

[18] Karnofsky (2013). [19] MacAskill (2015a, pp. 14–15). [20] Singer (2015b).

(4) Effective altruism is a research field which uses high-quality evidence and careful reasoning to work out how to help others as much as possible. It is also a community of people taking these answers seriously, focusing their efforts on the most promising solutions to the world's most pressing problems.[21]

(5) Effective altruism is a philosophy and social movement that uses evidence and reason to determine the most effective ways to benefit others.[22]

We can see some commonalities among these definitions.[23] All invoke the idea of maximization, and all are about the achievement of some value, whether that's the value of increasing wellbeing, or simply of achieving the good in general. However, there are differences, too. Definitions (1)–(3) talk about 'doing good' whereas definitions (4) and (5) talk about 'helping others' and 'benefitting others'. Unlike the others, definition (3) makes effective altruism a normative claim, rather than a non-normative project, such as an activity or research field or movement. Definitions (2), (4), and (5) invoke the idea of using evidence and careful reasoning, whereas definitions (1) and (3) do not.

The Centre for Effective Altruism's definition takes a stand on each of these issues, defining effective altruism as follows: effective altruism is about using evidence and reason to figure out how to benefit others as much as possible, and taking action on that basis.[24]

I led on the creation of this definition, with input from a wide number of advisors in the effective altruism community, and significant help from Julia Wise and Rob Bensinger. It and a set of guiding values that sit alongside it have been formally endorsed by the large majority of leaders in the effective altruism community.[25] There is no 'official' definition of effective altruism, but the Centre's definition is closer to being one than any other. However, this statement of effective altruism was intended for a general rather than a philosophical audience, so some

[21] 'Introduction to Effective Altruism' (2016).

[22] 'Effective Altruism.' *Wikipedia*.

[23] I'll treat each of these as definitions, although only the fourth had the right grammatical form to be one. All these statements are intended to be read by a general audience, so I don't place much weight on specific word choice like 'is about' or 'is based on'.

[24] This definition is accompanied by a set of guiding principles, that are intended to form a broad code of conduct for those in the effective altruism community. These principles are: commitment to others, scientific mindset, openness, integrity, and collaborative spirit. See 'CEA's Guiding Principles', Centre for Effective Altruism, https://www.centreforeffectivealtruism.org/ceas-guiding-principles/.

[25] This includes the following organizations: Impact Investing, 80,000 Hours, Animal Charity Evaluators, Charity Science, Effective Altruism Foundation, Foundational Research Institute, Future of Life Institute, Raising for Effective Giving, and The Life You Can Save. And it includes the following individuals (though not their respective organisations): Elie Hassenfeld of GiveWell, Holden Karnofsky of the Open Philanthropy Project, Toby Ord of the Future of Humanity Institute, Peter Singer of Princeton University and the University of Melbourne, and Nate Soares of the Machine Intelligence Research Institute.

precision was lost for the sake of accessibility. For that reason, I'd like to provide and then unpack a more precise formulation here. My definition is as follows:

Effective altruism is:

(*i*) the use of evidence and careful reasoning to work out how to maximize the good with a given unit of resources, tentatively understanding 'the good' in impartial welfarist terms, and

(*ii*) the use of the findings from (*i*) to try to improve the world.

(*i*) refers to effective altruism as an intellectual project (or 'research field'); (*ii*) refers to effective altruism as a practical project (or 'social movement').

The definition is:

- *Non-normative.* Effective altruism consists of two projects, rather than a set of normative claims.
- *Maximizing.* The point of these projects is to do as much good as possible with the resources that are dedicated towards it.
- *Science-aligned.* The best means to figuring out how to do the most good is the scientific method, broadly construed to include reliance on careful rigorous argument and theoretical models as well as data.
- *Tentatively impartial and welfarist.* As a tentative hypothesis or a first approximation, doing good is about promoting wellbeing, with everyone's wellbeing counting equally. More precisely: for any two worlds *A* and *B* with all and only the same individuals, of finite number, if there is a one-to-one mapping of individuals from *A* to *B* such that every individual in *A* has the same wellbeing as their counterpart in *B*, then *A* and *B* are equally good.[26]

I'll explain why these choices were made, in turn.

Two of the choices are uncontroversial. First, every proposed definition of effective altruism is maximizing, and this idea is baked into almost every explanation of effective altruist ideas, including the title of Peter Singer's book *The Most Good You Can Do*. However, there is an ambiguity that needs to be clarified. One can try to increase the amount of good one does in two ways: by increasing the amount of resources that one dedicates to doing good; and by trying to increase the effectiveness of the resources that one has dedicated to doing good. On the definition I suggest, effective altruism is about maximizing only in the

[26] Note that, read literally, the use of "benefit others" in CEA's definition would rule out some welfarist views, such as the view on which one can do good by creating good lives but that this does not involve benefiting those who would otherwise not exist. In this case, philosophical precision was sacrificed for readability.

latter sense. On other definitions this has not been clear; I explain the reasons for this choice in the next section.

Second, the idea that effective altruism involves relying on the scientific method, broadly construed, is also clearly a core part of the concept. All the major research organizations within effective altruism involve relying on data or scientific research where it is possible to do so, as well as on theoretical models and on clear and rigorous argument.

Again, however, a clarification is warranted. Sometimes critics interpret effective altruism's endorsement of the scientific method to mean that we rely solely on randomized controlled trials (RCTs). This, if true, would of course be naïve. But we should understand the 'scientific method' much more broadly than that. There are some issues that, for practical reasons, we cannot assess directly on the basis of an RCT, such as what the probability of human extinction is over the next two centuries. There are also a wide variety of ways of gaining empirical evidence other than RCTs, such as regressions, quasi-experiments, surveys, and simple fact-finding. And there are many issues for which experimental evidence in general is not relevant, such as in ethics, epistemology, and decision theory.

The two more controversial aspects of the definition are that it is non-normative, and that it is tentatively impartial and welfarist. I'll discuss these in turn.

2. Effective altruism as a project, rather than a normative claim

The definition of effective altruism I've given presents effective altruism as consisting of two projects: an intellectual project, of trying to figure out how to use resources in whatever way will do the most good with a given unit of resources; and a practical project, of putting the results from the intellectual project into practice and trying to use some of one's resources to improve the world.

There are two ways in which the definition of effective altruism could have made normative claims. First, it could have made claims about how much one is required to sacrifice: for example, it could have stated that everyone is required to use as much of their resources as possible in whatever way will do the most good; or it could have stated some more limited obligation to sacrifice, such as that everyone is required to use at least 10 per cent of their time or money in whatever way will do the most good.

There were three reasons why we didn't include an obligation to sacrifice in the definition. First, it was very unpopular among leaders of the effective altruism community: in a survey of such leaders in 2015, 80 per cent of respondents stated that they thought the definition should not include a sacrifice component and only 12.5 per cent thought it should contain a sacrifice component. Second, within the effective altruism community more broadly, only some members believe that one has an obligation to engage in effective altruism; others believe that engaging in effective altruism is part of a meaningful life for them, but that there is no obligation to do so. A 2017 survey of 1,843 members of the effective altruism community included the question, 'Do you think of Effective Altruism more as an "opportunity" or an "obligation"?' In response, 56.5 per cent chose 'moral duty' or 'obligation', and 37.7 per cent chose 'opportunity' (there was no option in that year to choose 'both').[27] In the previous effective altruism survey, in 2015, 42 per cent of respondents chose 'both' in response to the same question, 34 per cent chose 'opportunity' and 21 per cent chose 'obligation'.[28]

Third, it makes the concept far more ecumenical. Because effective altruism is not a normative claim, it's consistent with any moral view. But the project is still of interest to those with many different moral views: most plausible moral views would allow that there is a *pro tanto* reason to promote the good, and that wellbeing is of some value, and therefore that the question of how one can do the most to promote welfarist value with a given unit of resources needs to be resolved as one part of answering the question of how to live a morally good life. In contrast, any sort of claim about our obligations to maximize the good will be more controversial, particularly if we try to make a general statement covering people of very different income levels and personal situations. The public value of the concept of effective altruism therefore seems greater if it does not include a sacrifice component: it allows a wider range of people to engage in effective altruism, preventing the concept from being off-putting to those who don't believe that there are strong obligations of beneficence, in general or in their particular case. This is backed up by the anecdotal experience of those involved in Giving What We Can: those in the organization initially tried out both 'obligation' and 'opportunity' framings to encourage people to take the 10 per cent pledge, finding that the 'opportunity' framing was much more efficacious. This fact could also explain why Giving What We Can caused such a rise in the number of people taking Peter Singer's views on our obligations of beneficence very seriously, despite these ideas being around for decades prior.

Finally, it focuses attention on the most distinctive aspect of effective altruism: the open question of how we can use resources to improve the world as much as possible. This question is much more neglected and arguably more important than the question of how much and in what form altruism is required of one.[29] For this reason, most people within the effective altruism community are much more concerned with getting on with the project of figuring out *how* we can do

[27] McGeoch and Hurford (2017). Note that the sample was non-random: everyone who wanted to answer the survey was able to, and it was advertised as widely as possible within the community. As a result, all statistics drawn from this survey should be taken as suggestive but not definitive.

[28] Cundy (2015).

[29] For an argument that it is more important, see Chapter 2 of this volume by Toby Ord.

more good rather than asking to what extent, or in what way, we are required to do the most good.

The second way in which we could have made the definition normative is by appeal to conditional obligations. For example, the definition could have included the idea that if one is trying to use resources to do good, one ought to choose whatever action will maximize the good, subject to not violating any side constraints.[30]

I think that the case for being non-normative in this sense is not as strong as the case against including a sacrifice component, but we kept the definition entirely non-normative for much the same reasons that we did not want to include a sacrifice component. First, most EA leaders were against it: in the 2015 survey, 70 per cent of respondents stated that they thought the definition should be non-normative and only 20 per cent thought it should be normative.

Second, again, is ecumenicism. There are reasonable views on which, because it's permissible whether to use one's resources to do good, it's also permissible to aim to do some good, but less good than one could have done. Moreover, even if we think that sometimes conditional obligations of this form hold, there are also difficult questions about the scope of such obligations. We clearly would not want to commit to there being a conditional obligation to maximize the good in cases where doing so would violate someone's rights, but what about in conditions where it would violate the actor's integrity? Or in cases where one has already spent most of one's resources altruistically, but now wants to spend some of one's money on charities that are less effective but dear to one's heart? Any view on this topic will be highly controversial.[31]

We could dilute the normative claim by phrasing it merely in terms of reasons, for example, stating merely that one has some reason to do as much good as possible. But if so, then effective altruism would be a very weak claim, and not a very interesting one. The distinctive aspect of effective altruism is the choice to focus on asking how we can use some of our resources to do as much good as possible, and the conclusions we come to about how to do as much good as possible, not the very thin claim that one has some reason to do as much good as possible.

3. Effective altruism as tentatively impartial and welfarist

The second controversial part of the definition is that it is tentatively impartial and welfarist. It is tricky to delineate which axiological views should be counted as within the remit of effective altruism, and which should be counted as outside

[30] The idea of conditional obligations is explored by Pummer (2016), though the claim he defends is significantly weaker than this.

[31] See, for example, Pummer (2016); Sinclair (2018); McMahan (2018).

of effective altruism. On one end of the spectrum, we could define effective altruism as the attempt to do the most good, according to whatever view of the good the individual in question adheres to. On the other end of the spectrum, we could define effective altruism as the attempt to do the most good on one very particular understanding of the good, such as total hedonistic utilitarianism. Either choice faces severe problems. If we allow any view of the good to count, then white supremacists could count as practicing effective altruism, which is a conclusion that we clearly do not want. If we restrict ourselves to one particular view of the good, then we lose any claim to ecumenicism, and we also misrepresent the effective altruism community itself, which has vibrant disagreement over many areas of axiology.

Alternatively, one could attempt to restrict effective altruism to cover only 'reasonable' views of the good. But then, first, we face the difficulty of explaining what counts as 'reasonable'. And, second, we also misrepresent the practices of the effective altruism community, which is distinctive insofar as it is currently so focused on wellbeing, and insofar as all the analyses from the leading effective altruist research organizations count each individual's interests equally. What's more, I think that it is unlikely in the foreseeable future that the community will have people or projects focusing, for example, on art or biodiversity as ends in themselves. Similarly, it is unlikely that those in the community would focus on rectifying injustice in cases where they believed that there were other available actions which, though they would leave the injustice remaining, would do more good overall.

My preferred solution is tentative impartial welfarism, defined above. This excludes non-welfarist views on which, for example, biodiversity or art has intrinsic value, and excludes partialist views on which, for example, the wellbeing of one's co-nationals count for more than those of foreigners. But it includes utilitarianism, prioritarianism, sufficientarianism, egalitarianism, different views of population ethics, and different views of how to weight the wellbeing of different creatures.

This welfarism is 'tentative', however, insofar as it is taken to be merely a working assumption. The ultimate aim of the effective altruist project is to do as much good as possible; the current focus on wellbeing rests on the idea that, given the current state of the world and our incredible opportunity to benefit others, the best ways of promoting welfarist value are broadly the same as the best ways of promoting the good. If that view changed and those in the effective altruism community were convinced that the best way to do good might well involve promoting non-welfarist goods, then we would revise the definition to simply talk about 'doing good' rather than 'benefiting others'.

I believe that this understanding is supported by the views of EA leaders. In the 2015 survey of EA leaders referred to earlier, 52.5 per cent of respondents were in favour of the definition including welfarism and impartiality, with 25 per cent against. So the inclusion of impartial welfarism has broad support, but not as convincing support as other aspects of the definition.

What's more, this restriction does little to reduce effective altruism's ecumenicism: wellbeing is part of the good on most or all plausible moral views. Effective altruism is not claiming to be a complete account of the moral life. But, for any view that takes us to have reasons to promote the good, and that says wellbeing is part of the good, the project of working out how we can best promote wellbeing will be important and relevant.

Having explained what effective altruism *is*, let's now turn to what effective altruism *is not*, and address some common misconceptions.

4. Misunderstandings of effective altruism

4.1 Misconception #1: Effective altruism is just utilitarianism

Effective altruism is often considered to simply be a rebranding of utilitarianism, or to merely refer to applied utilitarianism. John Gray, for example, refers to 'utilitarian effective altruists', and in his critique does not distinguish between effective altruism and utilitarianism.[32] Giles Fraser claims that the 'big idea' of effective altruism is 'to encourage a broadly utilitarian/rationalist approach to doing good.'[33]

It is true that effective altruism has some similarities with utilitarianism: it is maximizing, it is primarily focused on improving wellbeing, many members of the community make significant sacrifices in order to do more good, and many members of the community self-describe as utilitarians.[34]

But this is very different from effective altruism being the same as utilitarianism. Unlike utilitarianism, effective altruism does not claim that one must always sacrifice one's own interests if one can benefit others to a greater extent.[35] Indeed, on the above definition effective altruism makes *no* claims about what obligations of benevolence one has.

[32] Gray (2015). [33] Fraser (2017); Bakić (2015); Gabriel (2015); Tumber (2015).

[34] In the 2017 effective altruism survey, 52.8 per cent of respondents chose 'utilitarianism' in response to the question 'What moral philosophy, if any, do you lean towards?' In addition, 12.6 per cent chose 'consequentialism (NOT utilitarianism)', 5.2 per cent chose 'virtue ethics', 3.9 per cent chose 'deontology', and 25.5 per cent chose 'no opinion, or not familiar with these terms'. As a caveat, however, it's not clear how well the respondents understood these terms. For example, in conversation I learned that one respondent thought that utilitarianism refers to any moral theory that can be represented by a utility function.

[35] On the demandingness objection to utilitarianism, see 'The Demandingness of Morality: Toward a Reflective Equilibrium' (Berkey 2016).

Unlike utilitarianism, effective altruism does not claim that one ought always to do the good, no matter what the means;[36] indeed, as suggested in the guiding principles, there is a strong community norm against 'ends justify the means' reasoning. This is emphasized, for example, in an 80,000 Hours blog post by Ben Todd and I.[37]

Finally, unlike utilitarianism, effective altruism does not claim that the good equals the sum total of wellbeing. As noted above, it is compatible with egalitarianism, prioritarianism, and, because it does not claim that wellbeing is the only thing of value, with views on which non-welfarist goods are of value.[38]

In general, very many plausible moral views entail that there is a *pro tanto* reason to promote the good, and that improving wellbeing is of moral value.[39] If a moral view endorses those two ideas, then effective altruism is part of the morally good life.

4.2 Misconception #2: Effective altruism is just about fighting poverty

The vast majority of the focus on effective altruism in the media and in critical academic discussion has been on the part of effective altruism that is about fighting poverty. For example, Judith Lichtenberg begins her article with the question, "How much money, time, and effort should you be giving to relieve dire poverty?"[40] Jennifer Rubenstein describes effective altruism as "a social movement focused on alleviating poverty," and Iason Gabriel describes effective altruism as encouraging "individuals to do as much good as possible, typically by contributing money to the best-performing aid and development organisations."[41]

It is, of course, true that fighting poverty is one core focus of those in the effective altruism community. In the 2017 EA survey, 41 per cent of respondents identified extreme poverty as their top priority cause area, and some effective altruist organizations such as GiveWell are exclusively focused on poverty alleviation[42] (just as some other organizations within effective altruism are focused exclusively on animal welfare[43] or existential risks).[44]

But two core parts of effective altruism are *cause-neutrality* and *means-neutrality*: being open in principle to focusing on any problem (such as global health, or climate change, or factory farming) and being open in principle to using any (non-side-constraint violating) means to addressing that problem. In every

[36] On utilitarianism and constraints, see Kagan (1989).
[37] Todd and MacAskill (2017).
[38] See Parfit (1997); Temkin (1993); Hurka (1993).
[39] Kagan (1998); Ross (1930).
[40] Lichtenberg (2015).
[41] Gabriel (2017).
[42] McGeoch and Hurford (2017).
[43] For example, Animal Charity Evaluators (ACE).
[44] For example, the Berkeley Existential Risk Initiative (BERI).

case, the criterion is simply what activity will do the most good. Cause and means neutrality follow straightforwardly from the assumptions of maximization and impartial welfarism. If, by focusing on one cause rather than another, or by choosing one means rather than another, one can do more to promote wellbeing (without violating any side constraints) then someone who is committed to effective altruism will do so.

And, in practice, members of the effective altruism community support many other causes, including animal suffering reduction, criminal justice reform, and existential risk mitigation. In the 2017 EA survey, in addition to the 41 per cent of respondents who identified extreme poverty as their top priority cause area, 19 per cent of respondents chose cause prioritization as the top priority, 16 per cent chose AI, 14 per cent chose environmentalism, 12 per cent chose promoting rationality, 10 per cent chose non-AI existential risk, and 10 per cent chose animal welfare. These results were broadly similar to the 2015 and 2014 surveys: poverty is the most common focus area for individuals in the effective altruism community, but is not the focus for the majority of individuals in the community.

This is mirrored when we look at the distribution of grants by the Open Philanthropy Project. In 2017, they spent:

- $118 million (42 per cent) on global health and development
- $43 million (15 per cent) on potential risks from advanced artificial intelligence
- $36 million (13 per cent) on scientific research (which cuts across other causes)
- $28 million (10 per cent) on biosecurity and pandemic preparedness
- $27 million (10 per cent) on farm animal welfare
- $10 million (4 per cent) on criminal justice reform
- $9 million (3 per cent) on other global catastrophic risks
- $10 million (4 per cent) on other cause areas, including land use reform, macroeconomic policy, immigration policy, promotion of effective altruism, and improving decision-making

The amount of money received by the Effective Altruism Funds—where individual donors can give to a fund managed by an expert for regranting within a particular cause area—tells a similar story. In 2017 it received:

- $982,000 (48 per cent) for the global health and development fund
- $409,000 (20 per cent) for the animal welfare fund
- $363,000 (18 per cent) for the long-term future fund
- $290,000 (14 per cent) for the effective altruism community fund

So, in contrast to the equation of effective altruism with poverty reduction only, a more accurate description would be that the effective altruism community currently focuses on extreme poverty, factory farming, and existential risk, with a small number of other areas of focus.

4.3 Misconception #3: Effective altruism is entirely about donations or earning to give

Most media attention focuses on the part of effective altruism that focuses on effective altruism as applied to donations, and a significant proportion has focused on the idea of 'earning to give'—that people should deliberately pursue a lucrative career in order to be able to donate a large proportion of those earnings to effective charities.[45]

This is also true for the criticism of effective altruism. Iason Gabriel described effective altruism as 'a philosophy and social movement that aims to revolutionise the way we do philanthropy', and focuses his discussion on effective altruism and charity.[46] Similarly, Jennifer Rubenstein's review of *Doing Good Better* and *The Most Good You Can Do* focuses on the charitable side of the effective altruism movement.[47]

There's no doubt that philanthropy is a major focus of the effective altruism community, and 80,000 Hours recognize that they promoted earning to give too heavily in their early marketing materials,[48] and so it's entirely reasonable for an article to focus on that aspect. But it means that a casual observer could think that this is *all* that the effective altruism focuses on, even though it is not the only focus.

The organization 80,000 Hours is entirely focused on helping individuals to use their career as effectively as possible. And they recommend that only about 15 per cent of altruistic graduates who would be happy in a wide variety of career paths should earn to give in the long term.[49] Similarly, in large part because of the success of the EA movement at raising philanthropic money, the primary focus of the Centre for Effective Altruism is to encourage people to move into working in particularly important causes, rather than funding those causes.[50] And in the 2015 EA survey, survey-takers were asked, 'What broad career path are you planning to follow?' Although earning to give was the most common response, receiving 36 per cent of responses, 13 per cent selected 'non-profit' work, 25 per cent selected 'research', and 26 per cent selected 'none of these'. It seems that most members of the effective altruism community, therefore, do not plan to use donations as their main path to impact.

[45] For examples, see Herzog (2016); Rubenstein (2015); Earle and Read (2016); and my own article arguing in favour of this position is 'Replaceability, Career Choice, and Making a Difference' (2014).
[46] Gabriel (2017). [47] Rubenstein (2015). [48] 'Our Mistakes' 80,000 Hours.
[49] MacAskill (2015b). [50] Hesketh-Rowe (2017).

4.4 Misconception #4: Effective altruism ignores systemic change

Of all the criticisms of effective altruism, the most common is that effective altruism ignores systemic change. For example, Brian Leiter comments that: "I am a bit skeptical of undertakings like [effective altruism], for the simple reason that most human misery has systemic causes, which charity never addresses, but which political change can address; ergo, all money and effort should go towards systemic and political reform."[51] This objection is also discussed by Amia Srinivasan,[52] Iason Gabriel,[53] and Jennifer Rubenstein.[54]

But effective altruism is clearly open to systemic change in both principle and practice.[55] We can distinguish a broader and a narrower sense of 'systemic change'. In the broader sense, a systemic change is any change that involves a one-off investment in order to reap a long-lasting benefit. In the narrower sense, 'systemic change' refers to long-lasting *political* change. Either way, the allegation is often that those in the effective altruism community have been biased by a desire for quantification away from difficult-to-assess measures such as political change.[56]

It's clear that effective altruism is open to systemic change in principle: effective altruism is committed to cause-neutrality and means-neutrality, so if improving the world in some systemic way is the course of action that will do the most good (in expectation, without violating any side constraints), then it's the best course of action by effective altruism's lights. More importantly, however, effective altruists often advocate for systemic change in practice, even in the narrower sense. An incomplete list of examples is as follows:[57]

- International labour mobility has been a focus area of members of the effective altruism community for some time. Openborders.info, run by a member of the effective altruism community, collates research on and promotes the option of dramatic increases in migration from poor to rich countries. Open Philanthropy has made grants in this area, including to the Center for Global Development, the US Association for International Migration, and ImmigrationWorks. The reason for this focus is that one of the structural reasons why people in poor countries are poor is that they are unable to move to countries where they could be more productive. In effect, they are being incarcerated in the country into which they were born by the joint migration restrictions of all other countries. For this reason, there are

[51] Leiter (2015). [52] Srinivasan (2015). [53] Gabriel (2017).
[54] Rubenstein (2015). Other instances of this criticism include Herzog (2016); Snow (2015); Earl and Read (2016). [See also Gabriel and McElwee, Chapter 7 of this volume].
[55] For further discussion of this issue, see Berkey (2018). [56] Clough (2015).
[57] For further discussion, see Wiblin (2015).

economic arguments that the benefits to people in poverty from greater freedom of movement across borders would be enormous.[58]

- The Center for Election Science promotes alternative voting systems, in particular approval voting; it's run by a member of the effective altruism community, and received a grant from the Open Philanthropy Project at my recommendation.[59]
- The Centre for Effective Altruism has provided advice for the World Bank, the WHO, the Department for International Development, and Number 10 Downing Street.
- 80,000 Hours' list of recommended careers includes party politics, policy-oriented civil service, and think tanks, and has an employee entirely dedicated to advising people who wish to work in policy and government in the area of technological risk.
- The animal welfare wing of the effective altruism community, including Mercy for Animals and The Humane League, has had astonishing success by lobbying large retailers and fast food chains to get them to pledge to no longer use eggs from caged hens in their supply chain.
- Organizations such as the Future of Humanity Institute and the Centre for the Study of Existential Risk are actively working on policy around developments of new technology, and advising organizations such as the US government, UK government and the UN.
- The Open Philanthropy Project has made numerous grants within the areas of land use reform, criminal justice reform, improving political decision-making, and macroeconomic policy.[60]

Once we consider the broader sense of systemic change, then an even larger proportion of effort from the effective altruism community is focused on systemic change. For example, all work addressing existential risks is in this category, as is the focus on scientific research and on improving science (such as through encouraging preregistration of trials), as is the focus on developing lab-grown meat and plant-based meat substitutes.

Of course, it's perfectly plausible that there are 'systemic' interventions that those in the effective altruism community are neglecting. Perhaps campaigning to create an international law banning the purchase of natural resources from dictatorships is an even more effective activity than any of the current activities of effective altruists.[61] But this is an in-house dispute, rather than a criticism of effective altruism per se. One could argue that it's in the nature of the way of

[58] Caplan and Naik (2015, ch. 8).

[59] See this introduction to voting theory by a board member of the Center for Election Science: Quinn (2018).

[60] Grant Database. Open Philanthropy Project.

[61] See Chapter 7 of this volume, 'Effective Altruism, Global Poverty, and Systemic Change'.

thinking of those in the effective altruism community that this idea is neglected. But there are ready alternative explanations: the chance of such a campaign being successful is astronomically low and, even if it were successful, even in the best case scenarios the legal change would occur decades hence, when the problem of extreme poverty will probably be far smaller and less severe than it is today.[62] Given this, and given the commitments to systemic change listed above, it's hard to see why we should think of this as a criticism of effective altruism per se, rather than simply a disagreement about the best ways of promoting wellbeing.

5. Conclusion

In this chapter, I've unpacked the Centre for Effective Altruism's definition of effective altruism, and explained some of the reasons why we chose that definition. I've then responded to some common misunderstandings of effective altruism. In doing so, I hope that I have helped to add clarity to future debates around effective altruism, allowing us to see which objections, if successful, would show that effective altruism has little or no place in our moral lives, and which are really just in-house debates about how to do the most good.

References

Bakić, Marko. 2015. 'How Is Effective Altruism Related to Utilitarianism?'Quora, December30.Availableathttps://www.quora.com/How-is-effective-altruism-related-to-utilitarianism.

Berkey, Brian. 2016. 'On the Demandingness Objection to Utilitarianism.' *Philosophical Studies* 173 (11): 3015–35.

Berkey, Brian. 2018. 'The Institutional Critique of Effective Altruism.' *Utilitas* 30 (2): 143–71.

Bollard, Lewis. 2016. 'Initial Grants to Support Corporate Cage-Free Reforms.' *Open Philanthropy Project* (blog), 31 March. Available at https://www.openphilanthropy.org/blog/initial-grants-support-corporate-cage-free-reforms.

Broome, John. 2012. *Climate Matters: Ethics in a Warming World*. New York: W.W. Norton.

Caplan, Bryan, and Vipul Naik. 2015. 'A Radical Case for Open Borders.' In *The Economics of Immigration: Market-Based Approaches, Social Science, and Public Policy*, Benjamin Powell, ed. New York: Oxford University Press, ch. 8.

[62] Poverty has decreased dramatically over the past two centuries, and we should expect this trend to continue. See Roser and Ortiz-Ospina (2017).

Clough, Emily. 2015. 'Effective Altruism's Political Blind Spot.' *Boston Review*, 14 July. Available at https://bostonreview.net/world/emily-clough-effective-altruism-ngos.

Cundy, Chris. 2015. 'The 2015 Survey of Effective Altruists: Results and Analysis.' Effective Altruism Forum, 29 July. Available at http://effective-altruism.com/ea/zw/the_2015_survey_of_effective_altruists_results/.

Davenport, Kelsey. 2018. 'Nuclear Weapons: Who Has What at a Glance.' Arms Control Association. Updated June 2018. Available at https://www.armscontrol.org/factsheets/Nuclearweaponswhohaswhat.

Dewey, Daniel. 2015. 'Potential Risks from Advanced Artificial Intelligence.' Open Philanthropy Project. Available at https://www.openphilanthropy.org/focus/global-catastrophic-risks/potential-risks-advanced-artificial-intelligence.

Earle, Sam, and Rupert Read. 2016. 'Why "Effective Altruism" is Ineffective: The Case of Refugees.' *Ecologist*, 5 April. Available at https://theecologist.org/2016/apr/05/why-effective-altruism-ineffective-case-refugees.

'Effective Altruism.' *Wikipedia* (Accessed 25 May 2018). Available at https://en.wikipedia.org/wiki/Effective_altruism.

Fraser, Giles. 2017. 'It's Called Effective Altruism—But is it Really the Best Way to Do Good?' *The Guardian*, 23 November. Available at https://www.theguardian.com/money/belief/2017/nov/23/its-called-effective-altruism-but-is-it-really-the-best-way-to-do-good.

Gabriel, Iason. 2015. 'The Logic of Effective Altruism.' *Boston Review* (forum review), 6 July. Available at https://bostonreview.net/forum/logic-effective-altruism/iason-gabriel-response-effective-altruism.

Gabriel, Iason. 2017. 'Effective Altruism and Its Critics.' *Journal Applied Philosophy* 34 (4): 457–73.

'GiveWell's Impact.' GiveWell (Accessed March 2018). Available at https://www.givewell.org/about/impact.

'The Giving What We Can Pledge.' Giving What We Can. Available at https://www.givingwhatwecan.org/pledge.

Gray, John. 2015. 'How & How Not to Be Good.' *The New York Review of Books*, 21 May. Available at http://www.nybooks.com/articles/2015/05/21/how-and-how-not-to-be-good/.

Herzog, Lisa. 2016. 'Can "Effective Altruism" Really Change the World?' openDemocracy, 22 February. Available at https://www.opendemocracy.net/transformation/lisa-herzog/can-effective-altruism-really-change-world.

Hesketh-Rowe, Larissa. 2017. 'CEA's 2017 Review and 2018 Plans.' Centre for Effective Altruism (blog), 18 December. Available at https://www.centreforeffectivealtruism.org/blog/cea-s-2017-review-and-2018-plans/.

'How Can We Accomplish as Much Good as Possible?' Open Philanthropy Project. Available at https://www.openphilanthropy.org/.

Hurka, Thomas. 1993. *Perfectionism*. New York: Oxford University Press.

Iason, Gabriel. 2017. 'Effective Altruism and Its Critics.' *Journal of Applied Philosophy* 34 (4): 457–73.

'Introduction to Effective Altruism.' 2016. Effective Altruism, 22 June. Available at https://www.effectivealtruism.org/articles/introduction-to-effective-altruism./

Kagan, Shelly. 1989. *The Limits of Morality*. New York: Oxford University Press.

Kagan, Shelly. 1998. *Normative Ethics*. Boulder, Colorado: Westview Press.

Karnofsky, Holden. 2013. 'Effective Altruism.' The GiveWell Blog, 13 August. Available at https://blog.givewell.org/2013/08/13/effective-altruism/.

Leiter, Brian. 2015. 'Effective Altruist Philosophers.' *Leiter Reports*, 22 June. Available at http://leiterreports.typepad.com/blog/2015/06/effective-altruist-philosophers.html.

Lichtenberg, Judith. 2015. 'Peter Singer's Extremely Altruistic Heirs.' *The New Republic*, 30 November. Available at https://newrepublic.com/article/124690/peter-singers-extremely-altruistic-heirs.

MacAskill, William. 2014. 'Replaceability, Career Choice, and Making a Difference.' *Ethical Theory and Moral Practice* 17 (2): 269–83.

MacAskill, William. 2015a. *Doing Good Better: How Effective Altruism Can Help You Make a Difference*. New York: Penguin Random House.

MacAskill, William. 2015b. '80,000 Hours Thinks that Only a Small Proportion of People Should Earn to Give Long Term.' 80,000 Hours, 6 July.

McGeoch, Ellen, and Peter Hurford. 2017. 'EA Survey 2017 Series: Distribution and Analysis Methodology.' Effective Altruism Forum, 29 August. Available at http://effective-altruism.com/ea/1e0/effective_altruism_survey_2017_distribution_and/.

McMahan, Jeff. 2016. 'Philosophical Critiques of Effective Altruism.' *The Philosophers' Magazine* 73: 92–9.

McMahan, Jeff. 2018. 'Doing Good and Doing the Best.' In *The Ethics of Philanthropy: Philosophers' Perspectives on Philanthropy*, Paul Woodruff, ed. New York: Oxford University Press, pp. 78–102.

Nordhaus, William. 2015. *The Climate Casino: Risk, Uncertainty, and Economics for a Warming World*. New Haven: Yale University Press.

Norris, Pippa, and Ronald Inglehart. 2018. *Cultural Backlash: The Rise of Populist Authoritarianism*. New York: Cambridge University Press.

Parfit, Derek. 1997. 'Equality and Priority.' *Ratio* 10: 202–21.

Pummer, Theron. 2016. 'Whether and Where to Give.' *Philosophy & Public Affairs* 44 (1): 77–95.

Quinn, Jameson. 2018. 'A Voting Theory Primer for Rationalists.' LessWrong (blog), 12 April. Available at https://www.lesswrong.com/posts/D6trAzh6DApKPhbv4/a-voting-theory-primer-for-rationalists.

Ross, David. 1930. *The Right and the Good*. Oxford: Oxford University Press, ch. 2.

Roser, Max, and Ortiz-Ospina. 2017. 'Global Extreme Poverty.' Our World in Data, 27 March. Available at https://ourworldindata.org/extreme-poverty.

Rubenstein, Jennifer. 2015. 'The Logic of Effective Altruism.' *Boston Review* (forum review), 1 July. Available at: https://bostonreview.net/forum/logic-effective-altruism/jennifer-rubenstein-response-effective-altruism.

Sinclair, T. 2018. 'Are We Conditionally Obligated to Be Effective Altruists?' *Philosophy and Public Affairs* 46 (1): 36–59.

Singer, Peter. 2015a. *The Most Good You Can Do: How Effective Altruism Is Changing Ideas About Living Ethically*. New Haven, CT: Yale University Press.

Singer, Peter. 2015b. 'The Logic of Effective Altruism' and replies. *Boston Review*, 1 July. Available at https://bostonreview.net/forum/peter-singer-logic-effective-altruism.

Snow, Matthew. 2015. 'Against Charity.' *Jacobin*, 25 August.

Srinivasan, Amia. 2015. 'Stop the Robot Apocalypse.' *London Review of Books* 37 (18): 3–6.

Temkin, Larry. 1993. *Inequality*. New York: Oxford University Press.

Todd, Benjamin, and William MacAskill. 2017. 'Is it Ever Okay to Take a Harmful Job in Order to Do More Good? An In-depth Analysis.' 80,000 Hours. Available at https://80000hours.org/articles/harmful-career/.

Tumber, Catherin. 2015. 'The Logic of Effective Altruism.' *Boston Review*, 1 July. Available at https://bostonreview.net/forum/logic-effective-altruism/catherine-tumber-response-effective-altruism.

UNICEF. 2017. 'Levels & Trends in Child Mortality.' Available at https://www.unicef.org/publications/index_101071.html.

United Nations Department of Economic and Social Affairs. 2015. *The World's Women 2015: Trends and Statistics*. New York: United Nations.

Wiblin, Robert. 2015. 'Effective Altruists Love Systemic Change.' 80,000 Hours, 18 July. Available at https://80000hours.org/2015/07/effective-altruists-love-systemic-change/.

World Bank Group. 2016. *Poverty and Shared Prosperity: Taking on Inequality 2016*. Herndon: World Bank Publications.

World Health Organization. 2016. 'Antibiotic Resistance Key Facts.' Available at http://www.who.int/mediacentre/factsheets/antibiotic-resistance/en/.

2
The Moral Imperative Toward Cost-Effectiveness in Global Health

Toby Ord

Cost-effectiveness is one of the most morally important issues in global health. This claim will be surprising to many, since conversations about the ethics of global health usually focus on more traditional moral issues such as justice, equality, and freedom. While these issues are also important, they are often overshadowed by cost-effectiveness. In this note, I shall explain how this happens and what it means for global health.

1. The cost-effectiveness landscape in global health

The importance of cost-effectiveness is due to the fact that it varies so much between different interventions. Let us start with a simplified example to show how this becomes a moral consideration. Suppose we have a $40,000 budget which we can spend as we wish to fight blindness. One thing we could do is to provide guide dogs to blind people in the United States to help them overcome their disability. This costs about $40,000 due to the training required for the dog and its recipient.[1] Another option is to pay for surgeries to reverse the effects of trachoma in Africa. This costs less than $20 per patient cured.[2] There are many other options, but for simplicity, let us just consider these two.

We could thus use our entire budget to provide a single guide dog, helping one person overcome the challenges of blindness, or we could use it to cure more than 2,000 people of blindness. If we think that people have equal moral value, then the second option is more than 2,000 times better than the first. Put another way, the first option squanders about 99.95% of the value that we could have produced.

This example illustrates the basic point, but it is also unrealistic in a couple of ways. Firstly, it is rare for treatments in the United States to be traded off against

[1] Guide Dogs of America estimate $19,000 for the training of the dog. When the cost of training the recipient to use the dog is included, the cost doubles to $38,000. Other guide dog providers give similar estimates, for example Seeing Eye estimates a total of $50,000 per person/dog partnership, while Guiding Eyes for the Blind estimates a total of $40,000.

[2] Cook et al. (2006, p. 954). Their figure is $7.14 per surgery and with a 77 per cent cure rate.

treatments elsewhere. A health budget is normally more restricted than this, with a constraint that it is only spent on people in a particular rich country, or only spent on people in a designated category of poor countries. Secondly, we often have a spectrum of options. Thirdly, and most importantly, the class of interventions under consideration is often broad enough that it is difficult to make direct 'apples to apples' comparisons between the effects of two interventions.

Health economists and moral philosophers have an answer to the third of these issues. They use measures of health benefits that are powerful enough to be able to compare the values of any two health benefits. The standard measure in global health is the Disability Adjusted Life Year (DALY). This measures the disvalue of health conditions in terms of the number of years of life lost due to the condition plus the number of years lived with disability multiplied by a number representing the severity of the disability. For example, a condition that caused one to die five years prematurely and to live the last ten years with deafness would be valued as $5 + (10 \times 33.3\%) = 8.33$ DALYs.

There are a number of complications and choices regarding the calculation of DALYs, which given rise to a number of subtly different versions of DALYs and the closely related units called QALYs. Chief among these is the question of the size of the weightings representing how bad it is on average to suffer from a particular disability. There are also considerations about discount rates and age weightings.

Different reasonable choices on these parameters could change the number of DALYs due to a condition by a few per cent or by as much as a factor of two. DALYs should thus be considered only as a rough measure of the disvalue of different conditions. It might seem that there would be little use for so rough a measure. This would be true if the difference in cost-effectiveness between interventions were also about a factor of two, but since it is often a factor of a hundred or more, a rough measure is perfectly adequate for making the key comparisons.

Let us now address all of the three concerns, by looking at a real-world example of funding the prevention or treatment of HIV and AIDS. Let us consider four intervention types: surgical treatment for Kaposi's sarcoma (an AIDS defining illness), antiretroviral therapy to fight the virus in infected people, prevention of transmission of HIV from mother to child during pregnancy, condom distribution to prevent transmission more generally, and education for high-risk groups such as sex workers. It is initially very unclear which of these interventions would be best to fund, and one might assume that they are roughly equal in importance. However, the most comprehensive compendium on cost-effectiveness in global health, *Disease Control Priorities in Developing Countries 2nd edition* (hereafter DCP2), lists their estimated cost-effectiveness as follows:[3]

[3] Jamison et al. (2006).

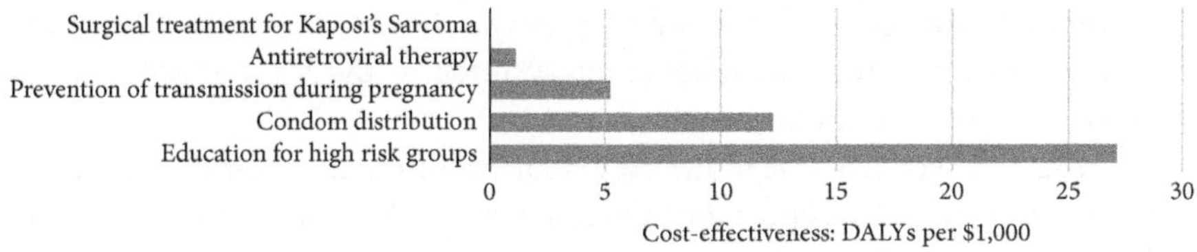

Note the wide discrepancies between the effectiveness of each intervention type. Treatment for Kaposi's sarcoma cannot be seen on the chart at this scale, but that says more about the other interventions being good than about this treatment being bad: treating Kaposi's sarcoma is considered cost-effective in a rich country setting. Antiretroviral therapy is estimated to be fifty times as effective as treatment of Kaposi's sarcoma; prevention of transmission during pregnancy is five times as effective as this; condom distribution is about twice as effective as that; and education for high-risk groups is about twice as effective again. In total, the best of these interventions is estimated to be 1,400 times as cost-effective as the least good, or more than 1,400 times better than it would need to be in order to be funded in rich countries.

This discrepancy becomes even larger if we make comparisons between interventions targeted at different types of illness. DCP2 includes cost-effectiveness estimates for 108 health interventions, which are presented in the chart below, arranged from least effective to most effective.[4]

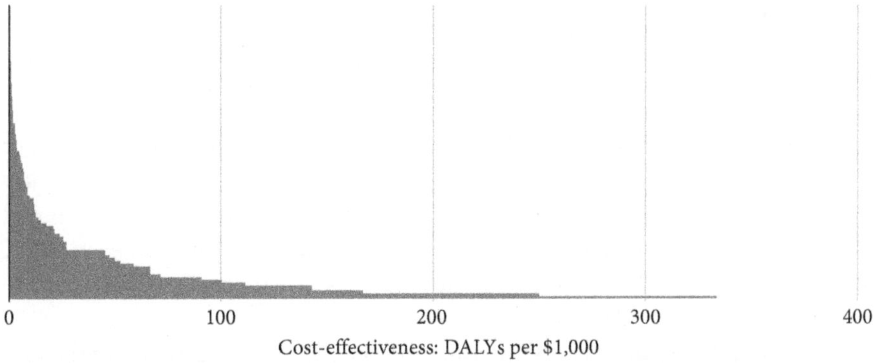

This larger sample of interventions is even more disparate in terms of cost-effectiveness. The least effective intervention analysed is still the treatment for Kaposi's sarcoma, but there are also interventions up to ten times more cost-effective than education for high-risk groups. In total, the interventions are spread over more than four orders of magnitude, ranging from 0.02 to 300 DALYs per $1,000, with a median of five. Thus, moving money from the least effective

[4] Jamison et al. (2006).

intervention to the most effective would produce about 15,000 times the benefit, and even moving it from the median intervention to the most effective would produce about sixty times the benefit.

It can also be seen that due to the skewed distribution, the most effective interventions produce a disproportionate amount of the benefits. According to the DCP2 data, if we funded all of these interventions equally, 80 per cent of the benefits would be produced by the top 20 per cent of the interventions.

It must be noted that these are merely *estimates* of cost-effectiveness and there may be less variance between the real, underlying cost-effectiveness values. However, even if the most effective interventions are a tenth as effective as these figures suggest and the least effective are ten times better than they appear, there would still be a factor of 150 between them.

Moreover, there have been health interventions that are even more effective than any of those studied in the DCP2. For example, consider the progress that has been made on saving lives lost to immunization-preventable illness, diarrhea, malaria, and smallpox, summarized in the following chart:[5]

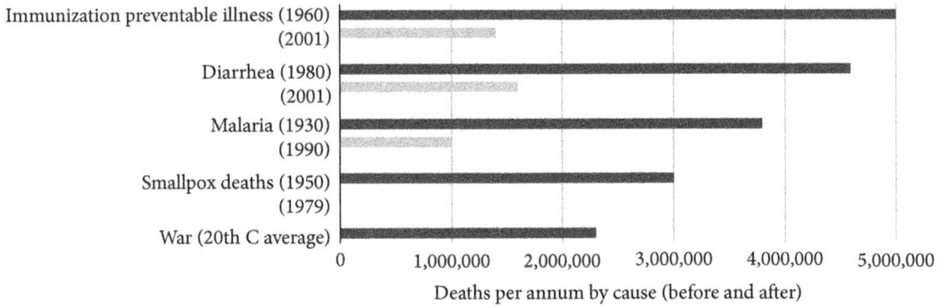

In all cases, our interventions have led to at least 2.5 million fewer deaths per year. To aid the reader in comprehending the scale of these achievements, I have added a final bar showing the average number of deaths per year due to war and genocide together over the twentieth century (2.3 million). Thus, in each of the four of these disease areas, our health interventions save more lives than would be saved by a lasting world peace.

Moreover, these gains have been achieved very cheaply. For instance in the case of smallpox, the total cost of eradication was about $1.5 billion in today's terms.[6] Since around 100 million lives have been saved so far, this has come to about $15 per life saved—significantly superior to all interventions in the DCP2. Moreover, the eradication also saved significant amounts of money. Approximately $0.5 billion

[5] The health estimates are from Jha et al. (2004, p. 1204). Estimates for the death toll from all acts of war and genocide in the twentieth century vary from about 160 million to 240 million, and differ in exactly which deaths they include. This estimate is from Leitenberg (2006, p. 1).

[6] Fenner et al. (1988, p. 1366). This and all other dollar figures in this paragraph have been adjusted to 2013 dollars.

was being spent across developing countries per year in routine vaccination and treatment for smallpox, and more than $7 billion was lost per year in reduced productivity.[7] Even just in the United States, smallpox vaccination and vigilance cost $1 billion per year before eradication.[8] The eradication programme thus saved more lives per year than are lost due to war, while *saving* money for both donors and recipients, paying back its entire costs every few months. It serves as an excellent proof of just how cost-effective global health can be.

2. The moral case

In these examples, we have seen how incredibly variable cost-effectiveness can be within global health. The least effective intervention in the HIV/AIDS case produces less than 0.1 per cent of the value of the most effective, and if we are willing to look at different kinds of disease, this fraction drops to less than 0.01 per cent. Ignoring cost-effectiveness thus does not mean losing 10 per cent or 20 per cent of the potential value that a health budget could have achieved, but can easily mean losing 99 per cent or more. Even choosing the median intervention can involve losing 85 per cent of the potential value.

In practical terms, this can mean hundreds, thousands, or millions of additional deaths due to failure to prioritize. In non-life-saving contexts it means thousands or millions of people with untreated disabling conditions.

Even when other ethical issues in global health are very important in absolute terms, they are typically much smaller than this. For instance, it may be worse on equity grounds to treat a million people in a relatively affluent city than to treat the same number of people spread between the city and the relatively much poorer rural areas. However, it is not *vastly* worse—not so bad that 99 per cent of the value is lost.

Learning how to correctly factor these other ethical issues into our decision-making is an important and challenging problem, but we are currently failing at a much more basic, more obvious, and more important problem: choosing to help more people instead of fewer people, to produce a larger health benefit instead of a smaller one.

3. Challenges addressed

Some people don't see cost-effectiveness as an ethical issue at all, since it is so cut and dried that it seems like a mere implementation issue. This is misguided.

[7] Fenner et al. (1988, p. 1364). [8] Fenner et al. (1988, p. 1365).

People who decide how to spend health budgets hold the lives or livelihoods of many other people in their hands. They are literally making life-or-death decisions. Most decisions of this sort take dramatically insufficient account of cost-effectiveness. As a result, thousands or millions of people die who otherwise would have lived. The few are saved at the expense of the many. It is typically done out of ignorance about the significance of the cost-effectiveness landscape rather than out of prejudice, but the effects are equally serious.

Some object that consequences are not the only thing that matters. For example, some people think that acting virtuously or avoiding violating rights matters too. However, all plausible ethical theories hold that consequences are an important input into moral decision-making, particularly when considering life or death situations, or those affecting thousands of people. Indeed these are precisely the types of cases in which people think that it may even become permissible to violate rights. However, in the cases under consideration, there is not even a conflict between producing a much greater good and acting virtuously or avoiding violating people's rights. The consequences are thus of great moral importance, with no serious moral factors counting in the opposite direction. Proponents of all ethical theories should therefore agree about the moral importance of funding the most cost-effective interventions.

People might also be concerned about the particular choices involved in estimating the benefits of different health interventions. For example, they may disagree about particular disability weights, or about the method for eliciting these weights, or about discounting health benefits, or weighting benefits depending on the age of the recipients, or whether other issues such as equality need to be factored in. However, none of this is in serious disagreement with the thrust of this note. Indeed I personally have many of the same concerns, but as mentioned earlier the practical choices we face often involve factors of ten or more between different interventions, so none of the modifications mentioned here will change the rankings very much. People who are concerned about the details of measuring cost-effectiveness should join with the cost-effectiveness community in improving these measures, rather than throwing out the baby with the bathwater, and leading to thousands of unnecessary deaths.

Another reason people might be initially suspicious of prioritization based on cost-effectiveness is through confusing it with *cost-benefit analysis* (CBA). The latter is an economic method for prioritization which involves determining the benefits for each person in terms of how many dollars they would be willing to pay, adding these up, and then dividing by the total costs in order to produce a benefit–cost ratio in units of dollars per dollar. This method is ethically suspect as it considers benefits to wealthy people (or groups) to be worth more than comparable benefits to poorer people (or groups) since the wealthy are willing to pay more for a given benefit.

However, the cost-effectiveness I have discussed in this note is very different, and is a type of analysis known as *cost-effectiveness analysis* (CEA). This doesn't convert benefits into dollars, but just provides a raw measure of the benefits in units such as DALYs per dollar, or lives saved per dollar. Thus the wealth of the recipients is not an input to the analysis and it doesn't discriminate towards interventions that favour the wealthy.

People might remain suspicious of cost-effectiveness since it makes a connection between dollars and health (or even life itself). Making trade-offs between so-called sacred values such as life with non-sacred values such as money strikes many people as morally problematic. However, no such trade-off is made in cost-effectiveness analysis. Instead there is a budget constraint of some fixed number of dollars. The cost-effectiveness ratios help one to see how much benefit could be causally produced if this money were spent on different interventions—for example, saving one thousand lives or saving ten thousand lives. The only comparison that is made is between these benefits. Whether or not it is worth spending the budget to save ten thousand lives is not part of the analysis.

4. Conclusions

In many cases, ignoring cost-effectiveness in global health means losing almost all the value that we could create. Thus there is a moral imperative to fund the most cost-effective interventions. This doesn't simply mean implementing the current interventions in the most cost-effective way possible, for the improvements that can be gained within a single intervention are quite small in comparison. It also doesn't just mean doing retrospective measures of the cost-effectiveness of the interventions you fund as part of programme evaluation. Instead, it means actively searching the landscape of interventions that you are allowed to fund and diverting the bulk of the funds to the very best interventions. Ideally it also means expanding the domain of interventions under consideration to include all those which have been analysed.

The main effect of understanding the moral imperative towards cost-effectiveness is spending our budgets so as to produce greater health benefits, saving many more lives and preventing or treating more disabling conditions. However, it also shows a very interesting fact about global health funding. If we can save one thousand lives with one intervention and ten thousand with another at an equal price, then merely moving our funding from the first to the second saves nine thousand lives. Thus merely moving funding from one intervention to a more cost-effective one can produce almost as much benefit as adding an equal amount of additional funding. This is unintuitive since it isn't the case when one option is merely 10 per cent or 30 per cent better than another. However, when one option is ten times or one hundred times better, as is often the case in global health, redirecting funding is so important that it is almost as good as adding new funding directly towards the superior intervention. In times of global austerity and shrinking budgets, it is good to know how much more can be done within existing ones.

References

Cook, Joseph et al. 2006. 'Loss of vision and hearing'. In Jamison et al., eds.

Fenner, Frank et al. 1988. *Smallpox and its eradication*. Geneva: World Health Organization.

Jamison, Dean et al. (eds.) 2006. *Disease control priorities in developing countries*, 2nd edn. Oxford and New York: Oxford University Press.

Jha, Prabhat et al. 2004. 'Health and economic benefits of an accelerated program of research to combat global infectious diseases', *Canadian Medical Association Journal* 171: 1203–8.

Leitenberg, Milton. 2006. 'Deaths in wars and conflicts in the 20th Century (3rd ed.)', Occasional Paper #29, Cornel University Peace Studies Program. Ithaca: Cornel University.

3

Evidence Neutrality and the Moral Value of Information

Amanda Askell

1. Introduction

Suppose we have decided to dedicate some proportion of our time and money to doing good in the world[1] and that we want to do the most good that we can with these resources.[2] We can choose to invest in a charity that has multiple randomized control trials indicating that it is among the most effective charities on our preferred measure of effectiveness. Alternatively, we can invest in a charity that may turn out to be very effective but is entirely new and untested. Many of us would be inclined to donate to the well-tested charity in these circumstances. It seems natural to think that we ought to invest our resources in a charity or intervention we have more evidence is effective over one that has little evidential support.

In this chapter, I will argue that if we want to do the most good with our resources then we should not favor interventions that have more evidential support over interventions that have less evidential support. In fact, I argue that we have reasons for investing in interventions with less evidential support over those with greater evidential support if the two interventions are comparable in terms of expected value.

In the Section 2, I will offer examples of interventions that have different levels of evidential support and introduce some key concepts. In the Section 3, I formulate the 'evidence favoring' view, which says that we should invest in interventions that we have more evidence about rather than those with less evidential support. I contrast this with the 'evidence neutral' view, which says that we should invest in whatever interventions produce the most expected value, regardless of how much evidence we have to support those estimates. I argue that, despite its intuitive appeal, we must reject the evidence-favoring view if we want to do the most good

[1] There has been a great deal of debate about what proportion of our time and money we are obligated to dedicate to altruistic causes. Singer (1972, pp. 231–5) and Unger (1996, ch. 6) argue that we are obligated to give all of our disposable income to those in need, while others (Noggle (2009); Timmerman (2015)) believe that our obligations to give are much weaker than this. I won't take a stand on this issue here: I merely assume that we have decided to dedicate.

[2] As Pummer (2016) argues, it may be the case that even if we are not obligated to donate to charity, if we choose to donate then we ought to donate to the most effective charities.

with our resources. In Section 4, I argue that research and evidence still play an important role in our ethical decision-making on the evidence neutral view. I argue that if two interventions are comparable in terms of expected value then we should prefer to invest in interventions with less evidential support because, in doing so, we can acquire valuable information about the effectiveness of that intervention.

2. Evidential weight and estimate resilience

If we are committed to doing the most good with our resources, we must estimate how much good will result from investing those resources in each of the interventions available to us.[3] The standard method for making such decisions under empirical uncertainty is to rank each investment opportunity based on the expected value of that investment: the value of the outcome of that intervention in each possible state of the world multiplied by our credence that the state in question is the true state of the world, given our evidence.[4] We can then invest in the intervention with the greatest expected value.[5] Ranking investments by their expected value does not require strong assumptions about how we should assign value to outcomes: it is consistent with utilitarian, egalitarian, prioritarian, or justice-based conceptions of the value of outcomes. In this chapter I will not commit to any particular view about how to assign value to outcomes, but I will generally assume a simple "maximizing lives saved" measure of value when discussing examples.[6]

Sometimes when we have to decide which of two interventions to invest in, we have very different amounts of evidence about how valuable each intervention is. For example, suppose that we are deciding whether to invest our resources into distributing long-lasting insecticidal nets (LLINs) or invest in research into an experimental genetic intervention (EGI) that might reduce or eradicate *Anopheles* mosquitoes, the main vector of malaria. The distribution of LLINs has been rigorously tested in multiple randomized control trials that have been subject to systematic review. It is estimated that for every $3,000 invested into distributing

[3] Here I will use the term "intervention" rather than "charity", to cover a broader set of possible targets of our resources. We might choose to spend our time in an ethical career, or we might choose to donate to political campaigns. These can be classed as interventions even though they are not charities.

[4] Credences are subjective probabilities in the [0,1] interval that obey the Kolmogorov axioms. Here I will generally use Savage's (1954) decision-making framework, though little rests on this choice.

[5] While we may also be normatively uncertain, as explored in MacAskill (2014), I will assume that we are not. Note that normative uncertainty may increase the value of information, discussed in the third section.

[6] I do assume that the value of outcomes can be measured on an interval scale. I also assume that we are risk-neutral, though we may be able to formulate a similar argument for risk-averse agents by replacing expected utility with risk-weighted expected utility as formulated in Buchak (2013, ch. 2).

LLINs, one life will be saved.[7] Our hypothetical EGI has not yet been tested in genetics labs, let alone in randomized control trials, but seems to have a plausible mechanism for action.[8] The EGI may be completely ineffective, but there is some chance that it will be even more effective than distributing LLINs.

The nature and amount of evidence we have supporting the cost-effectiveness estimate of these interventions is very different. In the case of LLINs, we have a great deal of high-quality evidence about how much value it produces across possible states. This includes our evidence about how malaria is spread, the plausible mechanism of action of LLINs based on this, and a large body of evidence about the effectiveness of LLIN distribution from randomized control trials. In the case of the experimental genetic intervention, we can estimate its effectiveness in possible states based on the existing evidence we have about how malaria is spread and the existing evidence we have from genetics that supports the hypothesis that this particular intervention would reduce or eradicate *Anopheles* mosquitoes. We may even have a promising result from an initial laboratory experiment. But we have no idea if the intervention will actually be effective in further laboratory experiments or once it is implemented in the real world.

It is helpful to distinguish between the *balance* and *weight* of our evidence for a given proposition: distinctions that are explored in detail by Joyce.[9] The balance of the evidence refers to how decisively the evidence supports the proposition. The weight of the evidence is the total amount of relevant evidence that we have. For example, suppose that a study is performed in which a large group of children is given a deworming medication and a large control group is given neither. The study indicates that the children in the first group miss twenty fewer days of school each year. Consider the proposition 'deworming increases school attendance'. This study shifts the balance of our total evidence so that it more decisively supports this proposition.[10] Since the study was not previously part of our evidence it also increases the total weight of the evidence we have for the proposition.[11]

As Joyce notes, the credence that we assign to a proposition reflects only the balance of our total evidence and not the weight of that evidence.[12] To take a variant of an example given by Popper,[13] we may have a credence of 0.5 that a given coin

[7] For more accurate estimates of the value of LLIN distribution, see GiveWell's analysis of the Against Malaria Foundation (including RCT data) in their cost-effectiveness model. Available at https://www.givewell.org/how-we-work/our-criteria/cost-effectiveness/cost-effectiveness-models.

[8] Although this is a hypothetical case, interventions to confer sterility in female *Anopheles gambiae* mosquitoes have already been successfully tested by Hammond et al. (2016). See Pugh (2016) for a discussion of the ethics of mosquito eradication.

[9] Joyce (2005).

[10] Of course, our total evidence still may not warrant a high credence in the proposition.

[11] A further concept is the *specificity* of our evidence. The specificity of the evidence is how much it favors only the proposition in question rather than this proposition plus alternatives. For example, the example study given here is more specific evidence for the proposition "deworming increases school attendance" than one in which the children receive the deworming medication and a multivitamin.

[12] Joyce (2005, p. 154).

[13] Popper (2005 [1959], pp. 436–46).

will land heads because our total evidence indicates that it is a fair coin or because we lack any evidence about whether the coin is biased and in what direction and thus appeal to the principle of insufficient reason.[14] The balance of our evidence is the same in both cases, but the weight of our evidence about the proposition 'the coin will land heads' is greater in the first scenario than it is in the second scenario. Similarly, the balance of the evidence may result in a comparable expected value estimate for both LLIN distribution and the EGI, even though the weight of our evidence for the estimate of the value of LLIN distribution is greater than the weight of our evidence for the estimate of the value of the EGI.

There is no accepted measure of evidential weight and the weight of our total evidence is not reflected in the particular credence we assign to it. This does not mean that there is no way to track evidential weight, however, since the weight of our total evidence is typically reflected in how *resilient* our credence about the proposition is as well as how *concentrated* our credences are across propositions. The resilience of our credence is a distinct property from the credence itself: it reflects the degree of stability we expect our credence to have in light of new evidence.[15] We might have a fairly high credence that it will rain tomorrow but believe that our credence could easily change in response to new evidence from the weather report, or we might have a credence of 1/6 that a fair die will land on five but be confident that our credence will not change much in response to new evidence prior to rolling it.[16]

The more evidence we already have in favor of (or against) a particular proposition, the less likely we are to update away from our current credence in that proposition based on some new datum. If the effectiveness of LLINs has already been established in multiple studies, then one new study is unlikely to radically change our credences about its effectiveness very much. But a single new study into the effectiveness of the EGI—for example, one showing that the EGI resulted in total eradication of malaria in a given test region—would have a more radical impact on our estimate of the effectiveness of this intervention. Let us say that an agent's estimate of the effectiveness of intervention X is resilient with respect to datum E to the extent that her estimate of the effectiveness of intervention X given E remains close to her unconditional estimate of the effectiveness of X.

In general, the more evidence we have about the effectiveness of an intervention, the more resilient our estimate of its effectiveness will be relative to a wide range of data.[17] Moreover, the greater the weight of our total evidence, the more

[14] See Jeffrey's (1965, p. 184) response to Popper, also discussed in Joyce (2010, p. 283–5).

[15] See Skyrms (1977, p. 705).

[16] See Joyce (2005, p. 161).

[17] This is not always the case, however. Consider some datum E indicating that bed nets tear at a higher rate than we previously thought. Our estimate of the effectiveness of the EGI is more resilient with respect to this datum than our estimate of the effectiveness of LLINs is, simply because E is relevant to the effectiveness of LLINs but is not relevant to the effectiveness of the EGI. As Behrens et al. (2007, p. 1,215) note, consistently receiving surprising evidence will increase uncertainty. This means that our credences may not be very resilient in such cases, even if we have a lot of evidence.

that our credences tend to be concentrated on a smaller set of hypotheses.[18] Therefore, the more evidence that we have that the cost-effectiveness of LLINs is in the region of $3,000 per life saved, the more our credences will be concentrated around estimates that are close to $3,000 per life saved. Since the weight of evidence regarding the EGI is low, our credences are likely to spread out across a much wider array of hypotheses about its cost-effectiveness: for example, we will probably have a higher (albeit low) credence that the cost-effectiveness of the EGI is in the region of $20 per life saved than we do for the hypothesis that the cost-effectiveness of LLINs is $20 per life saved.

To summarize: our credence that the cost-effectiveness of LLINs is $3,000 per life saved reflects the balance of our total evidence in favor of that hypothesis. This does not necessarily reflect the weight of our evidence that the cost-effectiveness of LLINs is $3,000 per life saved, which is instead reflected in how stable that estimate is in response to new evidence and how concentrated our credences are around a smaller set of estimates. Expected value calculations, the standard method for deciding between options under empirical uncertainty, use our credences about the value of investing in each intervention but do not take into account the weight of the evidence supporting those credences. In the next section, I will consider whether evidential weight should be a factor when deciding between interventions.

3. Evidence favoring and evidence neutral views

One very intuitive view is that it is better to invest in interventions that have more evidential support over those that have less evidential support. For example, Holden Karnofsky, co-founder of the charity evaluator GiveWell, states that GiveWell "generally prefer[s] to give where we have strong evidence that donations can do a lot of good rather than where we have weak evidence that donations can do far more good." In defense of this view, Karnofsky offers a thought experiment in which we must choose between a restaurant that has 200 reviews and an average of 4.75 stars and a different restaurant that has three reviews and an average of five stars. He argues that it would be better for us to go to the first restaurant rather than the second even if reviews are taken as a proxy for the expected value of the experience. He argues that, by analogous reasoning, it would be better for us to invest in interventions that we have strong evidence can do a lot of good rather than in intervention that we have weak evidence can do even more good.

Before addressing this argument, it is worth distinguishing between two quite different things one might mean by the claim that it is better to invest in

[18] Joyce (2005, p. 166).

interventions that have more evidential support over those that have less evidential support. First, we could mean that the interventions that are best in expectation will generally be those with more evidential support. We should invest in interventions for which we have more evidential support not because having more evidence that an intervention is effective adds value, but because the most effective interventions in expectation will be those that we have more evidence are effective. This will be the case if our prior about the effectiveness of interventions—our credence before receiving new evidence—is generally skeptical. If we have a skeptical prior in effectiveness, we will think that even if an intervention has a plausible mechanism for producing value, it is unlikely to produce value at a rate that is significantly above that of the mean intervention. In his book *Doing Good Better*, William MacAskill offers this kind of instrumental justification of favoring charities with greater evidential support:

> Often we should prefer a charity that has very good evidence of being fairly cost-effective to a charity that has only weak evidence of being very cost-effective; if the evidence behind an estimate is weak, it's likely that the estimate is optimistic, and the true cost-effectiveness is much lower.[19]

If people tend to give overly optimistic estimates of the effectiveness of interventions then we will have a strong prior that a randomly sampled intervention out of the set of 'plausibly effective interventions' will not be very effective.[20] To apply this to the restaurant thought experiment given above: suppose that our prior is that most restaurants are of three-star quality. If this is the case, then three five-star reviews might be enough to nudge us toward thinking that a restaurant is of 3.1 or 3.2-star quality in expectation. But 200 reviews with an average of 4.75 stars may be enough to make us confident that a restaurant is close to 4.75-star quality in expectation. Therefore, a skeptical prior about restaurant quality will cause us to prefer a restaurant with many reviews and a lower average over a restaurant with fewer reviews and a higher average. Similarly, a skeptical prior about interventions will cause us to have a lower estimate of the effectiveness of an intervention that lacks evidential support.

This is all consistent with the view that having more evidence that an intervention is effective does not provide any additional value. A stronger thing that we could mean when we say that it is better to invest in interventions that have more evidential support is that we have reasons to prefer investing in interventions with more evidential support even in cases where there is no such instrumental justification: i.e., even if the expected values of the interventions are comparable given

[19] MacAskill (2015, p. 113).

[20] Wiblin (2017) presents evidence that people do tend to give overly optimistic epistemic estimates of effectiveness.

our total evidence. I will call the view that we should favor interventions with more evidential support intrinsically rather than merely instrumentally the 'evidence favoring' view. We can formulate the central commitment of this view as follows:

The Evidence Favoring View: The total value of an investment is a function of the standard expected value of that investment and the weight of the evidence in support of the credences generating that expected value, such that investments supported by more evidence are better than investments supported by less evidence, all else being equal.

According to the evidence favoring view, if the standard expected value of investing in intervention *X* is the same as the standard expected value of investing in intervention *Y* but the estimate of the effectiveness of intervention *Y* is supported by more evidence of the estimate of the effectiveness of intervention *X*, then it is better to invest in *Y* than in *X*.

The evidence favoring view encourages us to make decisions about where to direct our resources in a manner that is analogous to a doctor deciding on the best treatment for their patient. There is increasing consensus that clinicians should select treatments that have been shown to be effective, where randomized control trials are generally considered 'gold standard' of evidence for treatment efficacy.[21] Even if they have a plausible mechanism of action, speculative treatments that have not been shown to be effective in clinical trials are generally not considered an acceptable first line of treatment.[22]

We can contrast the evidence favoring view with what I will call the 'evidence neutral' view, which simply says that we ought to invest in a way that maximizes expected value:

The Evidence Neutral View: The total value of an investment is just the standard expected value of that investment irrespective of the weight of the evidence in support of the credences generating that expected value.

According to the evidence neutral view, if investment *X* produces at least as much value as investment *Y* then investment *X* is at least as valuable as investment *Y* and if investment *X* produces more expected value than investment *Y* then investment *X* is more valuable than investment *Y*. This is true irrespective of the weight of the evidence we have about each intervention.

The arguments in favor of the evidence neutral view will mirror the arguments in favor of expected utility theory. For example, we could argue that, by the strong law of large numbers, we should expect the evidence neutral view to yield more

[21] For a definition and discussion of evidence-based medicine, see Sackett et al. (1996).
[22] Giving experimental treatments to patients is highly controversial. See Raus (2016).

value than the evidence favoring view in the long-run.[23] The evidence favoring view tells us to prefer to invest in interventions whose reward distributions we have more information about even if the expected rewards of these investments are equal to or lower than those of some alternatives that we have less evidence about. But the strong law of large numbers states that if we repeat the same choice scenario then the probability that the average outcome of those choices converges almost surely on its expected value. This indicates that we can expect to lose some amount of value in the long-run simply to avoid investing in interventions with less evidential support.

I will not attempt to assess such arguments for evidence neutrality here. Instead, I will attempt to show that evidence neutrality places sufficient value on evidence and research. In the next section I will show that research and new information is highly valuable in ethical decision-making even if we endorse the evidence neutral view.

4. Evidence neutrality and the moral value of information

If the evidence neutral view is correct, then we have no reason to invest in an intervention that has more evidential support over one that has less evidential support if both interventions produce comparable expected value. Accordingly, it may seem that the view causes us to undervalue research into the effectiveness of interventions. In this section, however, I will attempt to show that the evidence neutral view entails that we should place great value on acquiring new information about the effectiveness of interventions.

The difficulty of deciding which interventions to invest in arises because we do not know how much value a given investment in an intervention will produce. The problem of deciding where to assign limited resources when the expected value of our options is not known has been explored in some depth in the literature on multi-armed bandit problems.[24] A one-armed bandit (or slot machine) requires a certain amount of money to play and has a reward distribution that we can have more or less information about. Multi-armed bandit problems are problems that involve multiple one-armed bandits, where we have varying degrees of knowledge of the reward distribution of a given bandit and we gain information about the reward distribution by investing money to play it. The key question driving multi-armed bandit problems is whether and how we should 'explore' by playing different bandits in order to discover their reward distributions, and

[23] See Chapter 10 of Feller (1968). For worries about appealing to the law of large numbers to justify expected utility theory, see pp. 3–4, Easwaran (2014). Easwaran also outlines representation theorem arguments for expected utility theory (pp. 2–3).

[24] The multi-armed bandit problem was first described by Robbins (1952). For a comprehensive overview of the multi-armed bandit problem and its variants, see Bubeck and Cesa-Bianchi (2012).

when we should opt to 'exploit' the bandit that has the highest expected reward distribution by playing it rather than exploring.

If the process that generates the reward distribution of a one-armed bandit is deterministic but difficult to know then as we explore, our credences will become more accurate: we will have a higher credence in the true outcome of each play as we gain more evidence.[25] We can think of the interventions that we can invest in as one-armed bandits with reward distributions that we have varying amounts of evidence about.[26] The reward distribution of an intervention will almost always result from a deterministic but difficult to understand process. For example, the effectiveness of distributing LLINs in a given region depends on multiple factors such as the number of malaria-transmitting mosquitoes in the region, the cost of distributing to that region, the correct use of the LLINs, and so on.

The fact that the reward distribution of an intervention may vary depending on multiple factors may appear to be a problem for the claim that we can treat interventions like one-armed bandits. For example, suppose we discover that LLINs can be expected to save more than one life per $3,000 in a region *R1* while they can be expected to save less than one life per $3,000 in a region *R2* because the mosquito population is larger in region *R1* than in region *R2*. If we make such a discovery, then surely it does not make sense to treat the intervention 'distributing LLINs' as a single one-armed bandit. Instead, we ought to treat 'distributing LLINs in R1-like regions' and 'distributing LLINs in R2-like regions' as distinct one-armed bandits since these interventions have distinct reward distributions.

We can treat an intervention like a one-armed bandit only if, given our current evidence, the outcome of a given act of investment in that intervention is sampled from a single reward distribution. But this will result in a highly fine-grained concept of an intervention only if we have the option of investing in fine-grained interventions like 'distributing LLINs in R1-like regions'. We may not have the option of selecting which region will receive LLINs when choosing where to invest. If we can choose to invest $3,000 in a given LLIN-distributing charity but we will have no control over which regions the charity distributes LLINs, then we can treat this charity as a single intervention whose expected reward distribution depends on our credences about which regions the charity is likely to focus its efforts.

We can gain information about interventions in several different ways. We can perform relevant research into the intervention in question or its mechanism.

[25] Of course, if there are underlying factors that we cannot gain sufficient evidence about then we may never be able to have perfectly accurate credences in each outcome. Joyce (2005, p. 166) notes that if the process that generates the reward distributions of one-armed bandits is fundamentally stochastic then more evidence will make our credences be well-calibrated: closer to the objective probabilities.

[26] If we think of interventions as one-armed bandits, then the $3,000 per expected life saved for LLINs could be generated by various different reward distributions. For example, it may be the that LLIN one-armed bandit has probability 1 of saving one life every time we put $3,000 into the machine (and probability 0 of saving any lives until we put $3000 into the machine). Or it may be that it has a one-in-12,000 chance of saving four lives every time we put $1 into the machine.

An example of this would be assessing the effectiveness of the insecticides used to treat bed nets. This might be thought of as analogous to paying to see some small part of the mechanism generating the reward distribution inside the one-armed bandit. Alternatively, we can simply invest in the intervention and then note the outcome of this investment.[27] An example would be assessing the effectiveness of a deworming program in a given region after it has been implemented. This is analogous to simply paying to play the one-armed bandit and then finding out what reward we have received.

When we get more evidence about the mean reward of an intervention through research or by running trials, our credences in different expected value estimates generally become more heavily concentrated on a smaller set of possible reward distributions and, therefore, on a smaller set of possible mean rewards for a given intervention. By investing in an intervention, we get some information about what the reward distribution of that intervention looks like. It is easiest to illustrate this phenomenon by offering an example, albeit a highly idealized one. Suppose we have $6,000 to invest. We are certain that distributing LLINs will save one life per $3,000 invested based on extensive evidence, and so the expected value of investing $6,000 in this intervention is two lives saved. Since we have little evidence about the effectiveness of the EGI, we are equally uncertain about whether the expected value of investing $3,000 in the EGI is two lives, 1.5 lives, 0.5 lives, or zero lives (i.e. we have a credence of 0.25 in each of these hypotheses).[28] The expected value of investing $6,000 in the EGI is also two lives saved, but the mean variance of the possible reward distributions is higher.

In this scenario, both interventions save two lives in expectation per $6,000 invested. We might therefore believe that those who adopt the evidence favoring view would tell us to invest in LLINs, while those who adopt the evidence neutral view would be indifferent between investing in LLINs and the EGI. But this fails to take into account the value of the information that we receive from investing in each of these interventions. We can think of a given $6,000 investment as a trial of the one-armed bandit. If we invest $6,000 in the EGI—for example, by testing it in a very small region—and it saves four lives in that region, then this increases our credence that the EGI has a reward distribution that is of higher expected value than that of LLIN distribution. This information can be extremely valuable.

To once again offer an idealized example, suppose that a single trial could provide us with *perfect* information about the reward distribution of an intervention: i.e. three lives are saved in the region where the EGI is tested if and only if the

[27] One disadvantage of investing is that we may not be able to perform the kinds of controls required for us to receive the most robust evidence. Evidence we receive from investigation, however, such as randomized controlled trials (RCTs), may be more costly and fail to generalize. See Cartwright & Hardie (2012) for a full discussion of the merits and limitations of RCTs.

[28] It is obviously implausible to suppose that we would have a credence of 0.25 that the EGI will save two lives in expectation and a credence of 0.25 that the EGI will save 1.5 lives in expectation and a credence of 0 that the EGI will save 1.75 lives in expectation, but this simplifies the case.

expected value of the EGI is three lives per $6,000. Since we are assuming that LLIN distribution saves two lives in expectation and the EGI saves either four, three, one, or zero lives in expectation, the possible outcomes of investing $6,000 in LLINs or in the EGI are as follows:

	S1 (0.25)	S2 (0.25)	S3 (0.25)	S4 (0.25)
$6,000 in LLINs	2 lives saved	2 lives saved	2 lives saved	2 lives saved
$6,000 in EGI	4 lives saved	3 lives saved	1 life saved	0 lives saved

The expected non-information value of investing $6,000 in LLINs and the EGI is the same in this case: it is two lives saved. But we cannot gain any new information about LLINs from this trial, since we already know how many lives this intervention saves in expectation. We can, however, gain valuable new information about the EGI. How valuable this information is depends on how much we can invest in the EGI in the future. Suppose that after this trial we will have $600,000 remaining to invest in either intervention and that we do not expect the value of either intervention to diminish if we invest this full amount.[29] If we assume that this is a 'one-shot' trial opportunity then the information value of investing $6,000 in the EGI is 175 lives saved. This is because we have a credence of 0.25 that we will find out that the EGI saves four lives and so we can save 400 lives by investing $600,000 in the EGI. We also have a credence of 0.25 that we will find out that the EGI saves three lives and so we can save 300 lives by investing $600,000 in the EGI. Finally, we have a credence of 0.5 that the EGI will save one or zero lives and so we can save 200 lives by investing $600,000 in LLINs. So if we have only this one opportunity to trial the EGI, then an investment of $6,000 in the LLINs saves two lives in expectation while an investment of $6,000 in the EGI saves 177 lives in expectation. Therefore, the evidence neutral view would strongly favor investing in the EGI over the LLINs.

This case involves many idealizations. For example, the expected value of investing $6,000 in the EGI goes down a great deal if we assume that we can perform this trial at any later time. If we invest $6,000 in LLINs and then invest our next $6,000 in the EGI, the expected loss of the first investment relative to investing in the EGI is just 0.75 lives. But this only reduces the magnitude of the benefit of investing in the EGI: it is still the case that those who adopt the evidence neutral view will favor investing in the EGI. The same is true of many other idealizations made in this case. For example, it would hold in many cases in which our credences in the expected value of investing in each intervention are spread across a broader range of hypotheses if the EGI estimates are still higher

[29] It is likely that the value would diminish since not all regions will have the same rates of malaria. Diminishing returns would reduce the information value, but this does not undermine the general point.

variance and lower resilience than the LLIN estimates.[30] It would also hold even if we were to receive an information sample from only the $6,000 trial rather than perfect information as was assumed above.

When the difference in the expected non-information value of two investments is not great enough to counter the expected difference in the information value, the evidence neutral view will generally entail that we ought to invest in the intervention that has less evidential support over an intervention that has more evidential support. The information value we gain from investing in an intervention with less evidential support is generally greater because our estimates of the value of investing in these interventions are generally of higher variance (spread across more hypotheses) and of lower resilience (move more in response to new evidence). Investing in these more speculative interventions to get information about their value allows us to identify new sources of value going forward and avoid investing in less effective interventions going forward.

The evidence favoring view may also recommend investing in the EGI in the case above since the information value may be enough to outweigh any plausible penalty for the low evidential weight supporting the EGI. By favoring investments in interventions that have more evidential weight, however, the evidence favoring view recommends investments from which we expect to gain less information, not more. The evidence favoring view therefore prioritizes evidence and research in one sense: it rewards well-evidenced interventions by encouraging us to invest in those interventions. But in another sense the evidence favoring view fails to prioritize evidence and research: it encourages us to invest in interventions from which we have less to learn. The evidence neutral view, by contrast, prioritizes evidence and research by encouraging us to research and invest in interventions that we currently lack evidence about.

Because the evidence neutral view places less value on well-evidenced interventions, it may seem to create fewer incentives for organizations to use their own resources to produce evidence that they are effective and create fewer incentives for organizations that solve problems in ways that have been demonstrated to be effective.[31] In general, however, this effect will be minor and can be taken into account in our expected value calculations. It is also worth noting that the majority of speculative interventions will not be better than the most effective interventions that we have more evidence about, even when we take value of information into account.[32] And once we have sufficient evidence that an intervention is more effective than the alternatives, we will switch from exploring interventions to

[30] Gould (1974) demonstrates that the relationship between risk and information value is not as straightforward as greater risk resulting in greater information value. The relationship between increased variance and information value is explored in Stephens (1989).

[31] On the other hand, the information value of investments will be higher for interventions that are transparent and testable and so these properties are incentivized if we care about information value.

[32] In multi-armed bandit problems, it generally does not make sense not to waste resources to gain information about arms with sufficiently low expected value.

exploiting the best interventions for their non-information value. The evidence neutral view therefore does not create strong disincentives to produce evidence in favor of intervention.[33]

The question of exactly when we should switch from exploring to exploiting is a difficult one to answer. It depends on various factors, such as how far into the future we expect to be able to continue investing and how much, if at all, we discount future value. The value of exploration decreases the less we expect to be able to invest in the future. It also decreases the more we discount the future. This is reflected in the well-known Gittins index, which assigns a value to each one-armed bandit based on its record of wins and losses.[34] Selecting the option with the highest Gittins index has been shown to be the optimal policy in many circumstances if the reward distributions of the bandits do not change, there are finitely many options, and the rewards are within a bounded interval.[35]

How we should make the explore/exploit tradeoff in cases of ethical investments is a particularly difficult question for several reasons.[36] When it comes to many real-world interventions we may not be able to measure the reward output of a given intervention with accuracy. There are also many interventions that are available for only a finite period of time, the reward distribution of many interventions may not be independent, and some interventions we can invest in now may alter the resources and interventions available to us in the future. Finally, the expected rewards from each intervention plausibly change over time, making this question more analogous to the 'restless bandit problem'. Although selecting the option with the highest Gittins index may be a good heuristic in restless bandit problems, finding an optimal policy in such cases has been shown to be NP-hard.[37] The task of finding a good heuristic for how to decide whether to explore or exploit when investing in ethical interventions is an important one but is beyond the scope of this chapter.[38]

If valuing research and evidence does not require deviating from the evidence neutral view, we might wonder why we are inclined to avoid investing our resources in more speculative interventions even if the total expected value of investing in these interventions is marginally greater than the total expected value of investing in a more well-evidenced alternative (even if our skeptical prior means that this will not often be the case). This behavior could in part be explained by

[33] We might worry that the evidence neutral view will recommend that we invest in overly speculative interventions and leave us prey to 'Pascal's mugging' (Bostrom 2009). But, as I indicate above, the evidence neutral view does not entail that we should always invest in speculative interventions.

[34] Gittins et al. (2011 [1989]).

[35] See Tsitsiklis (1994) for a proof of the Gittins Theorem.

[36] On the other hand, some features of ethical decision-making may simplify the problem: for example, the problem is simpler if we do not discount future ethical value.

[37] Guha et al. (2010).

[38] A popular algorithm to use in multi-armed bandit problems is the upper confidence bound algorithm developed by Auer (2002). The upper confidence bound is, very roughly, the highest value a bandit could plausibly produce. The upper bound is high among bandits that we have not tested much and bandits that we have tested and shown to have high average rewards.

ambiguity aversion. Unlike risk aversion, which causes us to prefer gambles with less uncertainty over gambles with more uncertainty, ambiguity aversion causes us to prefer gambles where the probabilities are known over gambles in which the probabilities are not known. If we are averse to investing in interventions when we have less evidence about their reward distributions and so the reward probabilities are not known, we can expect that we would be willing to pay to research promising interventions—thereby increasing our information about their reward distribution—but unwilling to invest in those interventions. A similar result is borne out in at least one experiment by Anderson (2012) who notes that, where θ is the probability of success,

> Because ambiguity averse agents are willing to pay more than ambiguity neutral agents to learn the true value of θ, it appears that they overvalue information. On the other hand, when the information value question is presented in the arm choice frame, because their Gittins index is lower than optimal, ambiguity averse agents appear to undervalue information.[39]

In other words, ambiguity averse agents overvalue 'looking inside' the one-armed bandit and discovering its reward distribution and they undervalue playing a one-armed bandit with an unknown reward distribution even though this also provides information about its reward distribution. If this reflects our own response to ethical investments, then we may overvalue research into more speculative interventions and undervalue simply investing in those interventions.

5. Conclusion

In this chapter I have argued that although we may be inclined to favor investing in ethical interventions that have more evidential support over those that have less evidential support, we have no reason to favor such interventions. Indeed, all else being equal, we should expect to derive more value from investing in interventions for which we have less evidential support because doing so yields more information about the intervention's effectiveness. Of course, all else is rarely equal, and a skeptical prior about the mean effectiveness of interventions will prevent most speculative interventions from having greater expected value than interventions that have been shown to be highly effective. In general, however, we should be wary of underinvesting in interventions merely because they currently lack robust evidential support and thus miss opportunities to gain valuable information.[40]

[39] Anderson (2012, pp. 22–3).

[40] Recognizing the importance of information value may have important ramifications for ethical investments. For example, if the information returns on investments are high but diminish rapidly, this may constitute a reason to diversify our investments across several interventions.

References

Anderson, C. M. 2012. "Ambiguity aversion in multi-armed bandit problems." *Theory and Decision* 72 (1): 15–33.

Auer, Peter. 2002. "Using confidence bounds for exploitation-exploration trade-offs." *Journal of Machine Learning Research* 3 (3): 397–422.

Behrens, Timothy, Mark Woolrich, M.E. Walton, and Matthew Rushworth. 2007. "Learning the Value of Information in An Uncertain World." *Nature Neuroscience* 10 (9): 1,214.

Bostrom, Nick. 2009. "Pascal's mugging." *Analysis* 69 (3): 443–5.

Bubeck, Sébastien and Cesa-Bianchi, Nicolò. 2012. "Regret analysis of stochastic and nonstochastic multi-armed bandit problems." *Foundations and Trends in Machine Learning* 5 (1): 1–122.

Buchak, Lara. 2013. *Risk and Rationality*. Oxford: Oxford University Press.

Cartwright, Nancy, and Jeremy Hardie. 2012. *Evidence-Based Policy: A Practical Guide to Doing It Better*. Oxford: Oxford University Press.

Easwaran, Kenny. 2014. *Decision Theory without Representation Theorems*. Ann Arbor, MI: Michigan Publishing.

Feller, William. 1968. *An introduction to probability theory and its applications Vol. 1, No. 3)*. New York: Wiley.

Gittins, John, Kevin Glazebrook, and Richard Weber. 2011[1989]. *Multi-Armed Bandit Allocation Indices 2nd Edition*. New York: John Wiley & Sons.

Givewell. 2018. "GiveWell's Cost-Effectiveness Analyses." Accessed 5 June 2018. Available at https://www.givewell.org/how-we-work/our-criteria/cost-effectiveness/cost-effectiveness-models.

Guha, Sudipto, Kamesh Munagala, Peng Shi. 2010. "Approximation algorithms for restless bandit problems." *Journal of the ACM* 58 (1): 3.

Gould, John P. 1974. "Risk, stochastic preference, and the value of information." *Journal of Economic Theory* 8 (1): 64–84.

Hammond, A. et al. 2016. "A CRISPR-Cas9 gene drive system targeting female reproduction in the malaria mosquito vector Anopheles gambiae." *Nature Biotechnology* 34 (1): 78.

Jeffrey, Richard. 1965. *The Logic of Decision*. Chicago, IL: The University of Chicago Press.

Joyce, James M. 2005. "How probabilities reflect evidence." *Philosophical Perspectives* 19 (1): 153–178.

Joyce, James M. 2010. "A defense of imprecise credences in inference and decision-making." *Philosophical Perspectives* 24 (1): 281–323.

MacAskill, William. 2014. "Normative uncertainty." Doctoral dissertation. University of Oxford.

MacAskill, William. 2015. *Doing Good Better: Effective Altruism and a Radical New Way to Make a Difference*. Guardian Faber Publishing.

Noggle, Robert. 2009. "Give till it hurts? Beneficence, imperfect duties, and a moderate response to the aid question." *Journal of Social Philosophy* 40 (1): 1–16.

Popper, Karl. 2005 [1959]. *The logic of scientific discovery*. Abingdon, Oxon: Routledge.

Pugh, Jonathan. 2016. "Driven to Extinction? The Ethics of Eradicating Mosquitoes with Gene-drive Technologies." *Journal of Medical Ethics* 42 (9): 578–81.

Pummer, Theron. 2016. "Whether and Where to Give." *Philosophy & Public Affairs* 44 (1): 77–95.

Raus, Kasper. 2016. An analysis of common ethical justifications for compassionate use programs for experimental drugs. *BMC medical ethics* 17 (1): 60.

Robbins, Herbert. 1952. "Some Aspects of the Sequential Design of Experiments." *Bulletin of the American Mathematical Society* 55: 527–35.

Sackett, David L. et al. 1996. "Evidence based medicine: what it is and what it isn't." *BMJ* 312 (7023): 71–2.

Savage, Leonard J. 1954. *The Foundations of Statistics*. New York: Wiley.

Singer, Peter. 1972. "Famine, Affluence, and Morality." *Philosophy & Public Affairs* 1: 229–43.

Skyrms, Brian. 1977. "Resiliency, Propensities, and Causal Necessity." *The Journal of Philosophy* 74 (11): 704–13.

Stephens, D. W. 1989. "Variance and the Value of Information." *The American Naturalist* 134 (1): 128–40.

Timmerman, Travis. 2015. "Sometimes There is Nothing Wrong with Letting a Child Drown." *Analysis* 75 (2): 204–12.

Tsitsiklis, John. 1994. "A short proof of the Gittins index theorem." *The Annals of Applied Probability* 4 (1): 194–9.

Unger, Peter. 1996. *Living High and Letting Die: Our Illusion of Innocence*. New York: Oxford University Press.

Wiblin, Robert. 2017. "Most people report believing it's incredibly cheap to save lives in the developing world." *80,000 Hours* (Accessed 13 September 2018). Available at https://80000hours.org/2017/05/most-people-report-believing-its-incredibly-cheap-to-save-lives-in-the-developing-world/.

4

Effective Altruism and Transformative Experience

Jeff Sebo and Laurie Paul

1. Introduction

Effective altruists try to use evidence and reason to do the most good possible. However, some choices involve transformative experiences, which change what we care about in ways that we cannot fully anticipate. This limits our ability to make informed, rational, and authentic plans individually as well as collectively. In this chapter, we discuss the challenges that transformative experiences pose for effective altruists, given that such choices change us in surprising ways.

2. Effective altruism

Many effective altruists think about what to do in the following kind of way: First, they think about the *scale* of a problem. The more harm a problem causes, the higher priority it should have according to effective altruism all else equal. Second, they think about how *neglected* a problem is. The more neglected a problem is, the higher priority it should have according to effective altruism all else equal. Third, they think about the *tractability* of a problem. The more tractable a problem is, the higher priority it should have according to effective altruism all else equal. Finally, they think about *personal fit*. Given everything they know about their talents, interests, and backgrounds, what can they do individually in order to address the worst, most neglected, most tractable problems as effectively as possible?[1]

Many effective altruists try to answer these questions through impartial cost-benefit analysis. They try to collect as much evidence as possible, assign probabilities and utilities to different courses of action on the basis of this evidence, and then select the course of action that maximizes expected utility. Moreover, many effective altruists do not assign special weight to what they, as individuals, happen to think or feel. Yes, they care about personal fit, but only from an impartial standpoint.

[1] MacAskill (2015); Singer (2015).

They think that they should do the most good possible for everyone in the world, and so personal fit is relevant primarily insofar as it impacts productivity. Similarly, they care about deliberating about which course of action is best, but, again, only from an impartial standpoint. They think that they are only one of many people asking these questions, and that if they disagree with other, seemingly equally informed and rational individuals about the answers, they should seriously consider the possibility that they are wrong.

Given this commitment to informed, rational, impartial benevolence, effective altruists tend to agree about many issues. For example, they tend to agree that existential risk, global health and development, and animal welfare are high-priority cause areas.[2] They also tend to agree that certain interventions in these areas are more effective than others. Within the animal welfare category, for example, they agree that farmed animal advocacy is a higher priority than companion animal advocacy.[3]

With that said, effective altruists also disagree about some issues. For example, they disagree about some normative issues, such as whether one should attempt to maximize happiness or merely minimize suffering, and about whether one should do so by any means necessary or while respecting deontological side constraints. They also disagree about some descriptive issues, such as what kind of effective altruist movement is likely to produce the relevant desired outcomes, or what kind of political or economic system is likely to do so. (We will return to these issues below.) These methodological commitments, together with these areas of agreement and disagreement, raise several challenges for the effective altruist, two of which will be our focus here.

The first challenge concerns cost–benefit analysis. Effective altruists aspire to use cost–benefit analysis to decide what to do, yet they often lack essential information. In this kind of case, should they still attempt to apply cost–benefit analysis to all relevant options? Or should they apply cost–benefit analysis to a narrower range of options and/or use a different decision procedure?

The second, related challenge concerns impartiality. Effective altruists aspire to reason impartially, yet they do not always reach the same conclusions as other, seemingly equally informed and rational individuals. In this kind of case, should they assign weight only to the beliefs and values that they identify with, or should they assign weight also to other, seemingly equally informed and rational beliefs and values that they feel alienated from?

In what follows, we will explore how the possibility of undergoing a transformative experience can exacerbate these challenges for effective altruists, individually and collectively.

[2] Open Philanthropy Project (2018).

[3] Animal Charity Evaluators (2018).

3. Transformative experience

An experience can be transformative in at least two related ways. First, an experience is *epistemically transformative* when it teaches you something you could not have learned without having that experience. By having it, it teaches you what that kind of experience is like, and it also gives you the ability to imagine, recognize, and cognitively model new possible states. For example, you can learn what parenthood is like for you only by actually becoming a parent.[4] Second, an experience is *personally transformative* when it changes you in a personally fundamental way by changing a core personal belief, value, or practice.[5] For example, by becoming a parent, you can acquire an updated set of beliefs, values, and motivations. There can also be a certain amount of endogeneity. For instance, many parents find that, after having a child, they form a preference to have had that very child. In light of such changes, your pre-decision (*ex ante*) self and your post-decision (*ex post*) self might have different preferences, including different higher-order preferences.[6] A *transformative experience*, as defined by Paul, is an experience that is both epistemically and personally transformative.[7]

There are many ordinary examples of transformative experience. Some are relatively sudden, such as the experience of moving to a new city, starting college, starting a new job, having a baby, experiencing violent combat, or gaining a sensory ability. Others are gradual, such as the transformation from being ten years-old to being thirty years-old, from being a graduate student to being a tenured professor, or from being a Syrian refugee to being a U.S. citizen. Either way, these transformations are all in a certain sense irreversible. You can drop out of college, leave your job, and even leave your family, but these experiences will have affected you (in addition to having opportunity costs and changing your choice situation).

When a person thinks about what to do, they have to consider many possible things they could do, but in transformative contexts, they must also consider the many possible selves they could become. When these changes will be irreversible, a person has to decide what to do without having the opportunity to experience these different futures. So, if a person is making a decision that may involve transformative experience, they have to decide what to do without knowing what it will be like to take each available path. They also have to decide what to do even if this decision could change their core beliefs or values in a way that creates *ex ante/ex post* conflict.

[4] We think this problem, as it occurs in the real world, is both serious and often underestimated by philosophers. See: Paul and Quiggin (2018).
[5] Note that this sort of self-change need not entail a change in personal identity.
[6] Paul (2014); Pettigrew (2015); Paul (2015a); Paul and Healy (2017); Paul and Quiggin (2018).
[7] Paul (2014).

The possibility of transformative experience exacerbates the challenges for effective altruists that were considered in the previous section. First, it exacerbates the challenge to cost–benefit analysis, by raising the question of how to decide what to do if you will learn essential information only after the decision is made. For example, if you can accurately imagine parenthood only after becoming a parent, how do you decide whether or not to become a parent?

Importantly, the challenge is not merely that, prior to making your choice, you are uncertain about the probabilities and utilities of the outcome. The challenge is also that *you cannot assign value to the outcome with any accuracy.* Your value function for the outcome is undefined. This is because you cannot imaginatively represent an essential part of the outcome (the nature of the lived experience of being a parent) well enough to accurately assess its value.

Why, exactly, does your value function for the outcome go undefined? For the familiar reason that the relevant information carried by the experience cannot be grasped without having the experience. It is not possible, for example, for a person who has never seen color to know or accurately imagine what it is like to see red. She needs to have the experience before she can assign value to what the experience is like (at least, with any accuracy). Other transformative experiences are similar. In each case, we cannot know or accurately imagine what it is like to have a fundamentally new kind of experience until we have actually had it. And, insofar as we need to assign value to what the experience is like in order to assign value to an outcome involving that experience, our inability to make the former assignment with any accuracy will lead to an inability to make the latter assignment with any accuracy.[8]

This is therefore more than a case of uncertainty: It is a case of ignorance. And in many cases, this ignorance will never be fully resolved, not even after the fact. If you make one choice, you will bring about one future as a result, which you will then be able to accurately value and represent. But not only will you have already made your choice at this point, you will also still be unable to accurately value the other futures that you could have brought about through other choices. Therefore, you will still be unable to assess your choice relative to other choices that you could have made. The question, then, is: How should you decide what to do? Should you use cost–benefit analysis and consider all relevant options, even if you are unable to assess them? Or should you consider only options you are able to assess, or use a different decision procedure?[9]

Of course, to say that we lack essential information for first-person value assessment is not to say that cost–benefit analysis is always useless. Some cases

[8] This predicament is especially severe in real life cases, since we can't exploit the theoretical possibility that we could know what an experience is like simply by knowing, in complete detail, the neurological states that would realize that experience. For further discussion of the color vision case, see Jackson (1986). For further discussion of the parenthood case, see Paul (2014, ch. 2).

[9] For further discussion, see Pettigrew (2015); Paul (2015b).

are relatively easy to resolve without first-person value assessment, since they involve changes that are always good (or bad). Other cases are harder to assess, but we might still have at least some evidence to draw from, such as evidence about how other people react to this kind of change or how we react to other kinds of change. Alternatively, we might lack evidence but still have speculative estimates to draw from.[10]

However, it is not clear that these considerations will be enough to make cost–benefit analysis useful in the kinds of cases that we are discussing here. First, even when we do have evidence, it is not clear how representative this evidence is. Seeing how other people react to this kind of change will not necessarily tell us how *we* will react to it, and seeing how we react to other kinds of change will not necessarily tell us how we will react to *this* kind of change. Second, while speculative estimates can often be useful, it is not clear that they can be useful in many transformative cases, since, as noted above, we cannot assign value to all outcomes before having the experience and our preferences may be endogenous.

The possibility of transformative experience also exacerbates the challenge to impartiality, by raising a question about how to make decisions in cases where your core personal beliefs and values might change as a result. For example, if your preference for being a parent is endogenous to the process of becoming a parent, should you base your decision about whether or not to become a parent on an evaluative standpoint that excludes or includes this preference?[11] Moreover, if we suppose that you should do the latter, what happens if you expect to have *ex ante/ex post* conflicts arise? For example, what if you currently have one preference (e.g. to have one child), but you expect to form another if you end up remaining a non-parent (e.g. in the future you expect to prefer to have no children). What if you prefer to have one child now, but you expect to prefer to have twins (triplets…) if you end up having twins (or triplets)?

There are other reasons why one might care about the prospect of preference change. Some are, appropriately, existential in nature. For instance, you might resist making decisions that, in your view, would result in an elimination of your current self. Similarly, if you care about first-personal deliberation, then you might resist basing your decisions in part on preferences that you currently feel alienated from. But since many effective altruists care more about doing the most good possible than about avoiding self-elimination or alienation, we will not focus on that issue here.[12]

Other reasons for caring about the prospect of preference change are prudential, moral, or political in nature. For example, if you think that you have prudential, moral, or political duties to your future selves, then you might think that you

[10] See Askell, Chapter 3 in this volume. [11] Paul (2014); Paul (2015b).

[12] For discussion of the unimportance of the self and personal identity in prudence, morality, and rationality, see Parfit (1984).

should allow them to have a say in your decision as a matter of prudence, morality, or justice.[13] However, since effective altruists tend to care more about doing the most good overall than doing the most good for themselves (except insofar as they think that the ability to compromise and coordinate with past and future selves is instrumentally valuable), we will once again focus on other issues.

Importantly, groups may be able to have transformative experiences as well. Groups may not have phenomenally conscious mental states in the same kind of way that individuals do, but they can still have beliefs, values, and preferences in the relevant sense. For example, they can construct these states directly, by endorsing certain statements of fact, value, and priority. They can also construct these states indirectly, by pursuing courses of action that make sense in light of certain belief, value, and priority attributions. Either way, as in the individual case, groups will tend to form beliefs, values, and preferences that make sense in light of their actions and will tend to perform actions that make sense in light of their beliefs, values, and preferences. Moreover, as in the individual case, group members might sometimes face decisions that could change the group in ways that are difficult to anticipate, and which could result in *ex ante/ex post* conflict. For instance, if a company hires a new staff member or implements a new policy, they need to consider the possibility that this decision will result in preference change for the company as a whole.[14]

As in the individual case, the possibility of transformative experience exacerbates the challenges considered above. For example, when a company has to make a decision that may result in a transformative experience, should they use cost–benefit analysis and consider all relevant options, or should they consider fewer options and/or use a different decision procedure? Also, should they base decisions entirely on their current beliefs and values, or should they defer at least partly to other beliefs and values? Once again, one might care about these questions for many reasons. But we will here focus on the reasons for which an effective altruist will care about them.

Whether we confront cases involving transformative experience individually or collectively, we face the following kind of tension: Insofar as we restrict what we think about and how we think about such cases, we will be able to reason relatively accurately and authentically, but we will also limit our opportunities for doing good. Whereas insofar as we expand what and how we think about such cases, we will be able to consider more opportunities for doing good, but we will also recognize new limitations on our ability to reason accurately and authentically.

In what follows we will consider some examples that illustrate the challenges that choices involving transformative experiences raise for effective altruists.

[13] Briggs (2015); Sebo (2015a).

[14] For discussion of the idea of collective agency, see Schweikard and Schmid (2013). For discussion of the idea of collective self-narrativity, see Sebo (2015b). And, for discussion of the role of self-narrativity in self-constitution, see Dennett (1992); Schectman (1996); and Velleman (2009).

We will explore these challenges at both the individual and collective level, showing that analogous challenges arise at both levels, and suggesting that the stance effective altruists take toward such challenges will have a pervasive influence on their decision-making and impact.

4. Individual transformation

Effective altruists, like anyone else, face transformative choices such as what to do for a living, whether to get married, whether to have kids, and so on. Managing such choices can be especially challenging for an effective altruist, since in each case they are committed to using evidence and reason to do the most good possible, which requires deep assessment of a wide range of options. We will here focus on career choice as an illustration, but similar questions will arise for other choice situations as well.

Suppose that you are an effective altruist deciding what to do for a living,[15] and that you have three main options to consider: You can (*a*) go to grad school (so that you can work in research and education), (*b*) go to law school (so that you can work in law and politics), or (*c*) work in finance (so that you can earn to give). Suppose also, since grad school and law school would be more continuous with your college experience than finance would be, you have a better sense of what your life would be like in the first two scenarios than in the third.

In particular, the choice whether to work in finance strikes you as high risk/high reward. If it works out, you could earn millions of dollars per year and then donate that money to effective causes. But you wonder if you can expect it to work out. Here you may ask: Would I fail at investment banking? Would I succeed but lose my commitment to effective altruism? Would I retain my commitment to effective altruism but start to think that I need to spend more money on myself than I currently think I do? If I did change my mind in one or more of these ways, would I be rationally updating in light of new information and arguments? Would I simply be rationalizing the kind of self-interested behavior that I would have, at that point, been socialized into? Or might I change in other ways that I cannot imaginatively anticipate, and which might raise other possibilities for *ex ante*/*ex post* conflict?

With this in mind, consider the challenge that this kind of transformative choice can raise for cost–benefit analysis. For some people, the costs and benefits of these options might be easy to assess. For example, if you find that you have very little interest in material things and that your social environment has very little impact on your beliefs and values, then it might be rational for you to feel

[15] For some anecdotal information about how effective altruists think about career choice, see the resources at 80,000 Hours: https://80000hours.org/

confident that working in finance is the right choice for you. Likewise, if you find that you have a lot of interest in material things and/or that your social environment has a lot of impact on your beliefs and values, then it might be rational for you to feel confident that working in finance would be wrong for you. (Though even in these cases mistakes are possible.)

But for others, the costs and benefits of these options might be harder to assess. For example, if you find that you have a decent amount of interest in material things and/or that your social environment has a decent amount of impact on your personality, then it might not be rational for you to have much confidence one way or the other about whether finance would be right for you. For all you know now, if you worked in finance, you could be happy, productive, and committed to effective altruism and to earning to give. Or you could be happy, productive, and uncommitted. Or you could be miserable, productive, and committed. Or you could be miserable, unproductive, and uncommitted. And so on.

If you find yourself with this kind of question, how should you go about making this choice? A natural thought is to apply cost–benefit analysis to all of your options to the best of your ability. You can collect as much evidence as possible and then make the choice that maximizes expected value, given your evidence. In this case you have to ask: What kind of evidence is available to me?

One source of evidence comes from other people in this situation. Now that more people are earning to give, more information is available about successes and failures. But insofar as an effective altruist is interested in evidence-based estimates of value (as opposed to speculative estimates of value), what matters is not information in the form of anecdote, unvetted testimony, or emotional appeal. Rather, what matters is evidence drawn from long-term, empirically rigorous case studies. A problem here is that, since the effective altruism movement is fairly young, such evidence is not yet available.[16] Moreover, even if you were to have access to evidence from long-term, empirically rigorous case studies on other people, that might still not be enough to tell you what it will be like for *you* to be in this situation. As with any complex life experience, there is enough heterogeneity amongst individuals to raise worries about your ability to discover your reference class. That is, you need to know whether you are relevantly similar to other effective altruists to know whether working in finance would have the same impact on you as it did on those for whom data is available.

A second source of evidence comes from you in other situations. You might not have the experience of taking on the role of investment banker, but you have experience taking on other social roles, and then observing whether and to what degree these choices affect you. Perhaps in the past you remained happy, productive, and committed to effective altruism in the face of changing social environments.

[16] For related problems with the interpretation of observational data as well as with applying such results to one's own case, see Paul and Healy (2017) and Paul (2015a).

But once again, what matters is not information in the form of your own memory and self-narrativity, but *evidence*. You need evidence that rules out the possibility that there are relevant differences between this situation and other situations, differences that are opaque to you now, in virtue of which this choice would have a different impact on you than other choices did.

A third, related source of evidence is what John Stuart Mill called experiments in living.[17] You can dip your toes in the water by taking classes in finance, taking a summer internship in finance, spending time with people who work in finance, and so on, and, as a result you can collect evidence about yourself in this situation without yet committing to this path. This can certainly help. But insofar as these experiments are informative, they may also be transformative: You may already be changing your preferences as a result of the experience. And, insofar as these experiments are not transformative, they may also not be informative: You may still be making a decision about what to do in a state of ignorance about what it will be like to fully take this path.

Note that with respect to all three sources of evidence (especially the latter two), there is a risk of confabulation and cognitive dissonance that you will also need to address, insofar as you were committed to using evidence over anecdote, testimony, or hope when making important choices. There is also a risk that, if you have more familiarity with some options than with others, then your application of cost–benefit analysis will reflect bias. In some cases, this might mean a bias in favor of the status quo, resulting from the availability heuristic, status quo bias, sunk cost reasoning, and so on.[18] In other cases, it might mean a bias in favor of alternatives to the status quo, resulting from selective and wishful thinking about the nature and value of unknown possible futures.

Alternatively, you can try to decide in a different way. For example, you can use cost–benefit analysis while focusing only on options that you can accurately imagine, where presumably this means going to grad school or law school. You can err on the side of caution, where again presumably this means going to grad school or law school. You can do what makes you happy in the moment. You can make a radical choice, where this could mean any number of things. And so on.

To be clear, these decision procedures can be justified within an effective altruism framework. If evidence and reason indicate that you can do more good by using an alternative to cost–benefit analysis in some cases than by using cost–benefit analysis in all cases, then cost–benefit analysis at the meta level can endorse alternatives to cost–benefit analysis in some cases at the object level. If you reach this conclusion, then you would be a kind of indirect effective altruist, similar to indirect utilitarians who think that utilitarianism at the meta level endorses alternatives to utilitarianism in some cases at the object level.

[17] Mill (2004, p. 59).

[18] For more on cognitive biases, see Kahneman (2011). For related discussion of how these biases can be relevant to effective altruism, see Sebo and Singer (2018).

A challenge for this indirect approach, however, is that in cases involving transformative experience, you lack information about not only which *choice* will be best but also which *decision procedure* will be best. Granted, as above, you can ask what decision procedures tend to be useful for others in this kind of situation and for you in other kinds of situation. But you would still face the same challenges, only at a higher level. The kind of evidence you would need is difficult to collect. Moreover, evidence about which decision procedures work for others in this kind of situation will not tell you which decision procedure will work for you in this kind of situation, and evidence about which decision procedures work for you in other kinds of situation will not tell you which decision procedure will work for you in this kind of situation. And, insofar as this is true, you will once again be at risk of bias if you try to use intuition, speculation, anecdote, and so on to fill in the blanks.

Consider now the challenge that this kind of transformative experience can raise for impartiality. How should you go about making this choice if it might produce *ex ante/ex post* conflict? That is, how should you decide what to do if there is a reasonable chance that becoming an academic, a lawyer, or an investment banker will give you preferences that differ from your current preferences?[19] Should you base your decision entirely on your current preferences, or should you defer at least partly to your expected future preferences? Moreover, if there is no perspective-independent, higher-order way to resolve these differences, how can such a choice be rational?

One option is to endorse *the ex ante privilege view* and act only on the basis of your current preferences. On this view, you can consider the possibility of a change in preferences, but only to inform your current perspective. For example, if you expect your preferences to change, you can ask if your future self has preferences that your present self prefers (and, if so, you can update your current preferences accordingly). Similarly, you can reflect on how this change in preferences could be a problem for your current plans (and, if so, you can update your current plans accordingly). But beyond that, you should not, on this view, consider assigning any independent weight to your expected future preferences. For example, you should not think, "I reject my expected future preferences, and I do not see them as a threat to my current plans. But I will defer partly to them anyway." The benefit of the *ex ante* privilege view is that it coheres with standard decision theory, makes your deliberation relatively simple, and allows you to act only on preferences that you currently identify with. However, the cost of this view is that it arguably conflicts with the kind of impartiality that many effective altruists aspire to. After all, if you expect to have different preferences in the future from the ones you have now, and if you expect to be at least as informed and rational in the

[19] For a classic description of preference change in medical students see Becker et al. (1961).

future as you are now, then why does it make sense for you to privilege your current preferences over your expected future preferences when deciding what to do?

Another option, then, is to accept *the equal weight view* and act on the basis of an evaluative perspective that assigns equal weight to your current preferences and your expected future preferences. As with alternatives to cost–benefit analysis, this view can be justified within an effective altruism framework. In particular, if evidence and reason indicate that you can do more good by assigning weight to multiple, conflicting perspectives, then your current, pro-effective altruist preferences at the meta level can endorse this approach at the object level. Moreover, the equal weight view is arguably more impartial than the *ex ante* privilege view, since, again, it seems arbitrary for you to privilege your current preferences over later, equally legitimate preferences. At the same time, the equal weight view departs from standard decision theory, makes your deliberation more complicated, and may require you to act at least partly on preferences that you currently feel alienated from (including, possibly, non-effective altruist preferences).[20]

If you think that you should assign at least some weight to your expected future preferences, then you face additional questions about how extensive your epistemic humility should be. Consider three such questions as an illustration.

The first question concerns the distinction between actual and possible preferences. Recall that each choice you can make would bring about a different set of beliefs and values. This raises the question: Should you consider only the preferences that you would *actually* have, given the relevant choice, or should you consider also any preferences that you could *possibly* have, independently of the relevant choice? On the former, narrow view, you would consider your expected academic preferences when considering becoming an academic, your expected lawyer preferences when considering becoming a lawyer, and your expected investment banker preferences when considering becoming an investment banker. Whereas on the latter, wide view, you would consider all three sets of preferences when considering all three choices.

The narrow view simplifies deliberation, but it can also lead to bias. After all, why should you think that the preferences that you would have given your actual choices are more likely to be informed or rational than the preferences that you would have given other, possible choices? The narrow view can also lead to problems. For example, what should you do if your expected academic self prefers that you become a lawyer, your expected lawyer self prefers that you become an investment banker, and your expected investment banker self prefers that you become an academic? Meanwhile, the wide view avoids bias and paradox, but it complicates your deliberation.

[20] There are other views as well, including the *ex post privilege view* (act in accordance with your expected future preferences). But we will focus on the *ex ante* privilege view and the equal weight view here. See Pettigrew (forthcoming) for more sophisticated treatments.

The second question concerns intrapersonal versus interpersonal preferences. In particular, should you consider only the preferences that *you* would or could have, or should you consider also the preferences that *others* would or could have? On the former, narrow view, you would consider your actual and possible future preferences, but not others'. Whereas on the latter, wide view, you would consider others' as well. So, for example, even if you could never be from a different nation or generation, you might still have reason to consider the actual or possible preferences of individuals from other nations or generations when deciding what to do.

As with the previous issue, the narrow view simplifies deliberation. It also affirms the importance of personal identity, since it implies that you have reason to assign weight to your own preferences as such (assuming that you care about that). However, the narrow view can also lead to bias and paradox. Meanwhile, the wide view avoids bias and paradox, but it also complicates your deliberation. Granted, you might still have reason to assign extra weight to your own preferences in practice, since many of your plans will require cooperation from your future self. But this is a practical, not a theoretical, consideration, and it might apply more in some cases than in others.

The third question concerns how to determine whose preferences you should not only *consider* assigning weight to but *actually* assign weight to. Should you make use of your current beliefs and values while making this determination, or should you bracket them while doing so? On the former, narrow view, you might determine whose preferences count in part by asking if they share your commitment to effective altruism. On the latter, wide view, you would have to determine whose preferences count independently of whether or not they share this commitment, and so you would likely end up assigning weight to a wider range of preferences.

As before, the narrow view simplifies deliberation, in part by giving you a relatively clear basis for determining who counts. After all, if you bracket all your beliefs and values when stating and evaluating different sets of beliefs and values, then it is unclear how you can state or evaluate them at all. However, the narrow view can also lead to bias. After all, insofar as you require others to share your beliefs and values in order to count, you risk biasing your deliberation. Meanwhile, the wide view will not lead to bias, but it will also complicate your deliberation by raising questions about how you can evaluate other preferences without access to any particular standard of evaluation.

We cannot fully evaluate these issues here. However, we will note that, since narrow and wide answers to these questions tend to have similar pros and cons, we have at least some reason to expect that an effective altruist should take either a narrow or wide approach across the board. Moreover, since effective altruists tend to favor impartiality over partiality, we have at least some reason to think that effective altruists will tend to favor a wide approach to a narrow approach across the board. If this is right, then there is no special question about whether you should, say, assign weight to your expected investment banker preferences. Instead, the question is a much more general one: whether you should assign weight only to your own current preferences or also to many other preferences, actual and possible, future self and other, friend and enemy (where many effective altruists will likely prefer the latter option, perhaps within certain limits).

As this discussion shows, how we approach these problems involving cost–benefit analysis, impartiality, and transformative experience can have a significant impact on our decision-making, and there is no obvious or simple response. In our test case, insofar as you take a cautious approach by restricting yourself to options you can imagine and perspectives you can endorse, you will be able to reason relatively accurately and authentically, but you will not be considering all relevant possibilities. For instance, you might not consider finance or your expected future preferences at all, in spite of the fact that doing so might be necessary for doing the most good possible. Whereas insofar as you proceed more adventurously by allowing for other options and preferences, you will be considering all relevant possibilities, but you might not be reasoning accurately or authentically. For instance, you might decide to pursue finance based on partial deference to expected future preferences that you can barely imagine, let alone endorse.

5. Collective transformation

As noted above, groups can have transformative experiences too, many of which will be relevant for effective altruists trying to decide what to do. These transformative experiences can occur at many levels. For example, many effective altruists live and work together in small groups. They also, in part through these small groups, participate in the effective altruism movement. And they also, in part through the effective altruism movement, contribute to society as a whole.

In each of these cases (and many others), effective altruists are part of a group that has beliefs, values, and preferences in the relevant sense. And, in each case, group members might sometimes face decisions that could change the group in ways that are difficult to anticipate, and which could result in *ex ante/ex post* conflict. For example, you might be considering adding a new roommate to your apartment or implementing a new chore system in your apartment. You might be considering hiring a new staff member at work or implementing a new division of labor at work. You might be considering advocating to expand or redistribute power within the effective altruism movement. You might be considering advocating to open borders or redistribute benefits and burdens within your society. And so on. If so, then, in each case, you need to consider the possibility that these actions will result in transformative change for the group as a whole.

Granted, the details will vary from case to case. For example, the sense in which a household thinks and acts collectively is of course much different than the sense in which a society thinks and acts collectively. Still, insofar as these groups think and act collectively, and insofar as effective altruists can shape what these collective thoughts and actions are, effective altruists will face similar challenges with respect to these groups to those they face as individuals. In particular, in both cases, effective altruists will have many options to consider, where some of these options will be relatively continuous with the status quo and others will be relatively discontinuous with the status quo. And, the options that are relatively continuous with the status quo will be easier for effective altruists to imagine and less likely to result in fundamental change than options that are relatively discontinuous with the status quo. As a result, effective altruists will face the challenges concerning impartial cost–benefit analysis that we considered above.

First, effective altruists will have to decide whether to use cost–benefit analysis and, if so, whether to apply this framework to a narrow or wide range of options. Here they will face the same tension as before. Insofar as they apply cost–benefit analysis to a narrow range of options, they will be able to reason reliably about the options they consider, but they will not be able to consider all relevant options. Whereas, insofar as they use a different decision procedure or consider a wide range of options, they will be able to consider all relevant options, but they will not be able to reason reliably about them.

Second, effective altruists will have to decide whether to make these decisions only from the standpoint of their current preferences, or whether to at least partly defer to other preferences as well, including but not necessarily limited to their own expected future preferences. Here too they will face tension. Insofar as they consider only their current preferences, they will be able to reason authentically, but will not be able to consider all relevant preferences. Whereas insofar as they consider other preferences as well, they will be able to consider all relevant preferences, but they might not be able to reason authentically or rationally.

Of course, to say that we face similar questions in the individual and collective cases is not to say that we should answer them the same way in all cases. For example, it might be that we should take one approach in cases involving individual or small group change, and then another in cases involving medium or large group change. Still, we need to consider each case carefully. Otherwise we might find ourselves simply defaulting to a particular approach, either cautious or adventurous, without appreciating how sweeping its implications can be across cases. For example, at the cautious end of the spectrum, we might find ourselves placing strict limits on the goals that we pursue not only for ourselves but also for society as a whole, simply on the grounds that they happen to be the options we are currently able to imagine and endorse. Whereas at the adventurous end of the spectrum, we might find ourselves pursuing a deeply odd set of personal and societal goals, involving outcomes that we are unable to even imagine, let alone endorse.

6. Conclusion

This chapter has sketched some of the challenges that arise for decision-making in the context of individual and collective transformation, especially as such challenges can arise for the effective altruist. We hope we have shown that the question of how to make informed and rational decisions in transformative contexts is interesting and worth further study within the context of the effective altruism movement. The effective altruist should be concerned about these problems, since, if they act without understanding or managing them, they risk either missing the possibilities that they need to consider in order to do the most good possible, or losing the focus, empirical rigor, and philosophical sophistication that makes effective altruism distinctive.[21]

References

Animal Charity Evaluators. 2018. "Donation Impact." Available at https://animalcharityevaluators.org/donation-advice/donation-impact/.

Becker, Howard S., Blanche Geer, Everett C. Hughes, and Anselm Strauss. 1961. *Boys in White: Student Culture in Medical School.* Chicago: University of Chicago Press.

Briggs. 2015. "Transformative Experience and Interpersonal Utility Comparisons." *Res Philosophica* 92 (2): 189–216.

Dennett, Daniel C. 1992. "The Self as a Center of Narrative Gravity." In *Self and Consciousness: Multiple Perspectives*, F. Kessel, P.M. Cole, and D. Johnson, eds. Hillsdale, NJ: Erlbaum.

Jackson, Fred. 1986. "What Mary Didn't Know." *The Journal of Philosophy* 83 (5): 291–5.

Kahneman, Daniel. 2011. *Thinking, Fast and Slow.* New York: Farrar, Straus and Giroux.

MacAskill, William. 2015. *Doing Good Better.* Norwich: Guardian Faber Publishing.

Mill, John Stuart. 2004. *On Liberty.* New York, Barnes & Noble Books.

Open Philanthropy Project. 2018. "Focus Areas." Available at https://www.openphilanthropy.org/focus.

[21] Thanks to the editors of this book and to the organizers and participants of the 2017 American Philosophical Association Pacific Division Meeting, the Reading Group on Transformative Experience at UNC-Chapel Hill (especially Chris Blake-Turner), the Chapel Hill Workshop on Transformative Experience at UNC-Chapel Hill, and the Conference on the Ethics of Giving at the University of St. Andrews.

Parfit, Derek. 1984. *Reasons and Persons*. Oxford: Oxford University Press.

Pettigrew, Richard. 2015. "Transformative Experience and Decision Theory." *Philosophy and Phenomenological Research* XCI: 3.

Pettigrew, Richard (forthcoming). *Choosing for Changing Selves*. Oxford: Oxford University Press.

Paul, L.A. 2014. *Transformative Experience*. Oxford: Oxford University Press.

Paul, L.A. 2015a. "What You can't expect when you're expecting." *Res Philosophica* 92: 2.

Paul, L.A. 2015b. "Transformative experience: precis and replies." *Philosophy and Phenomenological Research* XCI (3): 760–5.

Paul, L.A. and Kieran Healy. 2017. "Transformative Treatments." *Nous* 52 (2): 320–35.

Paul, L.A. and John Quiggin. 2018. "Real World Problems." *Episteme* 15 (3): 363–82.

Schectman, Marya. 1996. *The Constitution of Selves*. Ithaca: Cornell University Press.

Schweikard, David, and Hans Schmid. 2013. "Collective Intentionality." *Stanford Encyclopedia of Philosophy*, Edward N. Zalta (ed.). Available at https://plato.stanford.edu/archives/sum2013/entries/collective-intentionality/.

Sebo, Jeff. 2015a. "The Just Soul." *Journal of Value Inquiry* 49 (1–2): 131–43.

Sebo, Jeff. 2015b. "Multiplicity, Self-narrative, and Akrasia." *Philosophical Psychology* 28 (4): 589–605.

Sebo, Jeff, and Peter Singer. 2018. "Activism." In *Critical Terms for Animal Studies*, Lori Gruen, ed. Chicago: Chicago University Press.

Singer, Peter. 2015. *The Most Good You Can Do*. New Haven: Yale University Press.

Velleman, J. David. 2009. *How We Get Along*. Cambridge: Cambridge University Press.

5

Should We Give to More Than One Charity?

James Snowden

This chapter examines recent work in normative decision theory to question whether and why a donor concerned with maximizing their expected impact has good reason to diversify their giving between different charities. I proceed in three sections.

In Section 1, I lay out a simplified version of the donor's question: how should a donor give to maximize their expected impact, given their beliefs about which charities are likely to be most effective? I show that, under certain assumptions, maximizing expected utility (MEU)[1] implies the donor should give to only one charity.

In Section 2, I consider whether MEU is a requirement of rationality. I argue that, while it may be *rational*, in the purely decision-theoretic sense, to violate MEU, it is not *reasonable* to do so in the simplified donor's question.

In Section 3, I review the assumptions underpinning the simplified donor's question, to determine what reasons we might actually have for donating to multiple charities, consistent with MEU.

I conclude that there are a number of reasons to donate to multiple charities, although in practice, the most persuasive reasons are more applicable to grant-making institutions giving large sums than the typical donor. This conclusion sits in tension with the observed behaviour of many donors, including those whose primary self-professed goal is to maximize the positive impact of their donations.

1. The simplified donor's question

A donor has just won $500 on a scratch card and decides to donate it all to charity, but is unsure which one will use her donation to the greatest effect.

[1] Throughout, I use 'utility' to refer to a donor's preferences (rather than necessarily self-interested welfare). I define a purely altruistic donor as one whose preferences (utility) are entirely determined by the welfare of others.

Two charities stand out. She can either donate to a charity promoting animal rights or a charity fighting malaria. The animal charity will use the money to significantly improve the lives of one hundred animals. The malaria charity will use the money extend the life of one person by ten years.

After some consideration, she decides that extending a human life is more important than improving the lives of one hundred animals so donates to the malaria charity.

The next day, she wins another $500 and, again, decides to donate it to charity. Which charity should she donate to? Assuming the charities experience no significant change to marginal returns over the interval of $1,000, her choice seems no different in the second case to the first. The amount of good done with the second donation is likely to be approximately the same as the amount of good done with the first. As the donor's beliefs and preferences are the same, her decision should also be the same. She therefore donates, once again, to the malaria charity.

Landsburg concludes from an analogous argument that, "if the problem remains unchanged, the solution should be unchanged as well."[2] If therefore, a donor decides to donate her first $500 to one charity, she should also donate her second $500 to the same charity (so long as her preferences and beliefs remain constant).

This is a compelling case for why a donor should donate to only one charity when she is certain of the outcomes, assuming she is not indifferent between them.

Charitable interventions, however, are often difficult to evaluate and there is always significant uncertainty over the marginal impact of a donation. How should she decide which charity to donate to when she is uncertain of the outcomes?

Decision theory gives us one answer: the donor should maximize expected utility (MEU).

Consider the decision when she is uncertain of the outcomes, i.e., the donor is not sure which charity is more effective. She believes the malaria charity, with each $500, has an equal chance of extending one human life, and having no effect. She believes the animal charity, with each $500, has an equal chance of improving one hundred animal lives, and having no effect. She still has the option of donating the whole $1,000 to one charity or donating $500 to each.

If we assume a cardinally significant utility function, we can assign numerical values to each outcome (unique up to positive affine transformation). If the donor prefers extending one human life to improving one hundred animal lives, the former outcome must receive a higher numerical value than the latter; without loss of generality, suppose the values in question are 1.1 and 1 respectively, with 0 the value of having no effect. If in addition we assume additive separability between the various goods, this data determines the value of the other relevant outcomes, as in the table below.

[2] Landsburg (2009, p. 165).

Table 5.1. State-consequence matrix of Bill's choice with numerical utilities

States: Actions	Both charities ineffective (25%)	Malaria charity ineffective; animal charity effective (25%)	Malaria charity effective; animal charity ineffective (25%)	Both charities effective (25%)	EU
$1,000 to **Malaria charity**	No effect 0	No effect 0	Extend two human lives 2.2	Extend two human lives 2.2	1.1
Split $500 to each	No effect 0	Improve one hundred animal lives 1	Extend one human life 1.1	Extend one human life; Improve one hundred animal lives 2.1	1.05
$1,000 to **Animal charity**	No effect 0	Improve 200 animal lives 2	No effect 0	Improve 200 animal lives 2	1

As donating to the malaria charity has the highest expected utility, MEU prescribes donating only to the malaria charity.

In Section 2, I consider whether MEU is a requirement of rationality. In Section 3, I return to the simplified donor's question, and consider what reasons we might have to give to multiple charities consistent with MEU.

2. Is maximizing expected utility a requirement of rationality?

While expected utility theory remains the dominant theory of rational choice, and a concave Bernoulli utility function remains the textbook explanation of risk aversion, other models, both descriptive and normative, have been developed which permit risk aversion over utilities. Rather than multiplying the realized utility in each state by the probability of that state occurring, these models apply a non-linear weighting to each of the states which depends on the global properties of the lottery, not just what happens in that state. Buchak calls this *global sensitivity*.[3] Prospect theory,[4] rank-dependent expected utility theory,[5] and risk-weighted expected utility theory[6] are three notable examples. If, for example, a globally sensitive decision rule led a donor to place more weight on the worst outcome than implied by its simple probability, it may explain (or even justify if it has normative force) a decision to split donations between charities. In this section I consider whether such a decision rule could be rationally permissible.

[3] Buchak (2013). [4] Kahneman & Tversky (1979). [5] Quiggin (1993).
[6] Buchak (2013).

Broome (1991) gives one line of argument asserting the rational requirement of MEU. He argues that disjunctive states are never simultaneously realized and so, unlike bundles of consumer goods, there can be no interaction effect between them. The value of the outcome in a particular state should not be sensitive to what happens in other disjunctive states. The outcomes in each disjunctive state can therefore be valued independently of each other and a rational agent should be insensitive to the global properties of a gamble.

The defender of global sensitivity would respond that what happens in each state is indeed valued independently of what happens in other states. Nevertheless, the value *contribution* this state-contingent outcome makes to the overall assessment of the lottery may be affected by the outcomes in other states. That is to say that the outcomes could be weighed differently based on global properties of the gamble. Buchak gives an analogy:

> Consider two scenarios, one which is better for one group of people and one which is better for a different group of people . . . One thing that might determine how these reasons are weighed is which people are the worst-off in each scenario: reasons concerning their well-being might count for more. Now let us introduce a third group of people, each of whom are benefitted equally by both scenarios. How things go for individuals in this third group does not change the reasons concerning the individuals in the first two groups, but it might directly affect how relatively well-off the members of each group are in each scenario: it might change which individuals are the worst-off and therefore which reasons should be weighted more heavily in determining which situation is better overall.[7]

The first thing to note is that the value in this analogy is located, not in mutually exclusive states, but in simultaneously occurring people. The egalitarian view, which Buchak puts forward, is equivalent to accepting global sensitivity when the value is located in people rather than states. On a non-instrumental egalitarian view, global considerations do matter. This view is justified not by appeal to the impact it has on the working of society but by a principle that inequality is objectionable for its own sake.

The strength of egalitarianism is that it appeals to our moral sense of distributive justice. People should be treated equally because it is unfair that they should have different outcomes based on no fault or choice of their own.[8] There does not however seem to be a corresponding moral intuition when the locations of the good are across probabilistic states rather than people.

The view that we have a reason to distribute welfare equally across mutually exclusive states (either prudentially or morally) therefore seems on less sure footing than the view that we have a reason to distribute welfare equally across

[7] Buchak (2013, pp. 167–8). [8] Cohen (1989); Arneson (1997); Temkin (2001).

society. According to Buchak, we may weigh outcomes in a non-linear way without violating *decision-theoretic rationality*. But in order to do so *reasonably*, there must be some substantive justification for doing so. When the value is located in people, this justification is an appeal to our sense of distributive justice. When the value is located in mutually exclusive states, it is not obvious what this justification might be.

I turn now to a special feature of the simplified donor's question which implies that the only justifiable choice is to donate to only one charity.

This feature is that the value which accrues from the lottery is other-regarding. What is at stake therefore seems to be a question of external value rather than her own subjective preference.

Consider a modified way of presenting the donor's question. The donor is choosing between donating all $1,000 to the malaria charity (malaria) or splitting between the malaria and animal charities (Split).[9] If she donates $1,000 to the malaria charity, two people will have a 50 per cent chance of benefitting (in the states in which the malaria charity is effective). If she chooses Split, one person will have a 50 per cent chance of benefitting (in the states in which the malaria charity is effective) and one hundred animals will have a 50 per cent chance of benefitting (in the states in which the animal charity is effective). These chances are independently determined.

Table 5.2. Outcomes across states and beneficiaries

Actions	States: Beneficiaries	Neither effective (25%)	Only Animal (25%)	Only Malaria (25%)	Both effective (25%)
Malaria	Person 1	0	0	1.1	1.1
	Person 2	0	0	1.1	1.1
	Animals 1–100	0	0	0	0
	Total	0	0	2.2	2.2
Split	Person 1	0	0	1.1	1.1
	Person 2	0	0	0	0
	Animals 1–100	0	1	0	1
	Total	0	1	1.1	2.1
Malaria*	Person 1	0	0	1.1	1.1
	Person 2	0	1.1	0	1.1
	Animals 1–100	0	0	0	0
	Total	0	1.1	1.1	2.2

[9] I set aside the possibility of donating only to the animal charity in this version of the question.

As the donor values helping each person more than one hundred animals, choosing malaria has higher expected value. But splitting her donation has a more equal spread of value across disjunctive states. If the donor is sufficiently risk averse, she has some reason to split her donation.

Now consider a hypothetical modification to the malaria action. Call it *malaria*. Rather than person 2 benefitting when only the malaria charity is effective, he instead benefits when only the animal charity is effective instead.

My argument is as follows:

1) If an action results in (weakly) higher expected welfare for each beneficiary than another alternative, it must be (weakly) preferred. (Premise).
2) For every beneficiary, the lottery faced is the same under malaria and malaria*. (Premise).
3) Malaria is just as good as malaria*. (From *1* and *2*).
4) *State-wise dominance:* if an action gives weakly better outcomes in every state, and a strictly better outcome in at least one state than another alternative, it must be strictly preferred. (Premise).
5) Malaria* gives a weakly preferred outcome than Split in every state, and a strictly preferred outcome to Split in at least one state. (Premise).
6) Malaria* is better than Split. (From *4* and *5*).
7) Malaria is better than Split. (From *3* and *6*).

The critical premise is (*1*); (*2*) is true by construction; (*4*) is widely accepted; and (*5*) is true by virtue of the donor placing more value in helping one person than one hundred animals.

(1) implies that a choosing agent should be indifferent between malaria and malaria*, as each person has the same expected welfare under each action.

Malaria is just as good as *malaria*, from the perspective of each beneficiary, regardless of their risk preferences. The fact that it is a different, equiprobable state in which these benefits accrue is of no importance to person 2 as he has the same probability distribution over benefits. But the risk-averse globally sensitive donor does in fact prefer malaria* to malaria, as her utility ("Total" in the table above) is more evenly spread across states.[10]

Risk-weighted expected utility theory implies that the value of states should be weighed differently depending on the rank order they receive within the lottery. But whose rank order should this be? Even if person 2 is globally sensitive, the malaria lottery is still identical for him to the *malaria* lottery. The rank-ordering therefore must be that of the choosing agent, once the value has been aggregated between beneficiaries. For the globally sensitive agent, there is therefore a

[10] I assume here that the donor's utility in each state is given by the sum of the welfare of the different possible beneficiaries. I later argue that the prescriptions are invariant to an egalitarian social welfare function. I consider other possible non-additive welfare functions in Section 3.

disagreement between the evaluation of the lotteries with respect to each of the beneficiaries taken individually, and the evaluation of the lottery taken as a whole across all beneficiaries.

Whether this disagreement is justified may depend on what kind of attitude global sensitivity is. Is it just a subjective preference capturing my own attitude towards risk? In prudential cases, if one's attitude towards risk is just a single preference among many, this may permit some degree of risk aversion. But in the altruistic case, where what is at stake is external value, it seems unjustifiable to distinguish between two actions resulting in the same probability distribution of value to each beneficiary, whatever one's own attitude to risk. To do so would imply that the donor's utility function is (at least partially) non-altruistic as decisions are informed by considerations unrelated to the beneficiaries' probability = distribution of welfare.

I note one common critique against (1). An *ex post* egalitarian may claim that what matters is not just the total value of welfare in each state, but equality of the ex post distribution of welfare. (1) therefore may not hold if it increases the likelihood of an unequal distribution of welfare.[11] This argument does not apply to the donor's question; Malaria is no more likely to result in less equal outcomes than *malaria*, and indeed is less likely to result in unequal outcomes if the value of distributional equality holds only over people, rather than including animals.

In sum, the prescription to donate to only one charity in this case relies on weaker principle than MEU; the principle that an altruistic donor should prefer an action over an alternative if that action results in higher expected welfare for each beneficiary.

3. When is it consistent with MEU to donate to multiple charities?

If splitting donations between charities is to be considered reasonable, it must be because the decision problem the donor faces changes in some way between the first $500 and the second $500.

Classical economists usually account for an investor splitting their spending between risky investments through the assumption of diminishing marginal utility of wealth. Alternatively, if we conceive of charities as firms producing an outcome the investor values, splitting may be justified by diminishing marginal returns. In both cases, the investor's behaviour can be explained consistent with the assumption that they are following MEU.

[11] Voorhoeve and Fleurbaey (2012).

There are therefore three broad possibilities, which might make splitting donations consistent with MEU:

1) At least one of the charities experiences diminishing marginal returns over the interval of the donation.
2) Donations to one charity increase the marginal returns of donations to the other charity.
3) The donor has diminishing marginal utility over the amount given to each charity, the outcomes produced by each charity, or the outcomes produced by the combined donation.

I consider each in turn.

3.1 At least one of the charities experiences diminishing marginal returns over the interval of the donation

Donations to one charity may make future donations to that charity less cost-effective. Suppose a charity prioritized financing the most important activities with the first $500, meaning the second $500 is less effective on the margin. Then it seems quite reasonable for the donor to split his donation between the two, prioritizing the most important activities of each. However, in reality, diminishing marginal returns are only likely to be substantial over the interval of a large donation, or for a small charity.[12]

But a donor may also value less direct outcomes from each donation, which experience diminishing marginal returns. Some possibilities are:

(i) **Value of information.** Suppose, by donating some to a charity, Bill finds out more about that organization, which allows him to make better decisions in the future. There is diminishing marginal information from donating to each charity.

(ii) **Incentives for engagement.** Suppose a foundation wanted to incentivize charities to go through the time-consuming process needed for a grant application. While the foundation is risk neutral, it knows the charities are risk averse and are more likely to apply for a greater chance of receiving some funding, than a smaller chance of receiving a lot of funding. There are diminishing marginal positive incentives to give to each charity.

[12] Although evidential decision theory (EDT) offers an exception. Under EDT, a donor's choice provides evidence of the choices that other donors will make in similar situations, meaning the world in which a donor gives all to one charity is a world in which other donors are also more likely to give only to that charity. If this is strong enough evidence, the difference in total donations may be enough to cause diminishing marginal returns.

(iii) **Signalling.** If an enthusiastic donor wants to advocate to others to donate to a charity, it may help to provide a strong credible signal that they believe it is a good donation target. There are diminishing marginal signalling benefits to giving to each charity.

Practically, each of these considerations seem most likely to be applicable to larger giving institutions or charity evaluators, who are likely to use additional information to make different decisions, have formal grant application processes, or invest in raising additional funds for their preferred charities.

3.2 Donations to one charity increase the marginal returns of donations to the other charity

Donations to one charity may make donations to the other charity more cost-effective. For example, one charity may improve correct diagnosis of pneumonia, and another might improve correct treatment given a correct diagnosis. The good outcomes from their combined work (correct treatment for people with pneumonia), is a multiplicative factor of each charity's work, and so donating to one charity makes donating to the other more valuable.

Again, this consideration seems most likely to be applicable to giving institutions, who may choose to invest in a particular focus area where the outputs of different charities interact in a meaningful way.

3.3 The donor has diminishing marginal utility over the amount given to each charity, the outcomes produced by each charity, or the outcomes produced by the combined donation

There are two possibilities:

(iv) **Non-altruistic preferences.** The experience of giving the second $500 to his first-preference charity may be less personally fulfilling than giving the first $500 to his second-preference charity. Or perhaps there is a large reputational benefit to being known to give to multiple charities. These preferences could be cashed out altruistically if the donor believes that greater personal fulfilment would cause them to donate more in the future.

(v) **Diminishing marginal moral value.** A donor may believe that it is particularly important (morally) that they have contributed some to a particular cause, and this importance does not scale linearly with the amount donated. For example, moral satisficing theories imply a requirement to contribute some to a cause, as may a commitment to meet particular deontological obligations, or requirements of being a virtuous person.

Analogously, for both non-altruistic preferences and diminishing marginal moral value, the donor may have diminishing marginal utility over the *outcomes* of each charity, rather than the *amount donated*. For example, they might have a particular desire (or duty) to save at least one life, or to help at least one hundred animals, that does not scale linearly with the quantum of the outcomes achieved. The donor might also experience diminishing marginal utility over the outcomes of the two charities combined. For example, they may experience particular regret (or fail morally) if they fail to create *any* positive outcomes.

In sum, there are several reasons an individual donor may choose to donate to multiple charities, each of which leads to diminishing marginal (relative) returns over each charity, or diminishing marginal utility over the amount donated to each charity, the outcomes created by each charity, or the outcomes of the combined donation.

While I leave it to the reader to think carefully about how each of these reasons might apply to their own situation, some general comments may be informative. It seems to me that (1) and (2) seem most likely to apply to larger giving institutions rather than the typical donor and (3) involves, at least in part, caring about features of the decision which are not directly related to the expected impact of one's giving. I therefore conclude that the typical donor trying to maximize their expected impact will most likely find the combination of reasons above insufficient to justify splitting their donations.

4. Conclusion

In Section 1, I showed that in a simplified decision problem, maximizing expected utility (under the assumptions of additive separability and a cardinally significant utility function) implies that donors should donate to only one charity, rather than diversifying their donations.

In Section 2, I argued that the prescription to maximize expected utility is particularly strong in the case of altruistic, rather than self-interested preferences, as it relies on the intuitively compelling principle that if an action results in (weakly) higher expected welfare for each beneficiary than another alternative, it should be (weakly) preferred.

In Section 3, I considered several reasons an individual might have for diversifying their charitable donations. I conclude that these reasons are unlikely to apply to the typical donor trying to maximize their expected impact, implying that the observed behaviour of many donors is either explained by non-altruistic motivations, or simply mistaken.

References

Arneson, Richard. "Egalitarianism and the Undeserving Poor," *The Journal of Political Philosophy* 5 No. 3 (1997), pp. 1–24.

Broome, John. 1991. *Weighing Goods*. Cambridge, Massachusetts: Blackwell.

Buchak, Lara. 2013. *Risk and Rationality*. Oxford: Oxford University Press.

Cohen, Gerald. 1989. "On the Currency of Egalitarian Justice." *Ethics* 99 (4): 906–44.

Kahneman, Daniel, and Amos Tversky. 1979. "Prospect theory: An analysis of decision under risk." *Econometrica* 47 (2): 263–91.

Landsburg, Steven. 2009. *More Sex is Safer Sex: The Unconventional Wisdom of Economics*. London: Simon and Shuster.

McClennen, Edward. 1983. "Sure-Thing Doubts." In *Foundations of Utility and Risk Theory with Applications*, B. Stigum and F. Wenstop, eds.

McClennen, Edward. 1990. *Rationality and Dynamic Choice*. Cambridge: Cambridge University Press.

Parfit, Derek. 1973. "Later selves and moral principles." In *Philosophy and Personal Relations*, A. Montefiore, ed. Montreal: McGill-Queens, pp. 137–69.

Quiggin, John. 1993. *Generalized Expected Utility Theory: The Rank-Dependent Model*. Netherlands: Springer Science+Business Media Dordrecht.

Temkin, Larry. 2001. "Egalitarianism: A Complex, Individualistic, and Comparative Notion." In *Philosophical Issues*, volume 11, Ernie Sosa and Enriquea Villanueva, eds. Oxford: Blackwell Publishers, pp. 327–52.

Voorhoeve, Alex and Fleurbaey, Marc. 2012. "Egalitarianism and the Separateness of Persons." *Utilitas* 24: 381–98.

Wenar, L. 2010. "Poverty is No Pond: Challenges for the Affluent." In *Giving Well: The Ethics of Philanthropy*, P. Illingworth, T. Pogge, and L. Wenar, eds. Oxford: Oxford University Press, pp. 104–32.

6

A Brief Argument for the Overwhelming Importance of Shaping the Far Future

Nick Beckstead

1. Introduction

The purpose of this chapter is to explain and illustrate the plausibility of the following argument:

1. There is a non-negligible chance that humanity will survive for millions, billions, or trillions of years.
2. If there is a non-negligible chance that humanity will survive for millions, billions, or trillions of years, then the expected value of the future is astronomically great.
3. Some of the actions humanity could take would shape the expected trajectory along which our descendants develop in non-negligible ways.
4. If the expected value of the future is astronomically great and some of the actions humanity could take would shape the trajectory along which our descendants develop in non-negligible ways, then what matters most (in expectation) is that we do what is best (in expectation) for the general trajectory along which our descendants develop over the coming millions, billions, or trillions of years.
5. Therefore, what matters most (in expectation) is that we do what is best (in expectation) for the general trajectory along which our descendants develop over the coming millions, billions, or trillions of years.

The argument considers only how *good* it is to shape the far future, in an impartial sense. It does not address deontological considerations. In Section 2, I defend the first premise of the above argument. In Section 3, I defend four normative assumptions which I will use to support the second premise. In Section 4, I defend the third and fourth premises of the argument, which concern how our actions might affect the far future.[1]

[1] This chapter is a succinct presentation of material from my PhD dissertation (Beckstead (2013)). The dissertation itself was in turn primarily influenced by Bostrom (2002, 2003, 2013), but also partly

2. How long could humanity survive?

2.1 How long could life on Earth last?

Consider the following passage from the end of *Reasons and Persons*. Derek Parfit writes:

> I believe that if we destroy mankind, as we now could, this outcome would be much worse than most people think. Compare three outcomes:
>
> (1) Peace.
> (2) A nuclear war that kills 99% of the world's existing population.
> (3) A nuclear war that kills 100%.
>
> (2) would be worse than (1), and (3) would be worse than (2). Which is the greater of these two differences? Most people believe that the greater difference is between (1) and (2). I believe that the difference between (2) and (3) is *very much* greater.
>
> ... The Earth will remain inhabitable for at least another billion years. Civilization began only a few thousand years ago. If we do not destroy mankind, these few thousand years may be only a tiny fraction of the whole of civilized human history. The difference between (2) and (3) may thus be the difference between this tiny fraction and all of the rest of this history. If we compare this possible history to a day, what has occurred so far is only a fraction of a second.[2]

What are the chances that we will last this long?

When I say "we," "civilization," or "humanity," I am not just talking about the species *Homo sapiens*. Very few species last for anything like 1 billion years, most dying off within 10 million years. I am asking, "How long will people exist in the future?" Here, I mean "people" in the sense of "sentient beings that matter," which, I am assuming, will include our descendants.

When we include our intelligent descendants, it is not absurd to consider the possibility that civilization continues for a billion years, until the Earth becomes uninhabitable. We cannot know the frequency with which civilizations like ours survive that long, or the "objective chance" that we will survive that long. But we can say something about what the reasonable betting odds would be with respect to the claim that our descendants will survive for at least 1 billion years.

Several potential catastrophes—including nuclear war, catastrophic climate change, asteroid impacts, and potential risks from synthetic biology and advanced artificial intelligence—have a reasonable chance of destroying all human life in the next century. How likely humans are to survive into the far future in the face

preceded and influenced by Parfit (1984, 2011) and Broome (1992, 2010). I am grateful to Theron Pummer and Pablo Stafforini for their extensive comments and suggestions on this version of the paper.

[2] D. Parfit (1984).

of these existential risks depends on what decisions society makes.[3] Given the great uncertainty involved, including uncertainty about what people will do to prepare for these risks, it would seem overconfident to have a very high subjective probability or a very low subjective probability that humans will survive for the full billion years. Having a very high or low probability in this claim, such as less than 1 percent or greater than 99 percent, would require much greater certainty about the future than it is reasonable to have. Obviously, choosing any specific number here would be arbitrary. To be conservative, I will assume that our subjective probability in this claim should be at least 1 percent. My argument would, of course, work only better if, as I believe, we are more likely to survive this long, since that would increase the expected value of preventing premature extinction or otherwise shaping the far future.

2.2 Beyond a billion years?

The lion's share of the expected duration of our existence comes from the possibility that our descendants colonize planets outside our solar system. There are many stars that we may be able to reach with future technology (about 10^{13} in our supercluster). Some of them will probably have planets that are hospitable to life, perhaps many of these planets could be made hospitable with appropriate technological developments. Some of these are near stars that will burn for much longer than our sun, some for as much as 100 trillion years.[4] If multiple locations were colonized, the risk of total destruction would dramatically decrease, since it would take independent global disasters or a cosmological catastrophe to destroy civilization. Because of this, it is possible that our descendants would survive until the very end, and that there could be extraordinarily large numbers of them.[5]

This scenario seems speculative and discussion of it may seem more fitting for science fiction than for serious academic philosophy. I readily acknowledge that we cannot be confident in very concrete predictions about the long-term future. At the same time, it would seem unreasonable to be highly confident that our descendants will not colonize space. After all, it is plausible that colonizing space is technologically possible, and that given 1 billion years of technological development our descendants would be able to do many of the technologically possible things they would be interested in doing. And as we've said, if our descendants *do* colonize space, the risk of extinction becomes much lower. In light of these

[3] See Bostrom (2002) for an introduction to the concept of existential risk. See Bostrom (2014) for a discussion of artificial intelligence as a potential existential risk.

[4] Adams (2008, p. 39).

[5] I am here bracketing questions that arise in connection with infinite populations. In addition to Chapter 7 of my dissertation, see Bostrom (2011), Askell (2018), and Clark (ms), for further discussion.

considerations, it is a live possibility that if our descendants do survive for the next billion years they will colonize many stars and survive for the full 100 trillion years ahead of us. As above, this doesn't tell us anything about the *objective* probability of our descendants eventually colonizing space, but it tells us that the *subjective probability*, in the sense of "reasonable betting odds," is not extremely low. Therefore, we should assign colonization and long-term survival a subjective probability greater than 1/100, conditional on surviving for a billion years.[6] We should therefore agree that the unconditional probability of this event is at least one in 10,000 (multiplying 1/100 and 1/100). Therefore, there are at least 1/10,000 × 100 trillion years = 10 billion expected years of civilization ahead of us.

3. A framework for estimating the value of a chance of a long future

The goal of this section is to outline a method of estimating the value of the future which would give approximately correct answers in some class of cases that lets us say something helpful about how good the future could be, supposing we were allowed to know everything about what happened in the future. We'll use this method, together with the conclusions of the previous section, to argue that a long future is extremely important.

I find it helpful to imagine we're designing a computer program that makes this estimate for us. What we want is a computer program that gets fed a possible history of the world, and then gives us an estimate of how good that history of the world is. We don't know exactly what this computer program should look like, but my idea is to say a few things about what it might look like, and then reach some conclusions on the basis of those assumptions.

First, the program would divide the history of the world into *periods*, chunks of time of some large duration (such as 100, 1,000, or 10,000 years). Second, for each of these periods, it would look at what happens during that period. On the basis of what happens during that period, it would assign that period a score which says how good that period was. This score could be a number, but in giving the value of a period a number we need not assume that periods could, in principle, be given precise values. Like Parfit, we might hold that only rough or imprecise

[6] Returning to this essay in 2018, I now believe that ≥1 percent credence is an even more overly modest estimate of the odds that our descendants will eventually colonize other stars than I used to (conditional on our long-term survival). In 2014, I surveyed the literature on this topic, conducted interviews with a handful of experts, wrote an overview Beckstead (2014), and spoke with the authors of Armstrong and Sandberg (2013), which put me in a position to make this case more strongly than I could when this piece was originally written as part of my dissertation. I have not edited the numbers throughout because the original claim is sufficient for my argument.

evaluation is possible, even in principle.[7] Third, it would use these scores to come up with an estimate of the value of the whole history.

Obviously, you might get different answers depending on how you carve up the world into periods of time, and there is no "privileged" way of carving up history into periods. This does not concern me because I am designing a method for making a rough approximation in a particular class of cases, rather than trying to provide a precise "final theory" of population ethics. It is not worrying if some approximation technique calls for judgment or might have been done any various ways that would give moderately different answers. Many valuable approximation techniques have these properties.

Equally obviously, it would be totally impractical to build something that could execute this computer program. Furthermore, if we were going to actually make this computer program, rather than just talk about its properties, we would need to do a lot more to spell out each of these steps. I am not going to try to spell out the second step much at all, and we'll see that this is a strength of my strategy. But I would like to propose some reasonable conditions for how the third step should go. These conditions imply that the third step should proceed by something like adding up the scores across periods.

3.1 Period Independence

The first, and most important, normative assumption that I will use is:

Period Independence: By and large, how well history goes as a whole is a function of how well things go during each period of history; when things go better during a period, that makes history as a whole go better; when things go worse during a period, that makes history as a whole go worse; and the extent to which it makes history as a whole go better or worse is independent of what happens in other such periods.

By "independent" I mean *evaluatively* independent, rather than causally independent. Obviously, what happens now can have profound causal impacts on the future. But when we ignore such causal effects, Period Independence claims that the additional value of things going better during a certain period can't depend on what happens in other periods.

It is easier to understand Period Independence if we're clearer about what it rules out. To do that, let's first consider an analogy. Some philosophers argue that how well a person's life goes depends on the "shape" of their life, and not just the

[7] Parfit (1984, p. 431) and (2016).

total amount of good that they enjoy at each moment. For instance, two lives might contain the same amount of moment-by-moment well-being, but in one of these lives the moment-by-moment well-being may increase over time, whereas in the other it would decrease over time. Some philosophers have argued that, in such cases, though each life contains the same amount of moment-by-moment well-being, the life with increasing moment-by-moment well-being is better because of its "shape".[8] Period Independence says that, in general, there is no such dependence on "shape" across different periods of history.[9]

For an illustration of Period Independence, consider the following possible histories of the world:

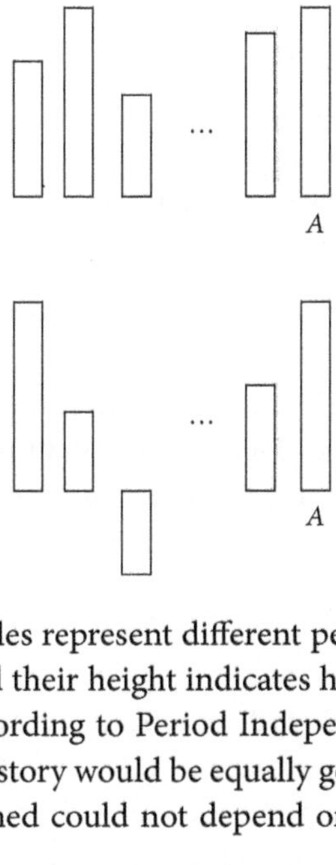

In this graph, the rectangles represent different periods of history. Their width indicates their duration, and their height indicates how well things go during the period (per unit time). According to Period Independence, adding or removing period *A* from the world's history would be equally good in either case. How good it was that period *A* happened could not depend on how well things go during other periods.

Therefore, we can calculate the value of the whole of history by starting from the beginning and asking how much the first period contributes, and then asking how much the second period contributes, and so forth. The result is that the value of the whole of history is, approximately, the sum of the value of what happens in each period. In saying this, I am not taking a stand on aggregative questions to do with whether many very small benefits can add up to a very large benefit.[10]

[8] Velleman (2000).

[9] The aforementioned shape-dependent view of lifetime well-being will, if true, introduce a margin of error into my calculations, insofar as some people live in more than one period. But again, I am here offering a method for rough approximation only.

[10] That is, I am not here endorsing what Temkin (2012) calls an "additive-aggregationist" approach.

3.1.1 A rationale for Period Independence

To appreciate the rationale for Period Independence, consider the following scenario:

Asteroid Analysis: World leaders hire experts to do a cost–benefit analysis and determine whether it is worth it to fund an Asteroid Deflection System. Thinking mostly of the interests of future generations, the leaders decide that it would be well worth it.

And then consider the following ending:

Our Surprisingly Relevant History: After the analysis has been done, some scientists discover that life was planted on Earth by other people who now live in an inaccessible region of spacetime. In the past, there were a lot of them, and they had really great lives. Upon learning this, world leaders decide that since there has already been a lot of value in the universe, it is much less important that they build this device than they previously thought.

On some views in population ethics, the world leaders might be right. For example, if we believe that additional lives have diminishing marginal value, the total value of the future could depend significantly on how many lives there have been in the past. Intuitively, it would seem unreasonable to claim that how good it would be to build the Asteroid Deflection System depends on this information about our distant past. Parfit and Broome appeal to analogous arguments when attacking diminishing marginal value and average views in population ethics.[11]

3.1.2 Objection: Period Independence ignores some important "shape" considerations

Some people may object to Period Independence on the grounds that how well history goes depends on averages across periods of time, how well things go at the best times, how badly things go at the worst times, whether things are getting better or worse, variety across periods of time, equality across periods of time, or shared traditions across periods of time. Defenders of Period Independence can count these holistic considerations *within* periods, but not *across* periods. I have a few responses to this.

First, we can reply that in variants of Our Surprisingly Relevant History, holistic concern for these ideals will have implausible implications, and insist that we are more certain that it would be irrational to change one's decision in Our Surprisingly Relevant History than we are that these concerns can rationally be applied across periods. By taking this strategy, we may fail to accommodate everything that certain people believe, but we might still have a more plausible view, all things considered.

[11] See Parfit (1984, p. 420) and Broome (2004, p. 197) for examples.

Second, we can reply that decreasing existential risk and shaping the far future generally are good with respect to at least some of these concerns. For example, if we avoid premature extinction, then there is reason to believe that the human condition will improve. And thus, there is reason to believe that the peaks of human achievement lie ahead of us. Therefore, recognizing a non-period-independent value which depends on how well things go during the best times or whether things are getting better would make it more important to improve the far future. Likewise, the worst parts of human history may be in the past anyway, so a focus on the worst periods of history would neither tell significantly in favor nor significantly against shaping the far future for the better. In addition, causing human civilization to last longer seems like it would probably make things better in terms of preservation of traditions.

Third, we can claim that the future is neither expectably good nor expectably bad with respect to some of these ideals, so we don't need to worry about those ideals. In the cases of equality and variety, it is hard to tell what the relevant values are, and even harder to predict the empirical facts that are relevant to the value assessments. So it's unclear that taking account of these factors would substantially affect the expected value of shaping the far future.

Finally, if we decide that some of these considerations are relevant and significant for some comparisons we would like to make, we can note that as a limitation of our analysis and try to adjust for it.

3.2 Additionality

If this argument is going to work, we need to establish that:

Additionality: If "standard good things" happen during a period of history—there are people, the people have good lives, society is organized appropriately, etc.—that makes that period go better than it would have if nothing good had happened.

If this were not true, then a future without prosperous future people might be no worse than a future with no sentient life.

What is the intuition behind Additionality? It goes back to our "computer program" analogy above. When we write the computer program that estimates the value of a possible future, it makes sense for that computer program to look at how well things go during each period in that possible future. And it seems that in order to know how well things go during a given period, the computer program should just have to look at qualitative facts about what happens during that period, such as what kind of "standard good things" are happening during that period. All the standard good things that are happening now make the present period better than if it had been a "blank" period in which no standard good things happen. So if similar good things happen in future periods, that should make them better as well.

According to strict Person-Affecting Views, the fact that a person's life would go well if they lived could not, in itself, imply that it would be in some way better to create them.[12] Why not? Many defenders of Person-Affecting Views argue that, since the person was never created, there is no person who could have benefited from being created.[13] On this type of view, it would be important to ensure that there are future generations only if it would somehow benefit people alive today or people who have lived in the past (perhaps by adding meaning to their lives). If one does not accept a view of this kind, I see no reason to think that it doesn't matter whether standard good things happen in the future, or to deny that the existence of people with good lives is one of these standard good things.

I think it would be very strange to respond to my arguments by appealing to a strict Person-Affecting View because these views have obviously implausible implications when considering cases involving human extinction. Consider this problematic case, for instance:

Mass Sterilization: Some terrorists engineer a highly contagious, incurable virus, and they spread it throughout the world. This virus causes sterilization in all people that are infected, but causes no other health problems. Within 150 years, no humans exist.

Although strict Person-Affecting Views can tell a story about why it would be bad for these terrorists to disperse this virus, it seems that they cannot tell the whole story. They can appeal to the fact that many people alive had an interest in having children or giving their lives meaning by perpetuating human civilization, but they cannot appeal to the fact that it is simply a great loss, in itself, for human civilization to come to an end. This is brought out by considering a variant of the case:

Voluntary Extinction: All people collectively decide not to have any children. No one is ever made upset, irritated, or otherwise negatively affected by the decision. In fact, everyone is made a little better off.

As Temkin points out, it seems like it would be bad if people opted for voluntary extinction when they could have produced a future filled with a lot of standard good things, the benefits to present people notwithstanding.[14]

[12] For discussion of strict as well as moderate Person-Affecting Views, see Chapter 4 of Beckstead (2013).

[13] For further discussion, see Roberts (2011); Arrhenius and Rabinowicz (2015); and Pummer (2019).

[14] Temkin (2008). For further relevant discussion, see the *Canadian Journal of Philosophy* Volume 47, Issue 2–3 (2017) on the theme "Ethics and Future Generations".

We can contrast strict Person-Affecting Views with *moderate* Person-Affecting Views. On these moderate views, creating people who would have good lives if they lived is good; it just often isn't as good as improving the lives of existing people by equivalent amounts. If this type of view is correct, it may be that additional future periods where standard good things happen might be less valuable than the current period with its standard good things. A fairly natural way to spell this out would be to say that these future periods have only some fraction of the value that they would have had if the value were calculated in a non-Person-Affecting way. If this fraction is not unreasonably small, it will not substantially affect our conclusions about the value of shaping the far future.

3.3 Temporal Neutrality

The next important assumption is:

Temporal Neutrality: the value of a particular period is independent of when it occurs.

This assumption is not very controversial among philosophers, but many economists reject it. In their view, we should count benefits that come in the farther future as intrinsically less important than benefits that come in the nearer future, and the value of future benefits should decrease exponentially with time. Since Parfit, Cowen, and Broome have convincingly argued against this position and few philosophers believe it anyway, I will only briefly explain why it should be rejected.[15]

Some rather obvious examples suggest that there is no fundamental significance to when future benefits and harms take place. To take an example from Parfit, suppose I bury some broken glass in a forest. In one case, a child steps on the broken glass ten years from now and is injured. In another case, a child steps on the broken glass 110 years from now and is injured in precisely the same way. If we discount for time, then we will count the first alternative as much worse than the second. If we use a 5 percent discount rate per year, we should count this alternative as over one hundred times worse. This is very implausible.

Economists often appeal to two arguments for pure temporal discounting. First, they argue that people want to discount the future and governments should echo the will of the people. As Parfit points out, there is a difference between the questions:

1. If people decide to do *A*, what should governments do?
2. Should people decide to do *A*?[16]

[15] Parfit (1984, Appendix F); Cowen and Parfit (1992); Broome (1992).
[16] Parfit (1984, Appendix F).

I am arguing about what people ought to decide, so the democratic argument has no clear relevance.

Second, some economists argue that if we do not discount future benefits, we would have to spend far too much of our resources on future generations.[17] This assumes that we are required to do whatever is best. It is a familiar fact that if we are required to do whatever is best, life will be demanding for us. That is a classic objection to the view that we are required to do whatever is best. If we want to avoid these demands, we should revise the view that we are required to do whatever is best, perhaps placing some limits on how much we should be required to sacrifice to promote good outcomes. We should not make implausible claims about the comparative badness of exactly when children step on glass in forests.

3.4 Risk Neutrality

My argument relies essentially on expected value considerations. I assume:

Risk Neutrality: The value of an uncertain prospect equals its expected value.

This assumption is important because, in all probability, any given project will do very little to affect the long-term prospects of civilization. I argue that, because the potential value of the future is extremely large, reducing existential risk even by a small probability (or having some small probability of creating some other positive trajectory change) is very important. The most straightforward way to do this is to use the Risk Neutrality assumption to argue that reducing existential risk by some fraction is as important as achieving that fraction of the potential value of the future.[18]

3.5 Objection: Don't these assumptions entail the Repugnant Conclusion?

What's true is that my argument rules out one way of avoiding the Repugnant Conclusion, namely, theories according to which there is diminishing marginal value of population across periods. Three strategies (lexical views, critical-level theories, and theories espousing diminishing marginal value across periods) cover most of the plausible ways of avoiding the Repugnant Conclusion within a broadly welfarist axiology. Since I am taking only one strategy off the table (diminishing

[17] Posner (2004).

[18] The argument would still go through if the assumption were revised to allow for a non-extreme degree of risk aversion. See Buchak (2013).

marginal value across periods), it does not follow that my assumptions entail the Repugnant Conclusion.[19]

4. What do these assumptions suggest about the value of shaping the far future?

In thinking about how we might shape the far future, I've found it useful to use the concept of a world's development trajectory, or just *trajectory* for short. As I use the term, a trajectory is a rough summary of the way the future will unfold over time. The summary includes various facts about the world that matter from a macro perspective, such as how rich people are, what technologies are available, how happy people are, how developed our science and culture is along various dimensions, and how well things are going all-things-considered at different points of time. It may help to think of the trajectory as a collection of graphs, where each graph in the collection has time on the x-axis and one of these other variables on the y-axis.[20]

With that concept in place, consider three different types of benefits from doing good. First, doing something good might have *proximate benefits*—this is the name I give to the fairly short-run, fairly predictable benefits that we think about when we cure some child's blindness, save a life, or help an old lady cross the street. Second, there are benefits from *speeding up development*. In many cases, ripple effects from good ordinary actions result in speeding up development in the sense that they make the world move along its trajectory more quickly. Saving a child's life might cause their country's economy to develop slightly quicker, or make certain technological or cultural innovations arrive more quickly. Third, in other cases, our actions may slightly or significantly alter the world's development trajectory. I call these shifts *trajectory changes*. If we ever prevent an existential catastrophe, that would be an extreme example of a trajectory change. There may also be smaller trajectory changes. For example, if some species of dolphins that we really loved were destroyed, that would be a much smaller trajectory change.

In this section, I'll argue that, on the level of global priorities, existential risk reduction is much more important than producing proximate benefits, in the sense that the opportunities to do good are much, much greater. A major qualification of this claim is that I don't mean to argue that benefits from feasible ways of reducing existential risk are much better than feasible ways of producing

[19] See Beckstead (2013, pp. 65–6) for my complete reply to this objection. Note that this argument is not ruling out diminishing marginal value of additional lives within periods.

[20] If the future does not evolve deterministically enough, then there are multiple potential future trajectories, so talking about "the" trajectory may be somewhat misleading. This difficulty could be avoided if I changed each occurrence of "trajectory" to "probability distribution over possible trajectories," but I would not find that sufficiently more enlightening to justify the repeated use of a cumbersome expression.

proximate benefits *once the ripple effects of proximate benefits are included* (in what follows I largely set ripple effects aside).[21]

4.1 How valuable is the far future, assuming it goes well?

Our assumptions imply that we can approximate the value of the far future by dividing the future of the world into periods, assigning value to each period in a way that is independent of when it happens, and adding up the value across the periods. To see where this leads, consider a possible history of the world where humanity survives for 100 trillion years as outlined in Section 2, and suppose we divide that history up into a trillion hundred-year periods. Then the whole history is a trillion times as valuable as what happens during an average hundred-year period. If we divided periods into a million years, the whole history would be 100 million times as valuable as one average million-year period. I prefer to think in terms of the hundred-year period, since I feel I have a better grip on what that's worth. We could run similar arguments with other proposed durations for periods.

In a world where humanity survives for an enormously long time, should we expect future periods to be, on average, better, worse, or about equally as good as current periods? I am inclined to think that if our descendants managed to create a vast civilization and they preserved a decent portion of the good aspects of our values, future periods would be, on average, much better than current periods. But even if average future periods were only about equally as good as the current period, the whole of the future would be about a trillion times more important, in itself, than everything that has happened in the last hundred years.

Indeed, even if future periods were on average worse than current periods, my argument could still go through. Could it go through if those in future periods lived lives that were very much worth *not* living? The higher our credence in the proposition that the future is net bad, the weaker the case for reducing preventing extinction scenarios. One might hold this view due to beliefs about what is likely to happen in this future, or if one uses a value system that assigns much greater weight to negative goods than positive goods. Both types of views seem weak to me, though I will not argue for that here. However, even if we were so pessimistic that we believed the future's overall expected value was negative, we would still be left with an astronomical number of expected future beings with lives that are suboptimal, and a future whose trajectory is potentially influenceable. Preventing extinction would no longer be a viable strategy, but seeking a trajectory with better lives would be, and that would become the new focal point for axiological considerations. In short, we can interpret the phrase "astronomically great" in premises 2 and 4 as "astronomically positive or negative," and run essentially the same argument. Having stated it, I will now set aside this pessimistic version of my argument.

[21] For more on the importance of ripple effects, see section 3.3.6 of Beckstead (2013).

4.2 How valuable is the far future, in light of our uncertainty about how long it will last?

To determine the value of a chance of humanity surviving for a very, very long time, we have to multiply by the chance of that happening. That tells us what the opportunity cost of premature extinction is, and it helps us determine how important it is to change our trajectory for the better. In Section 2, I argued that it is reasonable to assign at least a 1 percent probability to the possibility that humanity survives for 1 billion years, and at least a 1 percent probability to the possibility that humanity survives for 100 trillion years, given that humanity survives for 1 billion years. Therefore, the expected duration of humanity's existence is at least 1% × 1% × 100 trillion years = 10 billion years. And again, assuming that future periods are expected to go at least as well as the current hundred-year period, that's at least 100 million times more important, in itself, than everything that happened in the last hundred years.

4.3 How valuable is existential risk reduction in comparison with proximate benefits?

On a global level, what could feasibly be done to provide proximate benefits, and what could feasibly be done to reduce existential risk? A dramatic victory around the world might make this period go *twice* as well as it otherwise would. What kind of existential risk reduction would be required to produce comparable benefits? Given our assumptions from the above section, decreasing the probability of a particular risk by one in a million would result in an additional 10,000 expected years of civilization, and that would be at least hundred times better than making things go twice as well during this period.

It is not hard to believe that, collectively, humanity could do things that would decrease the risk of some existential catastrophes by one in a million. One major reason to believe this is that we've recently done a number of things that have reduced existential risk. We've made it through the Cold War and scaled back our reserves of nuclear weapons. We've tracked most of the large asteroids near Earth, so that we'd probably be able to respond if one were on track to collide with Earth.[22] We've built underground bunkers for "continuity of government" purposes, which might help humanity survive certain catastrophes.[23] We've instituted disease surveillance programs which would allow the world to respond more quickly in the event of a large-scale pandemic. We've identified climate change as a potential risk and developed some plans for responding, even if we've done rather little so far. We've also built institutions that reduce the risk of extinction

[22] NASA (2011). [23] See (Beckstead 2015) for details.

in subtler ways, such as decreasing the risk of war or improving the government's ability to respond to a catastrophe. For more detail on the general decline of violence, see Pinker (2011).

Another reason to believe that we could reduce existential risk by one in a million is that many of these efforts could be improved. We could track more asteroids, build better bunkers, improve our disease surveillance programs, reduce our greenhouse gas emissions, encourage non-proliferation of nuclear weapons, and strengthen world institutions in ways that may further decrease existential risk. We could also attempt to anticipate and prepare for potential existential risks that are yet to come, such as those from synthetic biology and advanced artificial intelligence. There is still a substantial challenge in identifying worthy projects, but it seems likely that such projects exist.

To sum up, relatively small reductions in existential risk are much more important, in themselves, than very large proximate benefits. This suggests that reducing existential risk is, in itself, a more important goal than providing proximate benefits.

4.4 How valuable is existential risk reduction in comparison with speeding up development?

For similar reasons, it is likely that existential risk reduction is more important, in itself, than speeding up development. As we saw in the above section, it is not unrealistic to consider scenarios in which humanity reduces existential risk by one in a million, and this results in an additional 10,000 expected years of civilization. In contrast, the amount that we could realistically speed up humanity's technological and moral progress in this period is much more modest, probably measured in decades at best. This suggests that existential risk reduction is more important than speeding up development.

4.5 Why "focus on trajectory changes," rather than "minimize existential risk" is the upshot of this discussion

I've now argued that proximate benefits and benefits from speeding up development are less important than benefits from reducing existential risk. Someone might argue, on this basis, that existential risk reduction is the most important way of shaping the far future. Bostrom has made roughly this argument.[24] He concluded:

> [T]he loss in expected value resulting from an existential catastrophe is so enormous that the objective of reducing existential risks should be a dominant

[24] Bostrom (2003, 2013).

consideration whenever we act out of an impersonal concern for humankind as a whole. It may be useful to adopt the following rule of thumb for such impersonal moral action:

Maxipok: Maximize the probability of an "OK outcome," where an OK outcome is any outcome that avoids existential catastrophe.[25]

This conclusion, however, does not follow because there may be other ways to have a large, persistent effect on the far future without reducing existential risk. Bostrom recognizes that it is possible for the future to be significantly flawed without human extinction, so it's worth emphasizing that he defines an existential catastrophe to include not only humanity's extinction, but also "the permanent and drastic destruction of its potential for desirable future development."[26] But there could be many positive or negative trajectory changes which would not be *drastic* curtailments of humanity's future potential. Some persistent changes in values and social norms could make the future one hundredth, one thousandth, or one millionth better or worse, without there being any drastic changes to the far future. And I see no knockdown argument that we should expect existential risks to be more worthy of our focus than these other trajectory changes. Sure, succeeding in preventing an existential catastrophe would be better than making a smaller trajectory change, but creating a small positive trajectory change may be significantly easier.

I do think my arguments support a more general rule of thumb: What matters most for shaping the far future is producing positive trajectory changes and avoiding negative ones. This is more general because preventing an existential catastrophe is one kind of trajectory change. It's supported by my arguments because:

1. The categories of "proximate benefits," "benefits from speeding up development," and "benefits from trajectory changes," appear to cover the most important categories for shaping the far future, and
2. I've already argued that one class of trajectory changes, existential risk reduction, is more important than providing benefits from speeding up development and proximate benefits.

4.6 A caveat: ordinary actions may systematically but unintentionally improve our long-term trajectory

I see great potential for increasing the expected good one accomplishes by carefully thinking about what factors are likely to determine our long-term trajectory for better or worse and how we can most effectively influence them for the better.

[25] Bostrom (2013, p. 10). [26] Bostrom (2013).

However, it would be a mistake to read the above arguments and conclude that actions aiming to create positive trajectory changes almost always do orders of magnitude more expected good than actions taken with more proximate benefits in mind. A simple illustration of this is that some people have done things that reduce existential risk while focusing on more proximate benefits, such as scientists who tracked near-Earth asteroids for the sake of curiosity or a desire to advance their discipline, or teachers who educated those scientists, or workers who made the paper the scientists used in their textbooks, or policymakers who voted to fund asteroid tracking programs, or people who voted for those policymakers, and so on. Perhaps some forms of social and moral progress have long-lasting effects on our long-term trajectory, with inputs from people in many directions. For reasons like this, I think that many people improve our expected long-term trajectory in subtle ways like this without knowing it and thereby do much greater expected good than one might think when contemplating these arguments, and much greater expected good than they realize themselves.

5. Conclusion

I have presented some normative and empirical considerations in favor of the conclusion that shaping the far future is overwhelmingly important. The key claims are that humanity could survive for a very long time, with an expected duration in the order of billions of years or more; that the future is overwhelmingly important if some plausible normative assumptions (Period Independence, Additionality, Temporal Neutrality, Risk Neutrality) are true; that we could potentially shape the future for the better by speeding up progress, reducing existential risk, or producing other positive trajectory changes; and that what matters most for shaping the far future is creating positive trajectory changes (including reducing existential risk as a special case). I have primarily aimed to illustrate the plausibility of these normative assumptions, and show that they lead to a striking conclusion that doing good is primarily a matter of creating positive trajectory changes. For a fuller, but still rather preliminary, defense of these premises from various possible objections, see Beckstead (2013).

References

Adams, Fred C. 2008. "Long-Term Astrophysical Processes." In *Global Catastrophic Risks*, Nick Bostrom and Milan M. Cirkovic, eds. New York: Oxford University Press, pp. 33–47.

Armstrong, Stuart, and Anders Sandberg. 2013. "Intelligent Life and Sharpening the Fermi Paradox." *Acta Astronautica* 89 (1): 1–13.

Arrhenius, Gustaf. Forthcoming. *Population Ethics: The Challenge of Future Generations*. Oxford: Oxford University Press.

Arrhenius, Gustaf, and Wlodek Rabinowicz. 2015. "The Value of Existence." In *the Oxford Handbook of Value Theory*, Iwao Hirose and Jonas Olson, eds. Oxford: Oxford University Press.

Askell, Amanda. 2018. "Pareto Principles in Infinite Ethics." PhD thesis. New York University.

Beckstead, Nicholas. 2013. "On the Overwhelming Importance of Shaping the Far Future." PhD thesis. Rutgers University.

Beckstead, Nicholas. 2014. "Will We eventually be Able to Colonize Other Stars?" Future of Humanity Institute. Available at https://web.archive.org/web/20180408181255/https://www.fhi.ox.ac.uk/will-we-eventually-be-able-to-colonize-other-stars-notes-from-a-preliminary-review/.

Beckstead, Nick. 2015. "How Much Could Refuges Help Us Recover from a Global Catastrophe?" *Futures* 72: 36–44.

Bostrom, Nick. 2002. "Existential Risks: Analyzing Human Extinction Scenarios and Related Hazards." *Journal of Evolution and Technology* 9 (1): 1–31.

Bostrom, Nick. 2003. "Astronomical Waste: The Opportunity Cost of Delayed Technological Development." *Utilitas* 15 (3): 308–14.

Bostrom, Nick. 2011. "Infinite Ethics. Analysis and Metaphysics." *Analysis and Metaphysics* 10: 9–50.

Bostrom, Nick. 2013. "Existential Risk Prevention as Global Priority." *Global Policy* 4 (1): 15–31.

Bostrom, Nick. 2014. *Superintelligence: Paths, Dangers, Strategies*. New York: Oxford University Press.

Broome, John. 1992. *Counting the Cost of Global Warming*. Cambridge, UK: White Horse Press.

Broome, John. 2004. *Weighing Lives*. Oxford: Oxford University Press.

Broome, John. 2010. "The Most Important Thing About Climate Change." In *Public Policy: Why Ethics Matters*, Jonathan Boston, Andrew Bradstock, and David Eng, eds. Canberra: ANU Press, pp. 101–16.

Buchak, Lara. 2013. *Risk and Rationality*. Oxford: Oxford University Press.

Clark, M. (ms). Infinite Classical Utilitarianism.

Cowen, Tyler, and Derek Parfit. 1992. "Against the Social Discount Rate." In *Justice Between Age Groups and Generations*, Peter Laslett and James S. Fishkin, eds. Yale University Press, pp. 144–61.

NASA. 2011. "NASA Space Telescope Finds Fewer Asteroids Near Earth." Available at http://www.nasa.gov/mission_pages/WISE/news/wise20110929.html.

Parfit, Derek. 1984. *Reasons and Persons*. Oxford: Oxford University Press.

Parfit, Derek. 2011. *On What Matters*. Oxford: Oxford University Press.

Parfit, Derek. 2016. "Can We Avoid the Repugnant Conclusion?" *Theoria* 82 (2): 110–27.

Pinker, Steven. 2011. *The Better Angels of Our Nature: Why Violence Has Declined*. New York: Viking.

Posner, Richard. 2004. *Catastrophe: Risk and Response*. Oxford: Oxford University Press.

Pummer, Theron. 2019. "The Worseness of Nonexistence". In *Saving People from the Harm of Death*, Espen Gamlund and Carl Tollef Solberg, eds. Oxford: Oxford University Press.

Roberts, Melinda A. 2011. "The Asymmetry: A Solution." *Theoria* 77 (4): 333–67.

Temkin, Larry S. 2008. "Is Living Longer Living Better?" *Journal of Applied Philosophy* 25 (3): 193–210.

Temkin, Larry S. 2012. *Rethinking the Good: Moral Ideals and the Nature of Practical Reasoning*. Oxford: Oxford University Press.

Velleman J.D. 2000. "Well-Being and Time." In *The Possibility of Practical Reason*. Oxford: Clarendon Press.

7

Effective Altruism, Global Poverty, and Systemic Change

Iason Gabriel and Brian McElwee

One of the main objections levelled against the effective altruism movement has been that it fails to address issues of systemic change.[1] On the face of it, this is surprising. There is no basic incompatibility between the central ideas of effective altruism and the pursuit of institutional reform. Moreover, given that systemic change is large-scale, one would expect that effective altruism, which aims at *doing the most good*, would be drawn to efforts to secure such changes.

In fact, effective altruists do support various systemic change initiatives.[2] However, the effective altruism movement is perhaps best known for its recommendations regarding severe global poverty. And in this area, effective altruist organizations have favoured, almost exclusively, small-scale high-confidence initiatives—in particular, health interventions and direct cash transfers—rather than efforts designed to alter global or national systems.

In this chapter, we will:

1. Argue that regarding global poverty, there is strong reason to believe that systemic initiatives will be amongst the very best bets in securing good outcomes.
2. Offer some diagnosis of why effective altruists have been reluctant to back poverty-related systemic change initiatives.
3. Suggest modifications of the evaluation methodologies deployed by effective altruists, so as to do justice to the promise of systemic change initiatives.

Without these modifications, effective altruism risks succumbing to the problem of the 'missing middle', focusing disproportionately on high-confidence low-impact interventions and low-confidence high-impact interventions, when there is evidence to suggest that equal—if not greater—positive impact can be achieved in other ways.

[1] See, for example, Srinivasan (2015); Herzog (2015) and (2016); Gabriel (2016); and various responses to "The Logic of Effective Altruism" forum (2015).

[2] See, for example, http://www.goodventures.org/our-portfolio and https://www.openphilanthropy.org/focus. For discussion of how effective altruism can and does support systemic change initiatives, see: Will MacAskill's Chapter 1 in this volume, and Berkey (2018).

1. Effective altruist evaluation

Effective altruists believe that we should use evidence and reason to figure out how to benefit others as much as possible, and take action on that basis.[3] High among the causes they prioritize are efforts to address global poverty.[4] Effective altruist organizations have provided public lists of charities they recommend—and have argued that giving a substantial portion of your income to these organizations is one of the best things you can do. To date, effective altruist meta-charities have tended to favour 'vertical' health interventions (interventions designed to treat specific diseases, such as malaria), and direct cash transfers to poor people.[5] In contrast, they have been reluctant to endorse political advocacy, citizen empowerment, or right-based initiatives as ways of improving the lives of the very poor. It may be true that these other activities are not as effective as those they recommend. But before we can have confidence in that judgement, it is important to examine the evaluative methods deployed, and to look at any assumptions on which calculations are based.

Effective altruism purports to be a movement that combines altruistic intentions and efforts with careful thought and attention to evidence. In practice, effective altruists tend to adhere to a thicker set of norms and assumptions that shape their understanding of the world and influence the advice they give. They generally interpret claims about 'impact' and the 'greatest good' in a distinctive way, adhering to an evaluative framework that is welfarist and consequentialist. Their aim, by and large, is to bring about the best possible state of affairs for human beings (and other sentient creatures) by reducing suffering and premature death. Questions have been raised about the dominance of this goal—we might wonder, for example, whether enough attention is given to considerations of justice or to other non-welfarist values.[6] For the purpose of this chapter, however, we lay such issues aside, and focus on whether effective altruists succeed on their own terms in identifying interventions with the greatest expected utility. In particular, we consider the epistemic standards they apply in assessing efforts to address severe poverty and its consequences, and the impact these standards have on their assessment of likely impact.

In order to be practically applicable, claims about evidence and reason must be understood in a specific way. The process of bestowing more concrete meaning on these terms has already taken place among the effective altruism community. With respect to what counts as 'evidence', the movement places a high premium

[3] See MacAskill (Chapter 1 of this volume).

[4] This is one of three principal current focal points of the effective altruism community, alongside factory farming and existential risk reduction. MacAskill (Chapter 1, this volume).

[5] See https://www.givewell.org/charities/top-charities and https://www.givingwhatwecan.org/giving-recommendations/ for ongoing recommendation updates.

[6] Gabriel (2016).

on information that is quantifiable and verifiable using scientific methods. While they do not discount the value of qualitative information altogether, effective altruists have often endorsed the view that there is a hierarchy of evidence types—one that has randomized controlled trials (RCTs) at the top.[7] GiveWell and Giving What We Can, effective altruist organizations which provide advice to donors about the effectiveness of charitable organizations, are yet to recommend any charity that does not do work that has been validated in this way.[8]

The appeal to 'reason' also means something quite specific. Effective altruists recommend that before deciding how to act, we should think seriously about three features of a problem: its *scale*, its *tractability*, and how *neglected* it is.[9] These three features serve as the primary heuristics for identifying which actions have the highest *expected value*. Rather than focusing on the issues that are most vivid, politically salient, or have the greatest emotional appeal, effective altruists encourage us to take the numbers seriously—and to seek out areas where we are likely to have the greatest marginal impact. A central claim made by the movement is that by acting in this way it is possible to identify specific activities that are *hundreds* of times better than the median intervention in a given area.[10] Indeed, many effective altruists believe that they have already identified activities of this kind.

Using these heuristics and insights, interventions can score highly in different ways which divide into three broad categories: low-value/high-confidence (LV/HC) activities; medium-value/medium-confidence (MV/MC) activities; and high-value/low-confidence (HV/LC) activities. When it comes to addressing global poverty, the recommendations made by effective altruist organizations tend to fall exclusively within the LV/HC category. (Note that this 'low' value is only low relative to the other sorts of initiatives mentioned; the good apparently achieved by the GiveWell-recommended organizations is very substantial indeed in absolute terms.) By striking contrast, when it comes to other causes, effective altruists frequently endorse MV/MC initiatives (e.g. criminal justice reform) and HV/LC initiatives (e.g. existential risk mitigation). This rough taxonomy suggests that estimates of evidential robustness or confidence, are potentially as important as questions surrounding the scale of impact, when it comes to working out which interventions to prioritize. What's more, if only certain kinds of evidence are accepted in some domains, while other forms of evidence are discounted, this could lead effective altruists' judgement astray.

[7] Singer, (2015); MacAskill (2015, p. 9). See Clough (2015) for critique.

[8] GiveWell offers some explanation of the link between evidential backing and advice to the public here: https://www.givewell.org/how-we-work/criteria#Whyisevidencesoimportant. Other effective altruist organizations, such as the Open Philanthropy Project and Good Ventures, endorse and support projects not validated by RCTs. However, they do not aim to advise the general public about where to give.

[9] See MacAskill (2015, part 1).

[10] Ord (2013).

In the following section, we explore the question of epistemic standards in relation to global poverty, with a particular value on the promise held by medium-value/medium-confidence efforts which aim at positive systemic change. Severe poverty is caused and sustained by harmful systems. These systems are of vast scale. And there is reason to believe that such systems are tractable. If this is correct, effective altruists should give stronger support to efforts to bring about some of the large-scale systemic reforms needed to address persistent severe global poverty.

2. Systemic change

In a complex and interdependent world, many of the most important aspects of our lives are governed by social, political, and economic *systems*. These systems—made up of large numbers of agents interacting in standardized ways to produce large-scale outcomes—create the social, political, and material basis for human flourishing. However, they also have the potential to do great harm. Global supply chains funnel massive flows of resources to authoritarian regimes that help to keep them in power.[11] Tax evasion deprives countries of vast capital flows that could be used to improve the lives of their citizens.[12] Reliance on fossil fuels already causes suffering and hardship to millions of people through climate change—a situation which looks set to worsen.[13] These facts lend credence to the following thought: the greatest positive impacts on the world can be achieved not through iterated small-scale interventions, but rather through systemic initiatives that alter the rules within which actors operate and that challenge the values that underpin them. Exerting even small leverage over very large systems could in principle have a much greater impact than efforts to optimize within the status quo.

Support for this conjecture derives from a number of sources. To begin with, we should note the *extraordinary scale* of the systems involved: they have global reach. Take the global tax system. Presently, one quarter of global GDP, or some $20 trillion dollars' worth of income, is untaxed.[14] Against this backdrop, research suggests that systematic efforts to crack down on illicit financial flows, close tax loopholes, and improve tax collection infrastructure, could generate trillions of dollars for governments to spend on their own populations.[15]

Equally striking are figures concerning the effects of the extractive industries. Countries with abundant natural resources tend to be less democratic, have high numbers of people living in severe poverty, and slow economic growth—the phenomenon known as the 'resource curse'. Many of the world's poorest people

[11] Wenar (2016). [12] Tax Justice Network: https://www.taxjustice.net/.

[13] Intergovernmental Panel on Climate Change: https://www.ipcc.ch/report/ar5/.

[14] Henry (2012).

[15] Even the most conservative estimates suggest that tax reforms could generate between $100 billion and $200 billion per year, of which $50 billion would accrue to sub-Saharan Africa (Forstater 2015).

live in countries, or regions, ravaged by conflict stemming from the actions of resource-rich authoritarian regimes.[16] Focusing on oil alone, Leif Wenar calculates that the average American family pays $275 directly into the pockets of corrupt and authoritarian regimes each year simply by filling up with gas.[17] This figure is two to three times more than their contribution to charities working in low-income countries. Improvements in how these 'systems' operate could therefore be expected have a huge positive impact.[18]

In addition to their size, there are four further reasons to think that systemic changes are especially promising bets from the perspective of expected value. First, the effect of leveraging systems is *likely to endure* over many lifetimes. The effects of large-scale institutional practices typically long outlive their creators. Second, and relatedly, institutions, including global institutions, evolve in *path-dependent* ways. This means that what we do now will determine the opportunities and constraints that people face in the future. Failure to act may foreclose valuable options for them, if we believe that there are promising opportunities that exist at the moment. Third, corrupt systems tend to be *subversive*. In ways that are not always apparent, they tend to frustrate attempts to bring about positive marginal change. Finally, there are some global challenges, climate change being a prominent example, for which there is presently no 'technical solution'.[19] When this is the case, catastrophic ruin is likely to be averted only by changing the parameters within which actors operate and the incentives they face. If systemic change is a *necessary* means to something of enormous value, then this fact has special significance for calculations about the greatest good.[20]

In light of this, we might wonder why have effective altruists been reluctant, in the case of severe poverty (and perhaps climate change), to endorse efforts to reform those societal structures that appear in urgent need of transformation. One possible answer would be that, though their scale is very large, the systemic issues discussed so far fail as good bets in promoting the good on the other two dimensions of neglectedness and tractability. If there are already a large number of actors working in these areas, the expected marginal return on additional effort could be small. Or if there is nothing that can be done in practice to bring about positive systemic change, then, again, we would be better turning our attention elsewhere. Neither claim is borne out, however.

To begin with, there are a plethora of systemic issues directly bearing on the plight of the world's poorest, including tax justice and clean trade, which continue to be relatively neglected given the high stakes involved. There are at most a handful of specialist NGOs working in these areas, operating with limited budgets

[16] Forty percent of people living in 'natural resource-rich' countries live on less than $2 per day. Wenar (2016, p. xv).
[17] Wenar (2016, p. xvi).
[18] It is also crucial to note, of course, that systemic changes may risk large-scale negative impacts.
[19] Hardin (1968). [20] Shue (2016).

which severely constrain their efforts.[21] Nor should we accept that these causes are intractable. The historical record provides numerous examples of advocacy movements achieving major social change through campaign work. It is notable too that few big social changes have occurred without this impetus.[22]

In recent decades, organizations working to improve the extractive industries or promote tax justice have achieved remarkable results while operating on a shoestring budget. One example is Global Witness, founded in 1993 to help tackle illicit financial flows to authoritarian regimes, including the trade in blood diamonds. Operating with an annual budget of several thousand dollars, the organization spearheaded efforts to establish the Kimberly Process for diamond certification and was nominated for the Nobel Peace Prize as a result of its efforts. More recently, it was the driving force behind the Extractive Industries Transparency Initiative (EITI), an endeavour which has led corporations to publicize trillions of dollars of previously hidden financial transactions.[23]

We should therefore ask whether there are alternative explanations for effective altruism's tendency to withhold support from such campaigning organizations. One possibility relates to their desire to have a high degree of confidence in the organizations they recommend. To achieve this confidence, effective altruists need indicators and metrics that reliably track the truth about impact. Just *how* tractable are the causes, relative to others? How good a bet is any particular campaigning effort? While many instances of large-scale social progress have resulted from campaigning efforts, many other worthy campaigns have, of course, had little success. Moreover, when it comes to campaigning efforts, the types of indicators used to assess vertical health interventions simply do not exist. If effective altruists judge there to be *no* sufficiently reliable indicators to guide judgement, they will withhold endorsement of organizations campaigning for systemic change. Most challenging for advocacy organizations is meeting the standard effective altruist preference in this field, for counterfactual validation. The efficacy of advocacy work cannot be tested using randomized trials: there is no other world we have access to where certain campaigns did not take place. And only rarely can a proxy be found that uses natural experiments. These considerations appear to loom large in this context.

In response to the charge of unwarranted neglect, it might be argued that an acceptable division of labour is at work here. GiveWell explicitly says that its

[21] See, for example, Tax Justice Network; www.cleantrade.org; Global Witness. The 2017 income of the Tax Justice Network was just £944,020.

[22] See Teles and Schmitt (2011).

[23] Another relevant example is the campaign by Oxfam to help the Ghanaian government invest its oil windfall wisely. About this Peter Singer writes that if 'Oxfam made it 1 percent more likely that an extra 15 percent of oil revenue would go to help Ghanaians in extreme poverty . . . the charity's actions still had an expected value of 1 percent of $116 million, or $1.16 million. For an outlay of $200,000, that indicates a return on investment of 580 percent.' Singer (2015, p. 159).

distinctive mission within the effective altruism movement is to highlight those charities which score highly according to a metric which places very high weight on rigorous evidence, without insisting that every altruist should act this way.[24] Indeed, other organizations within the movement support projects where the evidence of good effects is lower, and where quantitative evidence is supplemented with qualitative evidence. However, the question remains as to whether this high-evidence requirement is appropriate in guiding the donations of members of the general public, and whether there is sufficient justification for the dominance of LV/HC initiatives specifically when it comes to global poverty. If our analysis is correct, then there is reason to believe that the concern for evidential robustness deters some effective altruist organizations from endorsing what, from the perspective of expected value, may in fact be among the very best bets in addressing severe poverty. A further concern is that effective altruist organizations could do more harm than good, if the public responded to their recommendations by withdrawing support from systemic causes—such as efforts to promote human rights or combat climate change—adopting the view that the *only* interventions worth backing are those that show promise through testing which meets high-epistemic standards. In such circumstances, effective altruists can in principle adapt their recommendations, as what causes count as neglected changes. But clearly there is a need here for vigilant evaluation and critique of the recommendations made.

These problems need not be integral to the movement's outlook, if the movement allows different forms of evidence to inform its recommendations about how ordinary members of the public may best help tackle severe poverty—and this evidence allows effective altruists to identify important systemic opportunities to do good. When it comes to assessing the work done by advocacy organizations, some kinds of evaluation can be done using qualitative research methods. In the case of Global Witness, the fact that they were the predominant advocacy organization working on the projects in question, figuring prominently in narrative accounts of the projects, strongly suggests that they were influential, and that the results in question would not have happened without their efforts.[25] Importantly, given the nature and scale of the change effected, even rough probabilistic assessments may point towards the cost-effectiveness of such interventions.[26] We say more about this below.

[24] GiveWell. "Our Criteria for Top Charities." Available at https://www.givewell.org/how-we-work/criteria#Whyisevidencesoimportant

[25] For narrative accounts of the development of the Kimberley Process, see Bieri (2010); Ashgate (2010); and Haufler (2009).

[26] Effective altruists appear very willing to adopt such rough assessments elsewhere. In the case of global poverty, Singer appears to acknowledge the point in his discussion of the Oxfam/Ghana case mentioned in the note above.

These considerations highlight a tension between effective altruism's epistemic and normative aspirations. The emphasis on scientific rigour may allow them to identify organizations working in promising areas, but may also lead to the neglect of organizations that have the greatest impact. The issue of trade-offs between confidence in a positive impact and the scale of positive impacts is familiar to effective altruists. Many of them have after all proven willing to endorse *highly* speculative causes, such as efforts to reduce the risk of human extinction, on the basis that the scale and neglectedness in these cases are sufficiently high to counterbalance the comparatively small degree of confidence about having a positive impact. Investment in any specific effort to tackle 'existential risks' offers an extremely small chance of very great reward, and the evidential basis for any kind of probabilistic assessment is very thin.[27]

Yet the same methodology, namely calculation of expected value, should also clearly lead effective altruists to explore seriously the middle ground between extreme risk and vertical health interventions—including more prosaic systemic causes where we have evidence, but of only moderate strength, that a given effort will bear substantial fruit. At present, there appears to be something of a *missing middle* in the focus of the movement taken as a whole. The effective altruist meta-charities support many (relatively) low impact, but well-evidenced initiatives, whilst other effective altruist organizations prioritize extremely high impact, but very poorly evidenced, projects. Yet medium impact, moderately evidenced initiatives of the kinds highlighted above have received relatively little support. Surveying effective altruist areas of focus, it is striking that we observe so much support for LV/HC projects (e.g. health interventions) and HV/LC projects (e.g. existential risk), and relatively little support for MV/MC projects. Such projects are not *entirely* absent from effective altruism's areas of focus. Effective altruists efforts aimed at U.S. prison reform, and addressing animal welfare in food production, plausibly fall into the MV/MC category.[28] However, when it comes to addressing severe poverty, the cause for which effective altruism is most widely known, the low degree of support for MV/MC projects aimed at systemic change seems especially curious.

We believe that this anomaly can perhaps be explained by an aspect of many effective altruists' worldview which may lead them to underestimate the prospects of MV/MC efforts to secure systemic changes focused on reducing severe poverty: namely, their neglect of politics and preference for technical solutions.

[27] Commenting on straw polls that look at the risk posed by artificial intelligence, for example, Nick Bostrom writes that 'small sample sizes, selection biases, and—above all—the inherent unreliability of the subjective opinions elicited mean that one should not read too much into these expert surveys and interviews.' Bostrom (2014, p. 25).

[28] For a rough overview of effective altruism's cause areas, see Will MacAskill's 'The Definition of Effective Altruism', Chapter 1 of this volume.

3. Explanations and solutions: technical and political

Why does extreme poverty persist over time? It is highly unlikely that any single-factor explanation is correct. However, it is possible to identify certain explanatory paradigms that are especially relevant. Effective altruists tend to focus on two major impediments to alleviating severe poverty: (*i*) inadequate altruism, and (*ii*) a failure to apply evidence and reason to the challenges that confront us. The latter claim in particular is a central tenet of what we might term the *enlightenment worldview*. According to this viewpoint, a huge amount of avoidable suffering occurs because humanity has not yet sought out rational and scientific solutions to the problems we face. Once we do so, it is possible to secure gains in human well-being that have eluded past generations.[29] With regard to global poverty, effective altruists argue that there are a number of 'easy wins' that are within our reach.[30]

There is reason to be wary of these claims. To begin with, the information from RCTs upon which effective altruists base their recommendations is already widely used by the aid agencies and philanthropic foundations that fund the research.[31] The idea that this information should be made publicly accessible is new. But in stressing the importance of evidence and cost-effectiveness, effective altruists have been echoing a major trend already well underway in the sector. More importantly, simply adopting a more 'scientific' approach is insufficient to achieve serious progress in addressing severe poverty, unless this is understood very broadly indeed, in such a way as to include sensitivity to local conditions and to political factors.

There is a long history of seemingly scientific development projects undertaken in developing countries which have ended in failure.[32] Application of modernization theory, structural adjustment programmes, and attempts to modernize agricultural production all fall into this category.[33] In each case, no one ever thought that their approach was 'unscientific', irrational, or uninformed by evidence. Yet in each case, the attempt to reduce poverty reduction to something technical, based upon universalisable formulas, led practitioners to overlook variations in local context that caused their projects to fail.[34] Moreover, whether they met their formal goals or not, these development projects had a number of unintended

[29] See the now infamous claim that effective altruism might be the 'last social movement that we ever need.' Matthews (10 August 2015) Available at http://www.vox.com/2015/8/10/9124145/effective-altruism-global-ai

[30] See MacAskill (2015). See MacAskill (2015. ch. 2–4).

[31] These evaluations are generally donor-funded, rather than effective altruism funded. For the 'counterfactual problem' that this shared information gives rise to, see Gabriel (2016).

[32] Ferguson (1990).

[33] The idea that philanthropy should be scientific has an even longer history in a national context. It was a central tenet of nineteenth-century Victorian social reformers, who sought to distinguish their efforts from mere 'alms giving' McGoey (2012); Villadsen (2007).

[34] This critique has recently been levelled at RCTs by the Nobel Prize-winning economist Angus Deaton (Deaton and Cartwright 2017).

consequences—typically augmenting the power of non-democratic regimes and weakening chains of accountability to local populations.

To appreciate why this occurred, we need to look at the world through a different lens. According to what we might call the *political worldview*, neither donors, nor governments, nor poor people themselves suffer from any glaring deficit of rationality. In fact, the main causes of poverty arise from the operation of political power. At a global level, powerful nations have set rules in a way that advances their own interest at the expense of the poor. At a more local level, poor people remain poor because they are ruled by narrow elites who organize society for their own benefit at the expense of the majority.[35] Rent-seeking behaviour and 'extractive' national institutions subvert attempts to bring about positive social transformation by ensuring that resources continue to flow to those in power.[36]

If this political perspective is truer to the world than the enlightenment diagnosis, then two concerns emerge for effective altruism. First, the projects endorsed by effective altruist organizations are not immune to the effects of national power dynamics and institutions. While there may be less opportunity for rent-seeking behaviour with vertical health interventions and programmes that transfer funds directly, it is important to realize that the ability of charities to operate in these ways is conditional on government acquiescence—something that is problematic when working with undemocratic regimes.[37] The external funding of service delivery can reduce government accountability, and deter citizens from making claims on their government—which is problematic because such claim-making has been the main engine of progressive change in many low-income countries.[38]

Second, there may be interventions that have greater expected value that effective altruists overlook as a consequence of their focus on the technical over the political. In particular, the political worldview suggests that greater good can be achieved by focusing on citizen empowerment and rights-based initiatives. These approaches help people address the institutional arrangements that keep them poor. They also recognize that the poor are well placed to function as agents of positive change: they know more about their condition than foreign philanthropists, and they have a stronger interest in seeing it ended.[39] Many of those who work most closely with the poor believe that mobilization and empowerment of the poor themselves is needed to address poverty effectively.[40] What the poor require most is the capacity to exercise greater control over their own lives, to voice their needs and concerns in public, and to hold politicians accountable for their decisions. With this in mind, a central concern is that, by excluding empowerment and rights-based initiatives from the causes they endorse, effective altruists overlook highly promising opportunities to do good.[41] Moreover, such approaches more

[35] Acemoglu and Robinson (2012). [36] Acemoglu and Robinson (2012, p. 76).
[37] Rubenstein (2015). [38] Ferguson (2015). [39] Deveaux (2015).
[40] Green (2018); Ferguson (2015); Deaton (2013).
[41] We are not here calling into question effective altruism's focus on promoting the good at the expense of focus of rights or justice. Rather, the concern is that in practice, effective altruists may miss opportunities *to promote the good* by failing to endorse rights-based initiatives.

directly tackle directly the marginalization, shame, and powerlessness which form the core of poverty.[42]

Of course, it may be very hard to identify organizations with the strongest potential to be effective in areas where outside assistance is useful. But we are still left with a number of promising options. One is to provide support for watchdog organizations like Amnesty International and Global Witness which augment the capacity of local actors by sharing knowledge and providing new opportunities to voice and publicize their claims. Another significant implication of a more political perspective is that it encourages us to turn our attention to the role played by our own countries in perpetuating poverty overseas. In particular, it is important to resist a narrative which portrays affluent Westerners as mere generous benefactors of the needy, and instead to acknowledge them as beneficiaries of a network of institutions which actively contributes to the persistence of large-scale severe poverty.[43]

Effective altruists will rightly wish to take an evidence-based approach to assessing interventions which involve rights-based initiatives and political advocacy aiming at systemic change. What might an evidence-based approach to such evaluations involve? A central message of effective altruism is that it is difficult to predict what is effective on the basis of intuition alone; harder evidence is necessary. However, in 'The Elusive Craft of Evaluating Advocacy', Steven Teles and Mark Schmitt outline some distinctive features of political advocacy,[44] as compared to 'service delivery' projects, suggesting that appropriate evaluation of advocacy efforts may look quite different. Attempts to evaluate advocacy must take account of the fact that in politics, events unfold rapidly and in a nonlinear fashion. This differs from service delivery programmes, where benchmarks indicating steady progress are available. With advocacy, progress tends to come in fits and starts. Long periods of persistent effort and careful groundwork are required when no clear interim evidence of progress will be available. Moreover, '[a]dvocacy efforts almost always involve a fight against a strategic adversary capable of adapting over time' (41). The ability of organizations to react to unexpected opportunities for progress is a crucial indicator that an organization is a good bet.

Consequently, the authors argue:

> 'Advocacy evaluation should be seen...as a form of trained judgment—a craft requiring judgment and tacit knowledge—rather than as a scientific method. To be a skilled advocacy evaluator requires a deep knowledge of and feel for the politics of the issues, strong networks of trust among the key players, an ability to assess organisational quality, and a sense for the right time horizon against which to measure accomplishments' (39).

[42] Walker (2014). [43] See Pogge (2002, General Introduction).

[44] The authors note that the term 'advocacy' does not quite cover the scope and focus of what they have in mind. The point of advocacy is not simply to state the merits of the political changed being advocated, but to secure lasting political change.

They also propose that evaluation should be done not at the level of particular projects, but instead at the level of organizations, taking into account a whole portfolio of projects. Even the most successful organizations will pursue many projects which fail to achieve significant results. Such evaluation should involve 'using the longest feasible time horizon' (42).[45]

If Teles and Schmitt are correct in their analysis, then there is reason to guard against loading the dice from the start against political initiatives, and in favour of smaller-scale service delivery ones, by using evaluation methods which are appropriate for the latter, but not the former. A central goal of effective altruism is to incentivize charities to produce better results, and to garner, then publicize, better evidence of the results they produce. However, if the measures used to assess results are skewed in favour of service delivery over political advocacy, undesirable pressure may be put on organizations to abandon valuable longer time-scale efforts in order to prioritize the production of interim achievements.

4. Political neutrality and building alliances

The core ideas of effective altruism are compatible with both a first-person singular stance, which asks 'What difference can *I* make?' or with a first-person plural stance, which asks 'What difference can *we* make together?' The movement appears to be increasingly foregrounding the second stance.[46] In light of our observations about global poverty, this is encouraging. Positive *systemic* change is unlikely to result from the action of one individual alone.

Yet, important questions remain. Who is the relevant 'we' here? For a start, the people who are directly affected by global problem, such as poverty or climate change, and those who want to assist them. As the history of social movements can attest, building broad alliances with like-minded groups and individuals is essential to success. To that end, if the effective altruism movement is to have the positive impact it aspires to, it is imperative that aims to include people with different backgrounds and perspectives, and that it does not alienate organizations which could be potential partners. Public charity evaluation is hugely important, but it is crucial that such evaluations are couched in appropriate language, so as

[45] Some elements of this proposed approach have been adopted by effective altruism organizations in areas other than severe poverty. See, for example, the (evolving) methodology of the Open Philanthropy Project: https://www.openphilanthropy.org/blog/our-grantmaking-so-far-approach-and-process

[46] For example, the theme of the 2017 Effective Altruism Global conference in London was 'Doing Good Together'. See Stephanie Collins, 'Beyond Individualism', Chpater 13 in this volume, for related discussion.

to avoid undermining the coalition-building necessary for securing positive systemic change.[47]

Many effective altruists are already very aware of the importance of avoiding alienating potential recruits and allies. In light of this, a stance of *political neutrality*, endeavouring to avoid an appearance of partisanship which may serve to deter some who share their goals, has some attraction. However, if the foregoing discussion is correct, then severe global poverty is a thoroughgoing political matter. Its causes are, in very large part, political, and its solutions inevitably involve specific political commitments. Reform to political and economic institutions and practices are crucial to ending the most severe global poverty. As a consequence, a commitment to political neutrality threatens to alienate many of the most important players already in the field.

It is worth asking why, even with its attractive twin commitments of clear-headed rationality and concern for human welfare, the effective altruism movement has drawn substantial criticism in the media.[48] Much of the critique centres on a perceived stance of political neutrality. A perception persists that effective altruism is content to let large-scale systems remain as they are, while seeking merely to address some of their most iniquitous symptoms in the most efficient ways.[49] Whether or not this perception is just, there seem to be strong *strategic* reasons for effective altruists to eschew any commitment to political neutrality. We believe that effective altruists should be willing to voice criticisms of political institutions which abet the persistence of severe poverty, and to support overtly political attempts at reform. They must also address head-on a deeper dilemma: for their evaluations to be taken seriously, they must be perceived as impartial; yet to mobilize effectively, they must commit to a degree of partisanship and enter coalitions.

The effective altruism movement shows great promise in helping to address global poverty—through its attempts to raise public awareness, and through its recommendations to potential donors in the general public, based on careful

[47] Compare Singer (2015): 'to be a worthy recipient of our support, an organization must be able to demonstrate that it will do more good with our money or our time than other options open to us' (Singer 2015, inside cover). This bar is too high. Many organizations that *do* merit our support can do little to prove they will do more good than others, certainly by the current effective altruists-favoured metrics.

[48] See, for example, *Boston Review*, responses to: http://bostonreview.net/forum/peter-singer-logic-effective-altruism; Srinivasan (2015); Snow (2015).

[49] As noted already, effective altruist organizations have pursued overtly political projects in various domains, such as criminal justice reform and immigration reform. The perception of political neutrality has been encouraged by the movement's approach to severe poverty, along with the centrality of severe poverty in public consciousness about effective altruism. The perception has perhaps also been fostered by its public claims about *cause* neutrality, perceived as an indifference between causes.

evaluation of charities. We have offered some reasons, however, why the movement might be in danger of falling short on its own terms. Regarding global poverty in particular, there is reason to believe that the prospects for systemic change initiatives are greater than the movement has recognized hitherto. A more flexible approach to evaluation of initiatives may be needed to do justice to the promise of efforts to secure systemic change. The movement should take care not to overlook systemic changes which are difficult to evidence to a high degree of reliability; it should recalibrate its preference for technological solutions to global poverty over political solutions; and it should seek actively to build alliances with more political movements that share their goal of improving the lives of the world's poorest people.

References

Acemoglu, Daron, and James A. Robinson. 2012. *Why Nations Fail*. New York: Crown Business.

Berkey, Brian. 2018. "The Institutional Critique of Effective Altruism." *Utilitas* 30 (2): 143–71.

Bieri, Franziska. 2010. *From Blood Diamonds to the Kimberley Process: How NGOs Cleaned Up the Global Diamond Industry*. New York: Routledge.

Bostrom, Nick. 2014. *Superintelligence: Paths, Dangers, Strategies*. Oxford: Oxford University Press.

Collins, Stephanie. "Beyond Individualism." Chapter 13, this volume.

Deaton, Angus. 2013. *The Great Escape*. Princeton: Princeton University Press.

Deaton, Angus, and Nancy Cartwright. 2017. "Understanding and misunderstanding randomized controlled trials." *Social Science & Medicine* 210: 2–21.

Deveaux, Monique. 2015. "The Global Poor as Agents of Justice." *Journal of Moral Philosophy* 12 (2): 125–50.

Ferguson, James. 1990. *The Anti-Politics Machine: Development, Depoliticization, and Bureaucratic Power in Lesotho*. Minneapolis, Minnesota: University of Minnesota Press.

Ferguson, James. 2015. *Give a Man a Fish: Reflections on the New Politics of Distribution*. Durham, North Carolina: Duke University Press.

Forstater, Maya. 2015. 'Can Stopping "Tax Dodging" by Multinational Enterprises Close the Gap in Development Finance?' *CGD Policy Paper* 69, p. 32. Available at https://www.cgdev.org/sites/default/files/CGD-policy-paper-69-Forstater-tax-dodging-dev-finance_2.pdf.

Gabriel, Iason. 2016. "Effective Altruism and its Critics." *Journal of Applied Philosophy* 34 (4): 457–73.

Green, Duncan. 2018. "Peace has a PR Problem: How would you fix it?" In *From Poverty to Power*. Oxford: Oxfam GB/Practical Action Publishing.

GiveWell. November 2017. "Our Criteria for Top Charities." Available at https://www.givewell.org/how-we-work/criteria#Whyisevidencesoimportant.

Hardin, Garrett. 1968. "The Tragedy of the Commons." *Science* 162 (3,859): 1,243–8.

Haufler, Virginia. 2009. "The Kimberley Process Certification Scheme: An Innovation in Global Governance and Conflict Prevention." *Journal of Business Ethics* 89 (4): 403–16.

Henry, James S. 2012. *The Price of Offshore Revisited: New Estimates for "Missing" Global Private Wealth, Income, Inequality, and Lost Taxes*. Chesham: Tax Justice Network.

Herzog, Lisa. 21 October 2015. "(One of) Effective Altruism's blind spot(s), or: why moral theory needs institutional theory." *Justice Everywhere Blog*. Available at http://justice-everywhere.org/international/one-of-effective-altruisms-blind-spots-or-why-moral-theory-needs-institutional-theory/.

Herzog, Lisa. 22 February 2016. "Can 'Effective Altruism' Really Change the World?" *OpenDemocracy.net*. Available at https://www.opendemocracy.net/transformation/lisa-herzog/can-effective-altruism-really-change-world#.

MacAskill, William. "The Definition of Effective Altruism." Chapter 1, this volume.

MacAskill, William. 2015. *Doing Good Better*. New York: Penguin Random House.

Matthews, Dylan. 10 August 2015. "I spent a weekend at Google talking with nerds about charity. I came away...worried." *Vox Media*. Available at https://www.vox.com/2015/8/10/9124145/effective-altruism-global-ai.

McGoey, Linsey. 2012. "Philanthrocapitalism and its critics." *ScienceDirect* 40 (2): 185–99.

Ord, Toby. 2013. "The Moral Imperative toward Cost-Effectiveness in Global Health." *Center for Global Development*. Reprinted as Chapter 2 of this volume.

Pogge, Thomas. 2002. *World Poverty and Human Rights*. Cambridge: Polity Press.

Rubenstein, James C. 2015. *Between Samaritans and States: The Political Ethics of Humanitarian INGOs*. Oxford: Oxford University Press.

Shue, Henry. 2016. "Uncertainty as the Reason for Action: Last Opportunity and Future Climate Disaster." *Global Justice: Theory, Practice, Rhetoric* 8 (2): 86–103.

Singer, Peter. 2015. *The Most Good You Can Do*. New Haven: Yale University Press.

Snow, Matthew. 2015. "Against Charity." *Jacobin*. Available at https://www.jacobinmag.com/2015/08/peter-singer-charity-effective-altruism/.

Srinivasan, Amia. 2015. "Stop the Robot Apocalypse." *London Review of Books* 37 (18): 3–6.

Teles, Steven, and Mark Schmitt. 2011. "The Elusive Craft of Evaluating Advocacy." *Stanford Social Innovation Review* (Summer): 39–43.

Walker, Robert. 2014. *The shame of poverty*. Oxford: Oxford University Press.

"The Logic of Effective Altruism." 2015. *Boston Review*. Forum. Available at http://bostonreview.net/forum/peter-singer-logic-effective-altruism.

Villadsen, Kaspar. 2007. "The Emergence of 'Neo-Philanthropy': A New Discursive Space in Welfare Policy?" *Acta Sociologica* 5 (3): 309–23.

Wenar, Leif. 2016. *Blood Oil*. Oxford: Oxford University Press.

8
Benevolent Giving and the Problem of Paternalism

Emma Saunders-Hastings

This chapter asks whether attempts to promote welfare though voluntary giving can be objectionably paternalistic. I argue that they can be, and explicate the kinds of tradeoffs that addressing concerns about paternalism would require.

The argument does not depend on or recommend a more general rejection of attempts at promoting welfare (including attempts to improve the lives of poor people in either one's own or other countries). I proceed from the assumption that human welfare is of great moral importance, and that the possibility of welfare improvements (especially for people at very low levels of welfare) provides us with strong reasons to donate money and take other actions that we can reasonably expect to be effective in bringing those improvements about. In my view, theories of voluntary giving that require us to reject these claims are implausible.

In general terms, my claim is that paternalistic relationships are *pro tanto* morally objectionable and that avoiding paternalism is of significant (though not overriding) moral importance. This holds *even*, though of course not exclusively, when the conception of the good that the paternalist is attempting to promote is a reasonable and morally appropriate one (i.e. a conception of objective welfare). Some welfarist and consequentialist views fail to pay sufficient attention to the importance of anti-paternalism. However, as I try to show in what follows, the claim that paternalistic relationships are morally objectionable can itself have a consequentialist and even welfarist character. People who accept (as I think we should accept) the claim that welfare improvements are of great moral importance *thereby* have good reasons to worry about philanthropic paternalism and to adopt a presumption (though not a prohibition) against it. This is because even consequentialists should not, in promoting good outcomes (e.g. by pursuing welfare gains at the margins), neglect things that are of predictable and pervasive instrumental value, including non-paternalistic relationships. I also explain how accepting further, *non*-consequentialist reasons for objecting to paternalism would affect the argument and inform decisions about where to give philanthropically.

I begin in the next two sections by explaining my understanding of paternalism and of why it is objectionable, as well as how the charge of paternalism applies in the case of philanthropy (as opposed to the more familiar cases of interpersonal interventions and government legislation). I argue we have strong (though not always overriding) reasons to avoid paternalism, including philanthropic paternalism. In the third section, I discuss how different ethical theories of philanthropic giving can incorporate a concern with avoiding paternalism and balance that concern against other moral considerations. In particular, I consider the disagreements that can arise even given a shared (e.g. purely welfarist) conception of the good. In the fourth section, I argue that philanthropic paternalism often reflects a common inattention on the part of donors to the importance of egalitarian social and political relations and to the kinds of respect that are due to prospective beneficiaries.

1. Philanthropic paternalism in theory

The charge of paternalism is commonly made against both philanthropy in general and the actions of particular philanthropists. But for that accusation to have force, we need to know what paternalism is and why it is wrong. I therefore begin by explaining my understanding of paternalism and argue that our reasons to avoid it are grounded in the importance of egalitarian social and political relations, of which respect for autonomous agents is an essential component. As I go on to argue, even views that do not ascribe intrinsic value to egalitarian social and political relations should value them as instrumentally important and should avoid paternalism for that reason.[1]

I will use the term "paternalism" to refer to interventions that aim to restrict, manipulate, or circumvent an agent's choices, on the grounds that the agent's ability to choose or act well on her own behalf is deficient, or inferior to that of the paternalist, in some relevant respect or domain.[2] This definition is compatible

[1] That is, my general claim about the importance of egalitarian social and political relations is compatible with both consequentialist and non-consequentialist moral views, since it does not require us to attach *independent* weight to relations of equality or respect. The family of views that Martin O'Neill has usefully christened "non-intrinsic egalitarianism" provides a range of consequentialist reasons (including reasons referencing welfare) for valuing egalitarian political, economic, and social relations. See O'Neill (2008). It is consistent with this argument that the value of egalitarian social relations is entirely instrumental, and even that that value is instrumental to a purely welfarist conception of the good. On the other hand, an argument for the importance of relations of equality and respect for agents is also compatible with the claim that a welfarist conception of the good is too narrow as a fundamental matter and that we need to move to an alternative or pluralist conception of value.

[2] I elaborate and defend this understanding of paternalism further in Saunders-Hastings, "Welfare Paternalism and Objections from Equality" (working paper, available on request). For similar definitions in the philosophical literature on paternalism, see Shiffrin (2000) (whose influential motive-based definition focuses on the paternalist's attempt to substitute her judgment for that of the person paternalized); Quong (2011, p. 80); Cornell (2015); and Barnett (2015). The definition of paternalism that I offer here is, for the sake of argument, narrower in two ways than my preferred account. First, like Shiffrin and Cornell, I believe that actions whose primary motive is to benefit someone other than the person paternalized can count as paternalistic, but I try to avoid that question here in order to argue from a more widely accepted understanding of the paternalist motive. Second, like Cornell,

with a range of different conceptions of the good and of corollary judgments about when (if ever) paternalism can be justified: it includes, for example, paternalism that aims narrowly at the promotion of welfare and not at a broader or more controversial conception of good.[3]

My definition covers cases of coercive paternalism but is not limited to them. It is the effort to substitute one's judgment for that of the person (or persons) whose good one is trying to promote that constitutes paternalism—not the particular techniques that one uses to effect this substitution.[4] So I count as paternalistic some cases of non-coercive paternalism (sometimes called "libertarian" or "nudge" paternalism), where people are incentivized or manipulated, but not actually constrained or coerced, to take or forgo the actions that the paternalist thinks would be best for them. Philanthropic paternalism often takes such a non-coercive form, involving attempts to incentivize or otherwise shape beneficiaries' choices: philanthropic gifts that are consensually accepted can come with conditions and restrictions that usurp beneficiaries' judgment over time. Although there may be (and, I think, are) cases where the activities of philanthropists can count as coercive, we need not think that coercion is involved for the problem of paternalism to arise.

The claims that paternalism need not be coercive, and that it can be objectionable even when not coercive, are controversial. Dworkin defines paternalism as "the interference with a person's liberty of action justified by reasons referring exclusively to the happiness, needs, interests or values of the person being coerced,"[5] and the coercion criterion continues to enjoy broad acceptance. Defenses of "libertarian paternalism" have brought wider acceptance to the idea that paternalism may be non-coercive, but the corollary of that view is usually the claim that non-coercive paternalism is not morally objectionable.[6] In that sense, the traditional view and the revisionist "non-coercive paternalism" view agree on the point of

I believe that the external meaning expressed by the paternalist's actions is more significant than the paternalist's own motivations. Again, though, I avoid relying on that claim in order to begin from more widely shared assumptions about paternalism. This amounts to a joint requirement that the paternalist (1) aim to benefit the person(s) paternalized and (2) be motivated by a negative appraisal of the paternalized's judgment or will. Although I do not believe that this definition will include all cases of objectionable paternalism, it will include many relevant to a discussion of philanthropy, where donors often are trying to benefit the people they paternalize and where negative judgments about beneficiary competence are often made explicit.

---

[3] Proponents of welfare paternalism (including Cass Sunstein and Richard Thaler, Sarah Conly, and Esther Duflo) generally hold that paternalism is impermissible when aimed at people's moral improvement or perfection but that it can sometimes be justified if more narrowly tailored to promote what the people paternalized would themselves recognize as their own welfare, in ways that the people paternalized would fail to do for themselves, perhaps because of cognitive biases, errors, or weakness of will.

[4] I owe the idea that a "substitution of judgment" is constitutive of paternalism to Shiffrin (2000); note, however, that Shiffrin does *not* require that this substitution aim to benefit the person paternalized. See discussion in footnote 2 above.

[5] Dworkin (1972).

[6] See, for example, Sunstein and Thaler (2003) and Sunstein (2014).

normative importance even if they disagree on semantics: whatever we call it, "paternalism" that is not effected through coercion is not subject to the same normative objections as (genuine or coercive) paternalism. I argue both that we should accept a broad definition of paternalism (i.e. one not restricted to cases of coercion or liberty-infringement) and *also* that we have *pro tanto* reason to avoid paternalistic behaviors, interventions, or policies even when they are not coercive.[7] So two claims need argument: that paternalism can be non-coercive and—more importantly—that non-coercive paternalism may still be objectionable.

Although those claims can be distinguished analytically, I assume that their defenses should be closely linked: it is the fact that some non-coercive behaviors can be objectionable *in the same way that paternalism is objectionable* that gives us reason to classify those behaviors as paternalistic.[8] The important point, though, is normative rather than terminological: I am happy enough if someone agrees with my arguments about the reasons we have to avoid some (even non-coercive) behaviors, even if she prefers a narrower definition of paternalism.

Along with other authors, I believe that the normative significance of paternalism comes in part from the negative judgment or insult that paternalism expresses toward the person(s) paternalized.[9] This insult can be important from either intrinsic or purely instrumental moral perspectives (although those perspectives will of course differ in the particular features of paternalism, or of insulting behavior and its consequences, that they emphasize as normatively significant). Paternalism is insulting because (or when) it reflects, assumes, or attempts to put in place a hierarchical relationship, where the paternalizer exercises judgment or choice in domains appropriately under the control of the person paternalized. A paternalistic relational dynamic can exist independently of coercion or of defects in the consent of the person paternalized.[10]

Importantly, both the element of disrespect or insult and the attempt to create or reinforce a hierarchical relationship depend on the relational context in which

[7] Shiffrin, Cornell, and Barnett likewise accept this pair of claims.

[8] Or, alternatively: it is the fact that some non-coercive behaviors can be objectionable in the same way that paternalism is objectionable, *when paternalism is objectionable*, that gives us reason to classify those behaviors as paternalistic. This formulation allows for the possibility that some classes of paternalism are not even *pro tanto* objectionable (e.g. when directed at children, or in cases of serious impairment on the part of the paternalized).

[9] See, for example Shiffrin's claim that "paternalist doctrines and policies convey a special, generally impermissible, insult to autonomous agents" (Shiffrin 2000, p. 207) and Cornell's argument that "instances of paternalism are objectionable because of their expressive content. Paternalism is suspect because it implies that the other party is not capable of making good judgments for herself... According to the expressive view, paternalism is objectionable because it constitutes an insult" (Cornell 2015, p. 1,297). Cornell also makes the important point that assessing the degree and permissibility of paternalism in a given action depends on contextual factors that affect the action's meaning.

[10] However, coercion and the presence or absence of consent might nevertheless make an important moral difference in how we ought to respond to paternalism, or to whether or not we are justified in intervening to prevent paternalism.

paternalism occurs. Classifying instances of paternalism on the basis of dyadic interactions, abstracted from context, can be misleading. Suppose that the case under consideration is "*A* destroys *B*'s cigarettes, because she believes that *B* would otherwise be harmed by his choice to smoke." It may seem clear that this is a paternalistic intervention. But our intuition about that case may change if we learn that *A* is *B*'s eight-year-old daughter. The claim here is not just that the "paternalism" would be *excused* by the fact that an (ordinarily) wrongful act has been committed by a child who does not know better. Rather, I think we can make the stronger claim that *A*'s action is not a genuine case of paternalism at all. There may have been a coercive or judgmental intervention. But for a charge of paternalism to make sense, the putative paternalizer must either stand in a relation of *superior* power or status to the paternalized or else reasonably be interpreted as trying to put such a relation in place. To complain of being paternalized by one's eight-year-old child will generally sound like nonsense, for good reason: the complaint ignores the relational context that helps to distinguish paternalism from interventions of other kinds.

My claim is that paternalism is at heart about unequal and hierarchical relationships, which need not themselves arise from or involve coercion.[11] Paternalistic relationships may be structured by non-coercive forms of influence and control and be promoted in non-coercive ways (e.g. by the incentives created by background inequalities and injustices).[12] To motivate this intuition in people who do not yet share it, consider the following case. A woman believes (rightly or wrongly, and whether or not this is the result of background injustice) that her chances of a decent life depend on securing an eligible husband. Imagine further that her preferred (or only) suitor demands, as conditions of their marriage, that she turn over control of her property to him, allow him to exercise control over her work, and refrain from socializing without his permission. He makes these conditions because he believes that he will make better choices in these domains than she would, with a view to her happiness. Supposing that his conditions are not standard or legally enforceable, it does not seem that the suitor is coercing the woman. Nevertheless, I take it that he is exploiting an unfair, or at least asymmetrical, bargaining position, in an attempt to secure her consent into an inegalitarian relationship whose hierarchy is strongly paternalistic in character. This suggests, I believe, that our concern about paternalism is a concern about the quality of relationships, not just about particular acts (e.g. coercion or liberty infringement) ruled out of bounds by a lack of consent.

[11] This holds even in cases where we might think that paternalism is justifiable: for example, if we reverse the case and imagine a parent paternalizing her child. If paternalism is justified, it is because an asymmetrical or unequal relationship can be justified.

[12] One might think that forms of influence that are parasitic on background injustice *are* coercive—but the view that such forms of influence are paternalistic need not depend on that claim or on a controversially broad definition of coercion.

We can suppose, further, that the woman believes that she will be better off by consenting to a marriage on these terms than she would be if she married someone else or did not marry at all. We can even suppose that she is right about this: non-coercive behaviors (like coercive ones) can be objectionably paternalistic *even if they result in welfare benefits to the paternalized* (in this case, welfare benefits relative to the baseline situation under which the suitor declines—permissibly, let us grant—to marry the woman). What matters is the attempt to curtail the autonomy and shape the options open to the person paternalized, because of her presumed inability to judge well for herself. And the element of coercion or non-consensual liberty infringement is not necessary for a paternalistic relationship to arise: such a relationship could be one that the paternalized consensually opts into for lack (or perceived lack) of better options.

So far, I have not specified whether the inequality in the bargaining positions of the parties in this example results from background injustice. If it does, then perhaps the paternalized's position results from background circumstances that count as coercive or liberty-restricting. Even so, it is not *the paternalizer* who coerces the paternalized: we can suppose that he has no obligation to enter into a relationship with her at all, and so he does not threaten to make her worse off relative to that (permissible) baseline. At worst, he exploits rather than creates the injustice. But again, the element of *coercion* or liberty infringement *by the paternalizer* does not seem to make a difference to the effects on the paternalized. A proponent of a narrower definition of paternalism might hold that, against just background conditions, paternalism could only arise from coercion. Although I do not believe this, I am happy to concede it for the purposes of this argument, since the cases that interest me are not primarily ideal-theoretic ones but interactions occurring against the backdrop of unjust inequalities. At least in circumstances of background injustice (that the paternalist does not create but can exploit), coercion will fail to capture the full range of objectionable violations of, or constraints on, autonomy. I therefore count as paternalistic the exploitation of inequalities in order to incentivize constraints on autonomy, or relations of benevolent but hierarchical control. I believe that this is consistent with common intuitions about what is objectionable about paternalism. Even if we want to preserve paternalism as a relatively narrow category of impermissible motivations attaching to *already* wrongful actions, we should recognize the possibility that the relevant motivations could attach to *consensual* wrongs like exploitation.

The paternalistic marriage case has structural similarities to the kind of philanthropic paternalism that interests me.[13] In both cases, I claim, objectionable paternalism can exist even when the paternalized consents (at some stage) to conditions or restrictions on her autonomy. The incentives that the paternalizer

[13] Of course, there are also important differences, e.g. the greater intimacy of the relationship in the marriage case. Such factors are important but do not, I think, undermine the structural similarity.

extends to motivate that consent (whether in the form of philanthropic gifts, or the offer of a close personal relationship) may be benefits that he is entitled to withhold. Nevertheless, we can object to the paternalistic purposes for which he seeks to constrain the paternalized's autonomy and to the kind of relationship he attempts to put in place. The fact that the paternalized has opted into a paternalistic relationship makes *some* moral difference (i.e. it has important implications for the actions that governments and other actors can permissibly take to *prevent* paternalism), but this does not in general remove the moral objection to the conduct of the paternalizer.

2. Philanthropic paternalism in practice

Paternalism has a long history in the charitable sector: it has characterized giving of many kinds, including forms of charity that self-consciously aimed at maximizing the impact of assistance. The "scientific philanthropy" of the nineteenth and early twentieth centuries originated from a paternalistic complaint with earlier models of almsgiving: where aid went directly to poor people (and, especially, to the wrong kind of poor people), the giver could not ensure that his gift was put to worthy and efficient use.[14] The giver should retain continued control of the gift (e.g. by supplying public goods instead of distributing aid to recipients), because he knows better than those he is trying to benefit and can better avoid charitable funds going to waste. (Andrew Carnegie described this as an arrangement where "the millionaire will be but a trustee for the poor,"[15] and he did not seem to envision the trust ever being wound up.)

Another popular option was giving to recipients in ways that permitted other forms of control or otherwise limited their scope for choice. Some organizations offered in-kind relief instead of cash (which was dangerously fungible and easy for recipients to misspend). Others made opting in to tutelary or paternalistic social relations a condition of assistance. The British and American Charity Organization Societies of the late nineteenth century sent "friendly visitors" (often upper-class women volunteers) to visit poor people's houses, monitor the uses people were making of the assistance provided to them, and also to dispense moral and practical advice. Whether the *charity's* offer or conditions was coercive, or merely the exploitation of background injustice in order to exercise control, seems orthogonal to the charity's effects on the autonomy of recipients, especially over time.[16]

[14] See, for example, Zunz (2011, p. 19). [15] Carnegie (1901, p. 17).

[16] Paternalistic social relations were not, of course, confined to the charitable sector: there were parallel efforts to use government policy to constrain the poor for their own good (e.g. some arguments for Prohibition).

While there are significant historical and contemporary strands of philanthropy that engage in moralistic paternalism, and seek to make their intended beneficiaries more virtuous, other philanthropists are more likely to be tempted by welfare paternalism (if tempted to paternalism at all). While some moralists have argued for withholding assistance *entirely*, allegedly for people's own good, the important dilemmas for welfarists are generally about *how* (rather than whether) to give.[17]

The effective altruism movement is one contemporary, more rigorous successor to earlier movements for scientific philanthropy. The Centre for Effective Altruism defines effective altruism as "[the use of] evidence and reason to figure out how to benefit others as much as possible, and [the taking of] action on that basis."[18] While effective altruism is not exclusively a philosophy of voluntary giving, it has attracted public attention chiefly for its adherents' claim that we should donate in ways that maximize the good that we do with our charitable donations. MacAskill distinguishes two senses in which a theory of giving might be maximizing: "One can try to increase the amount of good one does in two ways: by increasing the amount of resources that one dedicates to doing good; and by trying to increase the effectiveness of the resources that one has dedicated to doing good."[19] On the definition of effective altruism endorsed by MacAskill in this volume and adopted by the Centre for Effective Altruism, effective altruism is maximizing only in the second of the two ways that MacAskill distinguishes.[20] Pummer likewise holds a view that is maximizing only in the latter sense: he argues that it can be (and often is) wrong to give to less effective organizations even in cases in which (for reasons of personal prerogative) it is morally acceptable not to give at all.[21] For any given amount of resources (i.e. holding the *amount* of a donation constant), effective altruism recommends maximizing the good that donation does (on what MacAskill calls a "tentatively welfarist" understanding of the good). It is this focus on maximizing on a donor-defined objective (and with an amount of resources likewise fixed by the donor) that links effective altruism

[17] Welfarist reasons might perhaps supply justification against giving cash to someone whom one knows will spend it on (say) cigarettes, or other addictive products with negative health impacts that would make the beneficiary worse off than she would have been without the donation, in terms of objective and perhaps also subjective welfare.

[18] See MacAskill "The Definition of Effective Altruism", Chapter 1 in this volume, p. 13. MacAskill characterizes effective altruism as "a project" rather than an obligation and denies that it is a normative claim (pp. 15–16). While it is conceivable that a person might engage in the project of benefitting others as much as possible for non-normative reasons, there is some risk of cryptonormativity in MacAskill's position: effective altruists are at least committed to the view that effective altruism is a permissible project, and generally also hold the view that we have strong normative reasons to act in ways that are consistent with the project of effective altruism (e.g. by seeking to "do the most good" with our charitable donations), rather than in ways that seem inconsistent with it (e.g. by donating to the Metropolitan Museum).

[19] MacAskill, "The Definition of Effective Altruism", Chapter 1 in this volume, p. 14.

[20] MacAskill, "The Definition of Effective Altruism", Chapter 1 in this volume, p. 14.

[21] Pummer (2016).

to earlier modes of philanthropic paternalism. On the conditionally maximizing views that MacAskill and Pummer endorse, the problem could in theory be especially acute (if paternalism is a welfare-efficient giving option), since the option of spending *more* in order to give in less paternalistic ways appears to be blocked: that surplus presumably counts as part of "the resources one has dedicated to doing good" and should therefore be spent more efficiently.

My claim isn't that evidence-based, outcome-oriented approaches *necessarily* produce more choice-constraining or paternalizing policies than other forms of philanthropy. Donors who are ineffective or even uninterested in effectiveness can of course act paternalistically too. But the main reason to expect *effective* altruists in particular to be tempted by welfare paternalism arises as a byproduct of effective altruism's greatest normative attraction: the fact that its adherents really do care about doing the most good possible with their charitable donations. This seriousness about outcomes, often coupled with stringent standards for measuring the benefits of donations, gives effective altruists incentives to monitor and regulate recipients' choices in hopes of extracting greater welfare returns than beneficiaries could produce for themselves. These incentives are (for better or worse) less pronounced for donors who take a more relaxed attitude toward the consequences of their donations.

Consider the ongoing debate around the merits of direct cash transfers. GiveDirectly is a charity that arranges unconditional cash transfers by cell phone to people in poor countries, targeting extremely low-income households. GiveDirectly has been one of GiveWell's top-rated charities since 2012. Giving What We Can, on the other hand, published blog posts criticizing GiveWell's recommendation, on the grounds that more efficiently welfare-promoting options are available.[22]

Effective altruists generally recognize cash transfers as a useful baseline against which to evaluate other interventions: as MacAskill puts it in his book, "we should only assume we're in a better position to help the poor than they are to help themselves if we have some particularly compelling reason for thinking so."[23] Here is how he now characterizes his view of GiveDirectly's effectiveness:

> The obvious first question to ask about GiveDirectly is: What do the recipients of these cash transfers do with the money? If they spend it on education, that sounds pretty good; if they spend it on drugs and alcohol, that's worrying. It turns out that the most common use of the transfer is to buy assets, typically farm animals, or to convert thatched roofs into iron ones; on average, recipients spent 39 percent of the transfer on assets. These purchases seem to have very high returns, potentially as high as 14 percent per year for at least a period of several years.[24]

[22] MacAskill (2012) and Mogensen (2014).
[23] MacAskill (2015, pp. 115–16).
[24] MacAskill (2015, p. 111).

MacAskill presents this mainly as evidence that poor people are performing relatively well according to objective standards for evaluating the value of alternative spending choices. Behavioral science research might give us reason to worry about the risk of irrational spending in the case of cash transfers, but the evidence that MacAskill presents suggests that the poor generally make good use of the funds. (It may also be evidence that poor people have different estimations of their most pressing needs than do donors and NGOs: as MacAskill points out, it does not seem that any charities are in the business of providing the metal roof upgrades that seem to be so highly valued by the poor.) But this amounts to only a qualified and contingent support for anti-paternalist interventions and, indeed, MacAskill continues to recommend other options in preference to GiveDirectly on the grounds of their greater expected welfare value. Other effective altruists show a similar ambivalence about cash transfers, grounded in the expectation that more welfare-promoting options are available. As Cari Tuna, the president of the effective altruist foundation Good Ventures puts it: "I am still optimistic that we can do better than just giving money to poor people."[25]

Tuna's hope need not be a paternalistic one. Even on non-paternalist grounds, cash transfers may not always be appropriate. Some public goods are unlikely to be provided by markets, and other goods (e.g. those subject to economies of scale) might need to be provided in-kind if at all. There can be a non-paternalist case for giving in-kind in cases where distributing cash would not be sufficient to provide a target population with access to the relevant good. This might justify the choice to provide, for example, some medical products in kind, without justifying the in-kind provision of goods that recipients could buy for themselves if they had the money (and where, as in the roof case, their choices might surprise outside observers).[26] Second, there may be a non-paternalist case for giving in-kind where we believe that this is necessary in order to get resources to people who might otherwise be deprived of them if cash were provided to families. One common argument against cash transfers is that benefits will be consumed by male heads of household and that cash aid will fail adequately or equitably to benefit women and children.[27] My claim is not that unconditional direct cash transfers are the uniquely justifiable anti-paternalist option for giving but rather that they can serve as a kind of non-paternalist baseline for evaluating interventions (as well as a welfarist one). A non-paternalist case might be made for other kinds of aid—but such a case does need to be made, and we should not be

[25] Quoted in Matthews (2015).

[26] For example, non-paternalist reasons might justify philanthropic efforts to supply insecticide-treated bed nets or deworming treatments, if supplying cash (or cash in combination with information) would not be sufficient to ensure access to the relevant preventive health measures.

[27] On the definition of paternalism that I am using, these attempts to benefit people other than the person paternalized would not count as paternalism. On Shiffrin's broader definition they might, *if* we consider them attempts to substitute the paternalizer's judgment about something (e.g. parenting choices) that properly lies within the paternalized's sphere of autonomy.

satisfied with a donor's confidence that her judgments will produce greater welfare returns than the recipients' otherwise would. The latter amounts to an attempt to justify paternalism rather than a rebuttal of the charge.

There is no reason to think that effective altruists *aim* at paternalism; I expect that, all else equal, they prefer to avoid it. But all else is unlikely to be equal for a movement so focused on measuring impact and distinguishing the very *most* effective interventions. Like earlier proponents of scientific philanthropy, effective altruists are likely to encounter tensions between the ambitious pursuit of highly specific outcomes and the promotion of non-hierarchal relations. Effective altruists, too, will face choices between merely benefitting the poor and acting as their "trustees": limiting beneficiaries' scope for choice (e.g. by making cash transfers conditional, or giving in-kind rather than cash), on the expectation that they will choose badly.[28] This raises the question of how alternative moral theories (or alternative ways of framing the same moral theory) handle the balancing of considerations involved in judging when and how far elements of paternalism can form a part of morally appropriate forms of giving. I turn to that question in the next section.

3. Incorporating concern for paternalism in consequentialist views

I have argued that there is something morally objectionable, *pro tanto*, about paternalistic relationships in general and hence about the relationships involved in philanthropic paternalism in particular. This is true despite the fact that philanthropic paternalism is often welfarist in its aims and non-coercive in its methods. What is the upshot for how philanthropists should act?

We might think that philanthropists have reason to avoid paternalism only to the extent that they are persuaded that there is something *intrinsically* objectionable about paternalism. But on the understanding of paternalism that I have advanced, one that pays particular attention to social and political relationships and their context, there are strong reasons for even consequentialists and welfarists to take account of concerns about paternalism.

Of course, most welfare consequentialists will quickly agree that philanthropists (and other actors) should avoid paternalistic actions or behaviors *when they result in welfare losses or undermine the goal of welfare-promotion.*[29] Many cases of

[28] This is not a *unique* failing of effective altruism: paternalism is a pitfall of many different ethical theories of voluntary giving. However, the paternalism complaint—unlike familiar criticisms of effective altruism on the grounds of its demandingness—will sometimes provide reasons *against* donating in the ways that effective altruists recommend (rather than just telling us that we are not obligated to donate in those ways or that other ways of donating are also permissible).

[29] One could easily adapt this claim to other forms of consequentialism, replacing "welfare" with an alternative formulation of the good to be promoted.

moralistic legislation (e.g. laws restricting sexual activity between consenting adults) are counterproductive in this way. But the objection need not attach only to coercive paternalism; non-coercive attempts to change a person's sexual preference (e.g. incentives offered by family members or nudges deployed by therapists) are likely to have similar welfare costs. Welfare losses could also result from welfarist interventions or nudges that misfire, and so welfare consequentialists will agree that any such interventions should be evidence-based and carefully designed.

The more controversial question will be whether philanthropists should (sometimes) avoid paternalistic actions or behaviors *even when they are welfare-promoting.* Clearly, welfare consequentialists will be inclined to reject this claim: because paternalism is not *intrinsically* wrong, we do not have a general duty to avoid it in cases where it really would promote welfare (nor do we need an independent stricture against paternalism to avoid the instances of it that are really worth avoiding). Estimating the consequences of alternative courses of action tells us all that we need to know about their relative moral value. And so, in cases where the same amount of money could be converted into anti-poverty resources in two (or more) different ways, one of which is more choice-constraining for recipients but expected to produce greater welfare improvements, many consequentialist views will recommend the paternalistic intervention. Of course, it is a delicate matter in practice which actions fit the description of "welfare-promoting," since many actions that naively *seem* welfare-promoting in fact might not be once the negative effects of paternalism have been appropriately taken into account.

But other consequentialist responses are possible, without attributing *intrinsic* wrongfulness to paternalism. One could agree that welfare, or some other consequence, is all that matters but reject the idea that donors calculating on a case-by-case basis is the best way of promoting the relevant conception of welfare. Perhaps the most obvious welfare consequentialist approach would seek to estimate the consequences of engaging in or refraining from *particular* instances of paternalistic behavior. But this is not the only way of framing a welfarist (or other consequentialist) objection to philanthropic paternalism.

Consider the following alternative: *Philanthropists should adopt a presumption against paternalism in their giving, and against creating or reinforcing paternalistic relationships, because adopting such a presumption will better promote welfare in general and in the long run.*

John Stuart Mill's anti-paternalism has this general form: he regards his liberty principle (which holds that appeals to an individual's "own good" is "not a sufficient warrant" for interference with her liberty of action) as justified ultimately in terms of utility.[30] Rather than calculating the utility of paternalistic behavior on a case-by-case basis, Mill adopts a rule against it. The rule is justified by our general

[30] Mill (2006, pp. 223–4).

confidence that individuals are the best judges of their own good and (crucially, for Mill) by the difficulty of quarantining paternalistic behavior to isolated interventions.[31] Mill has in mind here cases of (what he counts as) coercion, and thus the liberty principle's rule against paternalism is a strict one. But one could also adopt a more granular view, incorporating stronger and weaker strictures against paternalism of different kinds. While the liberty principle itself mainly presents a negative injunction against some kinds of paternalistic behavior, Mill also has a broader commitment to the *promotion* of egalitarian, mutually respectful relationships. It is partly for the sake of promoting such relationships, and the values that we expect them to help realize, that we are to refrain from paternalism even when it might look to have utility value if considered narrowly or as an isolated case.

Some of the reasons for adopting a presumption against paternalism are very broad and general. I argued in the first section that paternalism and paternalistic relationships are generally disrespectful and inimical to egalitarian social and political relationships, and we have good reasons to believe that egalitarian social and political relationships are of pervasive and important welfare value. They may themselves count as a component of welfare, if the experience of such relationships makes people happier than hierarchical ones. Egalitarian social and political relationships may also do a better job than hierarchical ones of promoting both material welfare (i.e. because people are generally the best judges of what is good for them) and psychological welfare (i.e. by promoting what Rawls called "the social bases of self-respect").[32] Of course, these claims are (at least to a very great extent) empirical and I do not claim to have provided adequate support for them here. Although I think we have good reason to believe that egalitarian social and political relationships promote morally important values (including welfare), the revised consequentialist claim would fail if the empirical assumptions on which it rests proved untrue. (Or rather, the claim would fail unless supplemented by further reasons to avoid paternalism).

But other reasons for avoiding paternalism apply with particular force in the philanthropic domain. Even if we accept (at least for the sake of argument) the claim that paternalistic and inegalitarian relationships generally fail to promote welfare, it seems overwhelmingly likely that *some* paternalistic interventions promote welfare. (For example, in cases of information asymmetries: perhaps beneficiaries do not have access to the data that would direct them to the most welfare-promoting

[31] For further discussion of this thread in Mill, see Saunders-Hastings (2014).

[32] For philosophical discussion of various ways that egalitarian relationships are instrumentally valuable (and hierarchical ones harmful), see, for example, Young (1990); O'Neill (2008); Rawls, (2001, pp. 130–1), and Scanlon (2018). Note that Rawls and Scanlon endorse deontological as well as instrumental reasons for caring about equality. For empirical studies supporting the relationship between egalitarian social and political relationships and well-being, see, for example, Drèze and Sen (1989) and Wilkinson and Pickett (2009).

courses of action and perhaps the difficulty or cost of communicating that information is very high. In such a case, paternalistic restrictions or nudges might promote what beneficiaries themselves would, from a different perspective, recognize as their own well-being.) There is a good chance that adopting a presumption against paternalism will sometimes cause philanthropists to refrain from paternalism in cases where it could be welfare-promoting.

For the presumption to hold, its instrumental value must outweigh its costs. There is good reason to think that this will be true (at least) in the case of philanthropic relationships. The alternative to a presumption against paternalism in the case of philanthropy is for donors to act paternalistically whenever *they* expect a more paternalizing giving option to produce greater good. But donors have cognitive limitations and biases too. To see the problem with a broad permission for philanthropic paternalism, we need not make the implausible claim that individuals are *always* the best judges or promoters of their own good. For the practice of philanthropic paternalism to make sense, we need to think not only that people will sometimes be wrong about how to promote their good but that philanthropists will, in general, judge better. Cautionary examples from past philanthropic experience suggest skepticism on this score. The narrower, welfare-oriented paternalism of some contemporary philanthropy does not entirely diffuse the worry. The errors of past philanthropists were not only the product of non-consequentialist conceptions of the good; they were predictable effects of the exercise of unaccountable power, including of *benevolent* unaccountable power. We can grant that some kinds of impartial third parties will sometimes do better than individuals at promoting welfare while denying that this is reliably true of philanthropists. In general, welfare paternalists focus on the case for paternalism in *public* policy which, when subject to democratic accountability, may be able to register and adapt to the preferences of the people affected in ways that philanthropy cannot. While the classic target of anti-paternalist arguments is government action, we are especially warranted in adopting a presumption against paternalism by unaccountable actors (whether public or private).

A presumption against philanthropic paternalism does not mean a prohibition, and the kind of presumption I have in mind is neither strict nor framed in wholly negative terms. Any plausible moral view that assigns value to anti-paternalism—*either* as having intrinsic value, or as a good instrumental rule of thumb—will also assign value to things that could potentially conflict with anti-paternalism (whether those are different values or just other important determinants of welfare). Anti-paternalism must be balanced against other moral and instrumental considerations, and so it might still be true that the morally best philanthropic interventions and opportunities are ones that involve an element of paternalism. In the domain of interventions that involve some paternalism, where does the line between morally appropriate and inappropriate interventions lie?

Here I will offer two candidate factors to assess in determining the justifiability of paternalist elements in philanthropic programs.

The first is the availability and cost of non-paternalist or less paternalist giving options (or options for conferring the relevant benefit, e.g. welfare). For consequentialist ethical theories of philanthropy, the interest is not primarily in distinguishing permissible from impermissible options but in making comparative judgments about the *most* morally appropriate forms of giving. Because that question is fundamentally a comparative one, the existence and cost of less paternalist options make a difference to how defensible paternalist options are. A presumption against paternalism would be less plausibly welfare-promoting if interpreted to mean that donors should prefer not to benefit others *at all* rather than to benefit them in (even slightly) paternalistic ways. So for welfare consequentialists, the presumption should rather be in favor of *minimizing* paternalism in philanthropic relationships and in favor of promoting egalitarian relations. At a minimum, this means choosing the least paternalistic option among comparably efficient ways of producing welfare benefits. But the longer-term and demonstration value of promoting forms of philanthropy (such as GiveDirectly) that register and respect beneficiary choice should also be taken into account, and should discourage donors from preferring paternalist forms of giving for the sake of small differences in naively expected welfare return.

The second consideration turns on the diachronic effects of philanthropic paternalism. It is worse for some kinds of relationships than others to be structured paternalistically. A one-off gift that offers the recipient limited choices but that does not create ongoing obligations or undermine valuable egalitarian social and political relationships is generally of less concern than paternalism that is enacted through or against close or durable social and political relationships. As I emphasized in the first section, the context against which paternalism occurs is crucial to its evaluation.

These guidelines are preliminary and subject to revision in light of evidence about the effects of different kinds of intervention and relationship. But even so, we can see how they might help guide judgments about the most morally appropriate forms of giving. For example, suppose we accept that the choice to provide bed nets or medical treatment instead of cash is not (at least in many cases) required to make those goods accessible, and that programs providing these goods therefore involve some element of paternalism. We might nevertheless think that such programs (e.g. projects by the Against Malaria Foundation and deworming initiatives) raise only minor concerns and can be justified on balance. While they do not give recipients the same range of options as cash transfers, these interventions do allow individualized opt-in by families and do not pose significant tradeoffs between promoting welfare and respecting beneficiaries' choices and judgment. Provided the relational consequences of interventions providing in-kind goods are minimal (i.e. that the benefits do not come with longer-term conditions attached), and that no *less* paternalistic interventions are available for producing comparable welfare benefits (i.e. because there is strong evidence that important health-related goods, even if they are already *accessible* and known to be so, will not be purchased or used unless provided in-kind), such interventions can plausibly be justified.

But these features are not built in to the domain of health interventions: more worrying cases, with more difficult tradeoffs, may lie on the horizon. We need guidelines for how to handle tradeoffs between maximizing welfare and respecting choice when interventions occur at the community or country-wide level, where designing interventions in ways that permit individualized opt-in or opt-out will often not be possible. Worries about paternalism become more significant as philanthropists increasingly focus on larger-scale impacts and "leveraging" donations to produce systemic change.[33] Even where their objectives are worthy, interventions involving public–private partnerships between philanthropists and host governments risk reorienting accountability from domestic populations to outside actors or blocking the formation of accountability relations in the first place.[34] Given our especially strong empirical reasons for believing that democratic accountability relationships are important contributors to welfare,[35] donors should resist subverting or crowding out such relationships even where it seems that doing so would produce marginal gains in welfare in particular cases. Effects on political relationships will likely be the most important class of cases where a concern for paternalism gives us reason to reject otherwise apparently justifiable interventions.

This section has tried to show that the tension between concern for paternalism and welfarist or consequentialist theories of voluntary giving may be overstated. Attention to the relational externalities of philanthropic interventions can be justified in consequentialist and welfarist terms. However, crude or naively applied conceptions of welfare consequentialism are unlikely to give relational concerns sufficient weight, and the unaccountability of philanthropic actors puts them at particular risk of engaging in short-sighted paternalism.

4. Philanthropy and relational obligations

The previous section argued that donors should adopt a presumption against paternalism as they go about promoting welfare. Since welfare features importantly

[33] See Gabriel and McElwee, "Effective Altruism, Global Poverty, and Systemic Change", Chapter 7 of this volume.

[34] For discussion of cases where philanthropic programs have arguably undermined state capacity and/or relationships of political accountability, see, for example, Waal (1997); Deaton (2015); and Clough (2015).

[35] See, for example, Sen (2000) and Drèze and Sen (1989) for the famous finding that a famine has never occurred in a democratic country with a free press.

in (even where it does not exhaust) consequentialist conceptions of the good, attention to paternalism would better help consequentialists to realize the values that they care about. But I do not wish to overstate the overlap between my argument against paternalism and consequentialist theories of giving. This is not only because the instrumental argument for adopting a presumption against philanthropic paternalism is vulnerable to empirical evidence showing *benefits* to paternalism and paternalist relationships. It also, in my view, fails to capture in full what is objectionable about paternalism. Paternalism is wrong not only for the welfare losses or opportunity costs that hierarchical and paternalistic relationships (often) entail; paternalism is also a disrespectful and intrinsically objectionable ways of treating autonomous agents. In this final section, I pursue some further implications of accepting the intrinsic wrongfulness of paternalistic treatment and relationships. Note, though, that the argument is modular: the instrumental reasons for attempting to minimize philanthropic paternalism apply independent of the argument in this section.

The set of issues that I consider in this final section is broader than paternalism. Paternalism is one way among many that philanthropists can demonstrate a mistaken understanding of the scope of their moral entitlement to pursue their own conceptions of the good (including through philanthropic donations). Paternalism can be symptomatic of a more general blind spot in theories of philanthropy that call for the promotion of an objective conception of the good in ways unmediated by relational duties; such theories risk instrumentalizing and subordinating the actual and prospective beneficiaries of philanthropy.

A single-minded focus on the promotion of an objective value can be disrespectful to the people *not* helped as well as to the people helped in inappropriately paternalizing ways. In the previous sections, I considered mainly cases where one could try to benefit a particular person or group in more or less choice-constraining ways. I did not count as paternalistic cases where a donor might choose to give to some recipients (or organizations benefitting some set of recipients) rather than others, on the grounds that she expected giving to one set of recipients to produce greater welfare benefits. Such a choice need not imply that the donor thinks that the disappointed prospective recipients are unable to choose or act well on their own behalf.[36] It might simply be the case that the first group can be helped more efficiently, so that donating to them will do more good overall.[37]

[36] Though it need not imply this, it might: if, for example, the motivation is concern *for the people denied aid*, e.g. if one believes that they will misuse aid in ways that will make themselves worse off relative to the no-donation baseline.

[37] Note that on Shiffrin's definition and ones influenced by it, which allow actions aiming to benefit third parties to count as paternalistic, this kind of decision might count as paternalistic if it is motivated by the relevant disrespect for the agency of the people denied aid: if, for example, the two groups currently occupy similar levels of welfare and the *reason* for expecting donations to one group to produce greater welfare returns turns on predictions about irrational or short-sighted behavior by the other group.

Though the use of efficient welfare promotion as a justification for giving to one group of people rather than another will often not count as paternalistic on the definition I have offered here, I believe that the issues are related.

Attempting to benefit people whom one expects to be able to help more efficiently than others and attempting to benefit people in paternalistic ways that one expects to produce greater benefits overall can presumably be justified (if at all) in parallel ways. In either case, a donor is pursuing an objective conception of the good and is using that to ground decisions about where and how to give. The question of whether a donor is justified in acting this way turns partly on whether the conception of the good is a morally appropriate one.

But it does not depend only on that. It also depends on the donor's entitlement to specify the good that she wishes to promote with her giving. And it is not clear that donors have this entitlement, *even* in cases where their aims are morally appropriate (e.g. the promotion of human health). The question depends on the kind of claim that prospective beneficiaries do or do not have on the donor. T.M. Scanlon gives a well-known argument that "a subjective criterion of well-being seems insensitive to differences between preferences that are of great relevance when these preferences are taken as the basis for moral claims."[38] He uses the example of duties of mutual aid:

> The strength of a stranger's claim on us for aid in the fulfilment of some interest depends upon what that interest is and need not be proportional to the importance he attaches to it. The fact that someone would be willing to forego a decent diet in order to build a monument to his god does not mean that his claim on others for aid in his project has the same strength as a claim for aid in obtaining enough to eat (even assuming that the sacrifices required of others would be the same).[39]

The fact that the example is of duties of mutual aid rather than justice is important for Scanlon's conclusion. If a stranger is *entitled* to some set of resources from me, then I am not permitted to dictate how she uses those resources. (If I owe her food, I may not stipulate that she eat it rather than use it to build a monument to her god.) This is true even if I am right and she is wrong about the use of resources that would most efficiently promote an objective conception of her good (or even her own subjective conception of her good). And so the claim that we are entitled to make distinctions, on the basis of objective criteria of well-being, between the strength of people's claims on us depends on the duties being ones of beneficence or mutual aid rather than justice.

Even when they take themselves to be acting on the basis of duties, philanthropists often understand the relevant duties as generalized ones of beneficence

[38] Scanlon (1975). [39] Scanlon (1975, pp. 659–60).

rather than as relational or justice-based obligations owed to particular people. On this interpretation, we have an obligation to promote welfare (or some other value), often understood in terms of objective criteria of well-being, not to transfer resources for people to use as they prefer. Acknowledging a general, even highly demanding, obligation to promote welfare can generate extremely fungible duties: it does not commit you to giving to any particular people or causes, and nobody has a complaint against you if you spend your time and money on something that produces greater welfare. You may, and should, donate to organizations working on the possibility of existential threats posed by artificial intelligence if that is where the greatest expected welfare benefits lie (even if that means investing in Silicon Valley start-ups rather than devoting resources to efforts to fight global poverty).[40]

Many people drawn to the effective altruist approach to global *poverty* are likely to feel that such recommendations miss something morally important about the claims of the living poor. People who see duties of beneficence as mediated by duties of justice (and structured in part by facts about background injustice) may doubt about their entitlement to discount the claims of some people on the grounds of greater expected welfare returns elsewhere or later. If I owe something as a matter of justice, it is not my place to attach conditions to returning it: any assertion of discretion on my part, or withholding of aid until my terms are met, would seem to compound the original wrong.[41] For some deontological theories, placing conditions on giving what I *owe* as a matter of justice is objectionable (perhaps even coercive) in a way that utilitarian theories do not register.

I think that this can help explain some diverging intuitions among people who share a general commitment to benefitting others, from different normative foundations.

A non-consequentialist who attributes intrinsic wrongness to relational wrongs like injustice and paternalism can of course still agree that promoting welfare (or doing good on some other conception of "good") matters, and that (among other things) this gives individuals strong moral reasons to donate money to charities that do good effectively. But she will see reasons to avoid paternalism that are not all instrumental to the goal of promoting welfare and that may mediate and constrain it. She will also see reasons *to* help some people—at least where significant welfare improvements are possible for people unjustly experiencing poverty and

[40] MacAskill (2015, pp. 193–4) provides some guidance on donating with a view toward mitigating global catastrophic risk. Organizations focused on existential risks (so-called "x-risks") include the Future of Humanity Institute at Oxford University and the Berkeley Existential Risk Initiative. The Open Philanthropy Project (a leading EA donor institution) makes grants in the areas of catastrophic risk and risks from artificial intelligence.

[41] For an argument along these lines applied to domestic philanthropy in affluent democracies, see Cordelli (2016, pp. 244–65).

deprivation—even without expecting those people to convert resources into good with maximum efficiency.

5. Conclusion

I have argued that there can be objectionable paternalism even where philanthropists adopt a morally appropriate goal (e.g. promoting welfare), and that consequentialists as well as those convinced of the intrinsic wrongfulness of paternalism should adopt a presumption against it. A focus on the marginal effects of *particular* paternalistic interventions or behaviors risks failing adequately to promote *relationships* that are of pervasive and important instrumental value. The problem is not specifically with promoting welfare: a similar point would apply to any donors who have a conception of the good that they are eager to promote (at least where that conception of the good is not exhausted by autonomy). The problem comes from assuming a donor's prerogative to maximally promote her own conception of the good. Whatever their specific moral views, donors should pay greater attention to the social and political relationships through which they try to do good—and that may limit the ways they can respectfully do it.

References

Barnett, Michael. 2015. "Paternalism and Global Governance." *Social Philosophy and Policy* 32 (1): 216–43.

Carnegie, Andrew. 1901. "The Gospel of Wealth." In *The Gospel of Wealth and Other Timely Essays*. New York: The Century Co.

Clough, Emily. 2015. "Effective Altruism's Political Blind Spot." *Boston Review* (online edition), 14 July (Accessed 11 June 2018). Available at http://bostonreview.net/world/emily-clough-effective-altruism-ngos.

Cordelli, Chiara. 2016. "Reparative Justice and the Moral Limits of Discretionary Philanthropy." In *Philanthropy in Democratic Societies: History, Institutions, Values*, Rob Reich, Chiara Cordelli, and Lucy Bernholz, eds. Chicago: University of Chicago Press.

Cornell, Nicolas. 2015. "A Third Theory of Paternalism." *Michigan Law Review* 113 (8): 1,295–336.

Drèze, Jean, and Amartya Sen. 1989. *Hunger and Public Action*. Oxford, UK: Oxford University Press.

Deaton, Angus. 2015. "The Logic of Effective Altruism." *Boston Review*, 1 July (Accessed 11 June 2018). Available at http://bostonreview.net/forum/logic-effective-altruism/angus-deaton-response-effective-altruism.

Dworkin, Gerald. 1972. "Paternalism." *The Monist* 56 (1): 70–6.

Gabriel, Iason and Brian McElwee. "Effective Altruism, Global Poverty, and Systemic Change." Chapter 7, this volume.

MacAskill, William. "The Definition of Effective Altruism." Chapter 1, this volume.

MacAskill, William. 2012. "GiveWell's Recommendation of GiveDirectly." *Giving What We Can blog*, 30 November (Accessed 11 June 2018). Available at https://www.givingwhatwecan.org/post/2012/11/givewells-recommendation-of-givedirectly/.

MacAskill, William. 2015. *Doing Good Better: How Effective Altruism Can Help You Make a Difference*. New York: Penguin Random House.

Matthews, Dylan. 2015. "You have $8 billion. You want to do as much good as possible. What do you do?" *Vox.com*, 24 April (Accessed 30 January 2017). Available at https://www.vox.com/2015/4/24/8457895/givewell-open-philanthropy-charity.

Mill, John Stuart. 2006. "On Liberty." In *The Collected Works of John Stuart Mill, Vol XVIII*, J. M. Robson, ed. Toronto: University of Toronto Press.

Mogensen, Andreas. 2014. "Why We (Still) Don't Recommend GiveDirectly," *Giving What We Can blog*, 27 February (Accessed 11 June 2018). Available at https://www.givingwhatwecan.org/post/2014/02/why-we-still-dont-recommend-givedirectly/.

O'Neill, Martin. 2008. "What Should Egalitarians Believe?" *Philosophy and Public Affairs* 36 (2): 119–56.

Pummer, Theron. 2016. "Whether and Where to Give." *Philosophy & Public Affairs* 44 (1): 77–95.

Quong, Jonathan. 2011. *Liberalism Without Perfection*. Oxford, UK: Oxford University Press.

Rawls, John. 2001. *Justice as Fairness: A Restatement*. Cambridge, MA: Harvard University Press.

Saunders-Hastings, Emma. 2014. "No Better to Give than to Receive: Charity and Women's Subjection in J.S. Mill." *Polity* 46 (2): 233–54.

Saunders-Hastings, Emma. "Welfare Paternalism and Objections from Equality" (working paper).

Sen, Amartya. 2000. *Development as Freedom*. New York: Anchor Books.

Scanlon, T.M. 1975. "Preference and Urgency," *The Journal of Philosophy* 72 (19): 655-669.

Scanlon, T.M. 2018. *Why Does Inequality Matter?* Oxford, UK: Oxford University Press.

Shiffrin, S. 2000. "Paternalism, Unconscionability Doctrine, and Accommodation." *Philosophy and Public Affairs* 29 (3): 205–50.

Sunstein, Cass R., and Richard H. Thaler. 2003. "Libertarian Paternalism Is Not an Oxymoron." *The University of Chicago Law Review* 70 (4): 1,159–201.

Sunstein, Cass R. 2014. *Why Nudge? The Politics of Libertarian Paternalism*. New Haven: Yale University Press.

Young, Iris Marion. 1990. "The Five Faces of Oppression." In *Justice and the Politics of Difference*. Princeton, NJ: Princeton University Press.

Waal, Alex de. 1997. *Famine Crimes: Politics and the Disaster Relief Industry in Africa*. Oxford, UK: Oxford University Press.

Wilkinson, Richard, and Kate Pickett. 2009. *The Spirit Level: Why Greater Equality Makes Societies Stronger*. New York: Bloomsbury Press.

Zunz, Oliver. 2011. *Philanthropy in America: A History*. Princeton, NJ: Princeton University Press.

9

Demanding the Demanding

Ben Sachs

1. Introduction

There's something curious about the public face of the effective altruism project. By "the public face", I mean the websites of the most prominent effective altruism organizations—specifically, Giving What We Can, Givewell, 80,000 Hours, and The Life You Can Save—and two books, William MacAskill's *Doing Good Better* and Peter Singer's *The Most Good You Can Do*.[1] When one reads those four websites and two books, one notices a curious thing: they don't *tell us that we should* give significant amounts to charity. Even Giving What We Can, the public face of which is its website on which people can make a pledge to give 10 percent of their income to charity, has nothing on its website by way of suggesting that people *ought* to do so. (Instead, the website says, "We *inspire* people to donate significantly.")[2] And in his contribution to this volume, MacAskill defends the Centre for Effective Altruism's choice to define effective altruism such that it excludes any claim about what people ought to do.[3]

Upon noticing this reticence, I began to wonder about its cause. Realizing that Singer, the founder of The Life You Can Save, and Toby Ord, the founder of Giving What We Can, both have strong act-consequentialist sympathies, and having read books and articles in which uncompromising act-consequentialists suggested that confronting people with uncompromising act-consequentialism's actual requirements would be counterproductive on account of their demandingness (see Section 2 of this chapter for details), I arrived at a hypothesis: The effective altruism movement's decision to not confront people with demanding requirements is based on a fear of the counterproductivity of doing so.[4]

I don't know whether this hypothesis is true. Even if it's basically true it's almost surely an oversimplification, since what I am calling "the effective altruism

[1] MacAskill (2015); Singer (2015).

[2] "About Us." Giving What We Can. (Emphasis added). Available at https://www.givingwhatwecan.org/about-us/.

[3] MacAskill. "The Definition of Effective Altruism." Chapter 1, this volume.

[4] Singer confirmed to me via email that he's an act-consequentialist. Ord confirmed to me via email that he believes in global consequentialism—i.e. he believes everything should be assessed directly in virtue of its consequences—which entails act-consequentialism, though he emphasized that he takes very seriously the possibility that his belief could be wrong and therefore he does not try to act in accordance with act-consequentialism.

project" is constituted by many institutions and actors, each of which has its own reasons for proceeding the way it does. But since this rationale for steering clear of confrontation has at least an initial ring of reasonability to it, and since, to my understanding, having spoken with some of the leaders of the effective altruism movement, it's at least part of the truth; and since there is a philosophical literature to look to in support of this rationale, it strikes me as ripe for investigating.[5]

Given this hypothesis, one question immediately presents itself: Is it true that confronting people with demanding requirements is likely to be counterproductive? Is it likely to be counterproductive to tell people, "Morally speaking, you should φ", where φ-ing is demanding? Or, if the ethical context goes without saying or has been made clear earlier in the conversation, is it counterproductive to tell people, "You should φ", or to just issue the imperative, "Φ"? I'll address one small part of this question—that part having to do with the ethical requirement to give to charity—and argue that on the current evidence we should not be at all confident that "demanding the demanding", as per the title of this chapter, is likely to be counterproductive.

A caveat before beginning: This chapter is not intended as a discussion of uncompromising act-consequentialism. I will, however, assume that the uncompromising act-consequentialists are right in holding that morality imposes very demanding requirements in the arena of charitable giving. Although this assumption is certainly disputable, it needs to be granted in order to get the discussion off the ground.

2. The empirical question

2.1 What the uncompromising act-consequentialists have said

Is it reasonable to be worried about what might happen if we were to go about confronting people with demanding requirements in the arena of charitable giving? As I said already, some philosophers who accept an uncompromising version of act-consequentialism are indeed worried about this. Specifically, they're worried that such confrontations will cause those who are confronted to fall farther short of giving what they ought to.[6] Shelly Kagan, Peter Unger, Katarzyna de Lazari-Radek, and Peter Singer have each expressed such a worry.

[5] MacAskill more or less admits as much in his contribution to this volume, where he says that one reason for defining the effective altruism project in a non-normative way is for the sake of "preventing the concept from being off-putting to those who don't believe that there are strong obligations of beneficence". (MacAskill, "The Definition of Effective Altruism." Chapter 1 of this volume).

[6] A natural question at this point would be: What's the baseline for comparison? I don't think that this question has a canonical answer to which most or all uncompromising act-consequentialists—or at least those of them who have expressed this worry—would sign on. So I'll have to leave this unspecified.

The question I am investigating in Section 2 is whether this is a reasonable worry. I'll examine the relevant empirical evidence on this. Since that body of evidence is far from conclusive (more on this later), though, I'll also take a second approach to tackling the question, namely asking whether there is a plausible psychological mechanism by which such confrontations *could* make the results (in terms of amount given) worse. Unfortunately, there is no canonical moral psychology implicit in the uncompromising act-consequentialists' expression of their worry. Kagan focuses on the economy of blame: His worry is that if the demands with which we confront people are so extreme that almost no one complies with them, then we will wind up spreading around blame so liberally that it will lose its motivational force.[7] De Lazari-Radek and Singer, meanwhile focus on the possibility of people becoming cynical about morality in response to overly demanding confrontations.[8] Peter Unger, by contrast, posits no mechanism at all.[9]

2.2 The evidence the uncompromising act-consequentialists have cited

My first task, as I have said, is to examine the evidence relevant to the uncompromising act-consequentialists' stated worry. I'll begin by asking this question: Have they offered any evidence to support their worry?

The answer is that precisely one of them has made an effort to do so, once. I refer to a passage in Singer's *The Life You Can Save*, in which he says:

> Over many years of talking and writing about this subject, I have found that for some people, striving for a high moral standard pushes them in the right direction, even if they—and here I include myself—do not go as far as the standard implies they should. The research by Shang and Croson referred to in chapter 5 [of *The Life You Can Save*], on how the amount donated by callers to American public radio stations can be increased by telling them about large amounts given by others, suggests the same conclusion. But Shang and Croson found that the

[7] "It might be plausibly suggested that if the standards that society held out were too high—so that, e.g. all who failed to make their maximal contribution to the good were subject to public moral condemnation—the net effect would be counterproductive: since few people would meet the standards, public criticism would by hypocritical and lose its motivating influence as a result of overexposure. It may be that more good overall would be produced if blame were not leveled against all those who fall short of doing all that they could" Kagan (1989, p. 387).

[8] "[I]t is . . . plausible to believe that, given the way human beings are, very few of them will respond to an appeal to give away everything they can spare to help the poor. In that case, such an appeal will do little to help the poor. Perhaps advocating so demanding a standard will just make people cynical about morality as a whole: 'If that is what it takes to live ethically,' they might say, 'let's forget about ethics, and just have fun.'" Lazari-Radek and Singer (2010, p. 37).

[9] Unger simply speculates that confronting people with highly demanding requirements "discourages" giving more to the poor and is "counterproductive". See Unger (1996, p. 156).

> method worked only within limits. Asking people to give more than almost anyone else gives risks turning them off, and at some level might cause them to question the point of striving to live an ethical life at all.[10]

And even this effort is to no avail.

To explain: First, Shang and Croson actually didn't study the effect of asking people to make donations. Rather, they studied the effect of telling people (over the phone or in a letter) that someone else has donated *X* amount and then saying "We invite you to join this member in renewing your membership today"[11] or "How much would you like to pledge today?"[12] As Shang and Croson themselves note, this constitutes studying the effect of providing information regarding what other people have donated.

And there is a second, more important, reason why Singer's citation of Shang and Croson's work doesn't help him to establish his point regarding the dangers of setting a high moral standard. Granting, for the sake of argument, that what Shang and Croson studied really was the effect of asking people to donate certain amounts of money, their studies provide no evidence that there is such thing as asking for too much money. Singer cites two now-published studies by Shang and Croson.[13] One of them[14] confirms Singer's claim that "the amount donated by callers to American public radio stations can be increased by telling them about large amounts given by others." (It was found that telling callers about others having donated $300 had a larger effect than telling callers about others having donated $180 or $75.)[15] Furthermore, in a published study by Shang and Croson that Singer didn't cite, it was found that asking people to give an amount that in fact corresponded to the 97th percentile of previous donations likewise increased the amount contributed over the control condition in which no information was provided.[16] But *neither published study supports Singer's claim that "the method worked only within limits."* It turns out that the pre-publication version of the one of the articles Singer cited,[17] which is the version that Singer was relying on and that he kindly provided to me in correspondence, reported some data that lent support to his claim—data that did not appear in the published version.

The take-home message is that Singer's claim that "the method worked only within limits" is not supported by any evidence that ever got published. Furthermore, the evidence that did get published supports the conclusion that

[10] Singer (2009, p. 151).

[11] Croson and Shang (2008, p. 228); Shang and Croson (2006, p. 149).

[12] Croson and Shang (2008, p. 227); Shang and Croson (2006, p. 147); Shang and Croson (2009, p. 1,428).

[13] Croson and Shang (2008); Shang and Croson (2009). Cited in *The Life You Can Save* (Singer. 2009, p. 186).

[14] Shang and Croson (2009).

[15] Croson and Shang (2009). Cited in *The Life You Can Save*, p. 186.

[16] Shang and Croson (2006).

[17] Shang and Croson (2009).

one can mention donations that are at least high relative to what others give (donations corresponding to the 97th percentile of those previously received) and, far from turning people off, receive high contributions as a result.

2.3 Other available evidence

Moving on from the question of what evidence the uncompromising act-consequentialists have offered in support of the reasonability of their worry, I'll now ask the broader question of what evidence there is, full stop.

The only other relevant evidence I am aware of is a set of experiments conducted by Mazar, Amir, and Ariely, the immediate subject of which was whether people will cheat on a test given the opportunity to do so. These six experiments, the results of which were published in a single article, all had the same basic setup. In the words of Mazar, Amir, and Ariely:

> The general setup of all our experiments involves a multiple-question task, in which participants are paid according to their performance. We compare the performance of respondents in the control conditions, in which they have no opportunity to be dishonest, with that of respondents in the "cheating" conditions, in which they have such an opportunity.[18]

It is very important to note that when Mazar, Amir, and Ariely refer to an "opportunity" to cheat, they mean a perfect opportunity—an opportunity that carries no risk of getting caught. To create such an opportunity, they had to rig the setup in the cheating condition so that *even they* would be unable to tell whether any particular person cheated. (To give you a flavor of the lengths to which they went: In some of the experiments the respondents, after using a pencil and paper to complete the multiple-question task, were told to check their own work using an answer key and then shred the paper on which they completed the task.) However, they had a method whereby they could determine whether cheating was going on: they compared the self-reported performance of the respondents in the cheating condition with the verified performance of the respondents in the control condition. And what they found is that self-reported performance in the former was better, to a statistically significant extent, than performance in the latter. This demonstrates that there was some cheating going on.

What makes this study interesting for our purposes, and what Mazar, Amir, and Ariely likewise hold out as their most interesting finding, is the breadth and depth of cheating that occurred. By "breadth", I mean the proportion of people

[18] Mazar, Amir, and Ariely (2008, p. 635).

who cheated; by "depth", I mean the amount by which those who cheated cheated. Regarding breadth, they found that most people in the cheating condition cheated. (Mazar, Amir, and Ariely know this because they observed a general shift of the distribution curve of correct responses in the self-reported performance condition from the baseline provided by the verified performance condition. If the mean performance improvement in the self-reported performance condition were a matter of a few self-reporting respondents drastically over-reporting their number of correct answers, no general shift would have occurred.) However, regarding depth, "the magnitude of dishonesty per person was relatively low (relative to the maximum possible amount.)"[19] Even with most people cheating in the cheating condition, the average score in the cheating condition wasn't a lot higher than the average score in the control condition. For instance, several of the experiments made use of a twenty-question quiz, and in those experiments the average number of right answers in the control condition was three to four (depending on which experiment) out of twenty while the average number of right answers in the cheating condition was four to seven (depending on which experiment) out of twenty.

What we can take away from these studies is that there is at least one setting, admittedly a contrived and controlled experimental scenario, in which the typical behavior is for people who have a perfect opportunity to violate an ethical standard to do so but by a small amount relative to the amount possible.

This strikes me as possibly relevant to our question of whether it is reasonable to worry about what will happen if people are confronted with the demand to devote large proportions of their resources to charity, because the basic contours of the two scenarios are the same. In both cases the agent has an opportunity to abide by an ethical standard or instead depart from it by anywhere from a little to a lot. This similarity and the results of the Mazar/Amir/Ariely studies give us a reason to believe that confronting people with the truth about what they are ethically required to devote to charity would have the result of the confronted people coming close to devoting the amount that they are ethically required to devote—a very good result, by any measure, and one that runs contrary to the worry that troubles the uncompromising act-consequentialists mentioned earlier.

The reason for belief that I have just posited is, I admit, extremely weak, not least because whereas the Mazar/Amir/Ariely experiments challenged people to conform to what might reasonably be considered a non-demanding ethical standard—don't cheat on a test—we are assuming that the true standard regarding charitable giving is demanding. I can imagine, however, that one might object that there is no reason at all for this belief, on account of two other important differences between the two kinds of scenario.

[19] Mazar, Amir, and Ariely (2008, p. 642).

Firstly, unlike the participants in the experimental conditions of the Mazar/Amir/Ariely experiments, people deciding whether and how much to devote to charity arguably aren't guaranteed to not get caught if they choose to not devote what they are ethically required to devote. Whether this dissimilarity is genuine will depend on the real-world situation in which a given potential giver finds him/herself and on what counts as "getting caught" not devoting the ethically required proportion to charity. But we can set aside these complications. For if the probability of getting caught is higher in the real-world situation of giving to charity than in the experimental situation Mazar, Amir, and Ariely set up, the effect one would expect that to have, if any, would be to cause the former set of people to depart *less* from the relevant ethical standard by comparison to the latter set of people. Consequently, it cannot support the uncompromising act-consequentialists' worry.

Secondly, whereas the Mazar/Amir/Ariely experiments tested how people respond to a purported ethical standard that it is reasonable to assume the respondents accept (i.e. the standard requiring them not to cheat), our question is how people would respond to a purported ethical standard that many people don't accept—namely that one should devote large proportions of one's resources to charity. By way of response I want to point out that those who believe that confronting people with demanding requirements would be counterproductive are banking, just as much as I am, on the idea that people could be effectively persuaded that devoting large proportions of their resources to charity is ethically required. The hypothesis that something bad would happen if we were to confront people with a demanding standard of giving makes sense only on the assumption that the people being confronted would actually accept that they are ethically required to do what we demand that they do. If most people's response to those demands were to simply dismiss them as ethically mistaken then the confrontations would probably have no effect, as opposed to a bad effect.

2.4 What we can infer from armchair moral psychology

To say the least, the available empirical evidence—or at least those bits of it of that Singer and I have invoked—is inconclusive as to whether the uncompromising act-consequentialists are right to worry about what would happen if we were to confront people with demanding requirements of charitable giving.[20] Consequently,

[20] One body of empirical literature with which I won't engage is the set of studies on the effect of social norming on human behavior in ethically laden contexts. (One recent paper, which cites much of this literature, is "The Effects of Feedback on Energy Conservation: A Meta-Analysis." Karlin, Zinger, and Ford (2015). This literature indicates that our decision-making about whether to conform to certain norms is highly sensitive to our beliefs about the frequency with which other people violate those norms. It would be difficult to incorporate that literature into my discussion here,

we might as well engage in a bit of informed speculation. Specifically, since the available evidence regarding how people *do* behave when confronted with demanding requirements is limited, we should ask ourselves this question: What does common-sense moral psychology suggest as to how people *would* behave in such situations?

It is not an unusual experience to find oneself in a situation in which one accepts the validity of an ethical standard that issues demanding requirements in the context of one's own life. I assume that most people who are in a relationship in which monogamy is the mutually agreed rule accept the validity of the ethical standard forbidding them to pursue romantic relationships with other people and that many such people also sometimes find themselves tempted to do just that. As another example: many people subscribe to an ethical standard forbidding the consumption of meat and make it a practice to so abstain, and I assume that a significant proportion of those people often find themselves tempted to indulge in meat eating.[21]

How do we cope with these situations? My impression, based on my own experience in such situations and my observation of others' behavior, is that we generally cope reasonably well with them. Specifically, we mostly abide by the injunctions that we're tempted to violate. We're good, but not perfect.

Indeed, it seems to me that certain religions are built around this very view of human nature. Most religions have action-guidance at their core; they are systems of norms. And among the religions that are like that, many of them have the following two features: 1) Their set of norms is very demanding, and 2) they have processes built in for dealing with the inevitable liability of people to occasionally violate those norms. This suggests that these religions are founded on the image of humans as able to conform their behavior to demanding norms but also liable to succumb to temptation from time to time.

One example here is Roman Catholicism. Famously, this religion is very demanding regarding the circumstances in which it's permissible to have sexual intercourse. But it also has a process whereby one can seek absolution for one's sins: confession.

because the studies don't control for moral belief. In particular, it's left open whether beliefs about others' behavior changes our decision-making by way of changing our moral beliefs (i.e. "if everyone's doing it then surely it can't be wrong") or by some other mechanism. It tells us nothing helpful, therefore, about how people are likely to act with regard to norms that they believe are true ethical requirements.

[21] One might object that one can be strongly tempted to violate an ethical injunction without that injunction being demanding. (On this issue, see Brian McElwee, "What is Demandingness?", in Ackeren and Kühler (2015)). But insofar as we are interested in the possible counterproductivity of confronting people with what we believe to be the true ethical requirements in the arena of giving, surely we should be interested in how people react when confronted with injunctions that they accept and are tempted to violate, regardless of whether acceptance plus temptation are jointly sufficient for demandingness.

Judaism fits the bill as well. There are 613 commandments in this religion, so its normative standard is demanding by sheer volume, to say nothing of particular parts of it (like the injunction not to break a vow). And, like Roman Catholicism, it has a process for atoning for sins: observance of Yom Kippur.

Something similar holds for Islam. Muslims are required to pray five times a day and to abstain from food, drink and sexual activity during daylight hours for the entire month of Ramadan. These requirements, obviously, are ones that it would be difficult to obey without fail for one's entire life. Fortunately, Islam holds that forgiveness from God can be obtained through prayer, sincere remorse, and changing one's ways.

Admittedly, a theory of how people respond to the requirements I've been discussing can't apply directly to the requirement to devote a certain proportion of one's resources to charity. The temptation to cheat on one's spouse or to eat meat (if one is committed to vegetarianism) is episodic; that is to say, the temptation manifests itself in the form of spatiotemporally separable objects (*this* other man/woman; *this* piece of meat) that are available for indulgence for discrete, limited periods of time (until I've walked away from him/her; until I've satisfied my hunger by eating something else). By contrast, devoting a certain proportion of one's resources to charity is a way of life. This is true, one might say, in both the ethical and the practical nature of the requirement. As an ethical matter, it is reasonable to think, what one is required to do is to devote a certain proportion of one's *lifetime* resources to charity. And as a practical matter, it seems one spends a *lifetime* abiding by or violating this requirement, because one is constantly making decisions that either directly or indirectly constitute decisions as to whether to follow it. Consequently there is a sense in which one's response to this requirement, whatever it is, has to be all-or-nothing, since each of us lives only one life.

But we should be careful not to draw a hasty inference from this. In particular, we should not infer that there is consequently only one mechanism by which taking a requirement seriously can lead to action in cases where the response to the requirement is a way of life: namely, via the agent adopting an intention to conform to it. I speculate that the uncompromising act-consequentialists cited above may have made an inference of this sort on the way to arriving at their worry about confronting people with demanding requirements. And since they're skeptical of the likelihood of anyone adopting an intention to conform to the demanded standard of charitable giving, they arrive at the conclusion that people will respond to the confrontation by adopting an intention to give much less to charity.

The reason we should not make this inference is that there are other available psychological mechanisms even in way-of-life cases. And given that in cases of episodically demanding requirements people seem to make it a priority (though not a trumping priority) to conform to those requirements, the following mechanism suggests itself: People will respond to the demand to devote large proportions of their resources to charity by adopting an intention to *come close* to devoting what they are exhorted to devote. Not only does this moral psychology fit with how people seem to respond to episodically demanding requirements, it also dovetails with observed behavior in the Mazar/Amir/Ariely experiments. Most of those respondents, given the chance to conform entirely, not at all, or somewhat to the ethical injunction not to cheat decided to come close to conforming: Specifically, the performance they reported for themselves was close to their actual performance.

Of course, calling this a "moral psychology" is a bit generous, since psychology (like any other science) is supposed to be explanatory and there is more explanation needed here. In particular, it is entirely reasonable to ask why it is the case, assuming it is the case, that most people when confronted with a demanding ethical standard that they accept come close to conforming to it. Mazar, Amir, and Ariely have an answer: they call it the theory of *self-concept maintenance*. On this theory, one's response to situations in which conformity to a moral standard would be costly is to find an approach that balances two motivating factors. The first factor is the obvious one: the desire to avoid incurring costs. The second factor is one's desire to maintain one's self-concept. Mazar, Amir, and Ariely cite studies that (according to them) demonstrate that "people have strong beliefs in their own morality, and they want to maintain this aspect of their self-concept."[22] Sometimes, however, one is forced to update one's self-concept in a negative direction because one has done something immoral. This is experienced by the agent as costly, which makes plausible a moral psychology that represents agents as making the decision of whether to abide by a demanding moral standard by balancing the cost of conformity against the cost (in reduced self-concept) of non-conformity. If this is an accurate moral psychology, and if Mazar, Amir, and Ariely's further empirical finding, that people are able to hold their self-concept constant even while departing from moral standards by a little bit, is accurate, then we should predict that when confronted with moral standards conformity to which is costly, we should predict that people will come close to conforming to them.[23] In another context, Ariely has labeled this the "fudge factor" theory.[24]

2.5 Taking stock

I began this section by asking whether the uncompromising act-consequentialists have identified any empirical support for their worry about what will happen if we confront people with demands to devote large proportions of their resources to charity. I reported that just one of them, Singer, has, and I reviewed the two studies he cited, plus another study on the same topic by the same two authors.

[22] Mazar, Amir, and Ariely (2012, p. 634). [23] Mazar, Amir, and Ariely (2012, p. 630).
[24] Ariely (2012, pp. 26–9).

I concluded that, contrary to what Singer said, those studies provide no support at all for the worry and if anything undermine it.

I then broadened the inquiry, asking whether there is any evidence at all, one way or the other, regarding the worry. I suggested that the series of experiments conducted by Mazar, Amir, and Ariely on dishonesty constitutes such evidence, and points against the reasonability of the worry. What that series suggests is that ethical standards that we accept but to which we are not willing to conform can nevertheless exert a pull on us *in the direction of* conformity to them.

Finally, I engaged in some armchair moral psychology, asking what a common-sense understanding of human nature predicts about how people will respond when confronted with a demanding ethical standard that they accept. I noted that the general phenomenon of conforming for-the-most-part-but-not-always to ethical standards that are experienced as demanding is quite familiar and that certain prominent religions seem built around the expectation that people will behave this way. Starting from this observation, and bringing in some of Mazar, Amir, and Ariely's own speculative (albeit somewhat evidence-supported) moral psychology, I arrived at a moral psychology whereby people when confronted with a demanding ethical standard that they accept will respond by *mostly* conforming to it. This moral psychology, the "fudge factor" theory, predicts that when confronted with a demand to devote a large proportion of their resources to charity will (assuming they accept its validity) respond by adopting an intention to come close to donating the ethically required proportion.

3. Practical upshot (or lack thereof)

There is no strong basis for the fear that confronting people with demanding requirements of charitable giving would be counterproductive. If anything, I've argued, we should believe that the more we demand when we confront, the closer people will come to giving what they're ethically required to give.

What is the practical upshot of all this? In my judgment it's too soon to extract any lessons. Obviously if what I've argued here is correct then one major objection to demanding the demanding is thereby disarmed. But that's a big "if". The evidence that exists—or at least the evidence of which I am aware, all of which I mentioned in Section 2—constitutes too meager a basis on which to conclude with confidence that demanding the demanding is not likely to be counterproductive. Hopefully further empirical studies on this topic will be conducted.

Furthermore, there are other objections to demanding the demanding. The one that immediately comes to mind is the hypocrisy objection. Given that few if any of us give as much to charity as morality (*ex hypothesi*) requires, it would seem hypocritical for us to confront others with demands to give as morality requires. My own inclination is always to set aside hypocrisy worries, since I don't think hypocrisy is much of a moral failing; but there is a literature on this and so for now I simply defer to it.[25] It's worth noting, however, that to the extent that hypocrisy is a serious moral failing its badness can surely be mitigated by doing as Singer does—i.e. being candid about one's own failure to do what one is saying ought to be done.[26]

Even if demanding the demanding is not objectionable, we still might not be able to muster much of an argument for doing it, as the question would remain whether demanding the demanding is better than the alternatives. Perhaps, after all, some other kind of demanding would elicit even better behavior in its targets than demanding the demanding, on the present evidence, seems likely to.[27] It would help, then, if we could raise a serious moral objection against demanding anything other than precisely what one believes is morally required (call this "morally imprecise demanding"). The best hope for mounting such an argument is surely the idea that demanding anything else is deceptive on grounds of predictably leading the demander's audience to adopt a mistaken belief about what they (the demander) believes is morally required. Whether such an objection could be substantiated depends on whether the empirical claim and the implicit theory of morally objectionable deception embedded within it are sound. And whether such an objection is strong—strong enough to make morally imprecise demanding always and ever wrong—depends on how much weight the correct normative ethical theory gives to concerns about deception.

Finally, even an argument in favor of demanding the demanding as against other kinds of demanding isn't on its own an argument for demanding the demanding, full stop. For we still need to compare demanding as against other kinds of communicative acts targeted at the same outcome. In particular, we need evidence regarding the relative effectiveness of demanding as opposed to other strategies—such as the (what might be called) "invitational" strategy that currently predominates in the effective altruism websites and books cited at the beginning of this chapter—as ways of eliciting donations. I hope that the leaders of the effective altruism movement come to see the value of the research that would need to be done to generate such evidence, just as they've enthusiastically embraced the need for empirical investigation of the effectiveness of various charities and indeed the effectiveness of their own efforts.[28]

[25] Cohen 2013; Szabados 1979; Wallace 2010. [26] Singer (2009, p. 151).

[27] Given "fudge factor" moral psychology, this would seem to be a distinct possibility. That psychology suggests that a good strategy for getting people to donate X percent of their resources to charity would be to confront them with a demand to give $[X+Y]$ percent, with "Y" being the fudge factor—in other words, to demand *more* than morality actually requires!

[28] GiveWell, Giving What We Can, and The Life You Can Save each conduct empirical research both on the effectiveness of various charities and on their own effectiveness in redirecting donations from less effective to highly effective charities. 80,000 Hours conducts empirical research into its own effectiveness as well. None of these organizations, however, nor any organization of which I am aware, has researched the comparative effectiveness of demanding strategies as against other strategies aimed at increasing the size of people's charitable donations.

References

"About Us." Giving What We Can (Accessed 23 January 2018). Available at https://www.givingwhatwecan.org/about-us.

Ackeren, von Marcel, and Michael Kühler. 2015. *The Limits of Moral Obligation: Moral Demandingness and Ought Implies Can (Routledge Studies in Ethics and Moral Theory)*. New York: Routledge.

Ariely, Dan. 2012. *The (Honest) Truth about Dishonest*. New York: Harper.

Cohen, G.A. 2013. "Casting the First Stone: Who Can and Who Can't Condemn the Terrorists?" In *Finding Oneself in thCE: Reference Lazari-Radek and Singer. (2010 has not been provided in the Bibliography. Please check.e Other*, G.A. Cohen and Michael Otsuka, eds. Princeton: Princeton University Press.

Croson, Rachel, and Jen (Yue) Shang. 2008. "The Impact of Downward Social Information on Contribution Decisions." *Experimental Economics* 11 (3): 221–33.

Kagan, Shelly. 1989. *The Limits of Morality*. New York: Oxford University Press.

Karlin, Beth, Joanne F. Zinger, and Rebecca Ford. 2015. "The Effects of Feedback on Energy Conservation: A Meta-Analysis." *Psychological Bulletin* 141 (6): 1,205–27.

Lazari-Radek, Katarzyna, and Peter Singer. 2010. "Secrecy in Consequentialism: A Defence of Esoteric Morality." *Ratio* 23 (1): 34–58.

MacAskill, William. "The Definition of Effective Altruism." Chapter 1, this volume.

MacAskill, William. 2015. *Doing Good Better*. London: Guardian Books and Faber & Faber.

Mazar, Nina, On Amir, and Dan Ariely. 2008. "The Dishonesty of Honest People: A Theory of Self-Concept Maintenance." *Journal of Marketing Research* 45 (6): 633–44.

McElwee, Brian. 2015. "What is Demandingness?" In *The Limits of Moral Obligation: Moral Demandingness and Ought Implies Can*, Marcel van Ackeren and Michael Kühler, eds. New York: Routledge.

Shang, Jen, and Rachel Croson. 2006. "The Impact of Social Comparisons on Nonprofit Fund Raising." *Experiments Investigating Fundraising and Charitable Contributors: Research in Experimental Economics* 11: 143–56.

Shang, Jen, and Rachel Croson. 2009. "A Field Experiment in Charitable Contribution: The Impact of Social Information on the Primary Provision of Public Goods." *The Economic Journal* 119 (540): 1,422–39.

Singer, Peter. 2009. *The Life You Can Save*. New York: Random House.

Singer, Peter. 2015. *The Most Good You Can Do*. New Haven: Yale University Press.

Szabados, Béla. 1979. "Hypocrisy." *Canadian Journal of Philosophy* 9 (2): 195–210.

Unger, Peter. 1996. *Living High and Letting Die*. New York: Oxford University Press.

Wallace, R. Jay. 2010. "Hypocrisy, Moral Address, and the Equal Standing of Persons." *Philosophy & Public Affairs* 38 (4): 307–41.

10

On Satisfying Duties to Assist

Christian Barry and Holly Lawford-Smith

Most effective altruists and indeed most ordinary people think that we have duties to assist people in severe need, and that these duties can be satisfied. They think that a person is morally required to do something to help others in need, but that at some point she can refuse to do more on the grounds that she has already done enough. They may allow that some emergencies and instances in which agents can prevent catastrophic risk are exceptions to this: it may always be wrong to refuse to help in situations of this type, at least when one can do so without significant additional sacrifice. But what makes it the case that a person has satisfied her duties to assist in other kinds of cases? This question is of practical importance: determining how we can satisfy our duties to assist is important for each of us who is working out what we ought to do, as well as for gauging whether others may be liable to moral criticism or other sanctions on the grounds that they are not doing enough.

Duties to assist are justified by the importance of the end of helping those in severe need, so one natural thought is that a person has satisfied her duties to assist when she has succeeded in securing enough good for such people. Such a position is suggested by Frances Kamm. Kamm observes that a "moral moderate" may, at least in cases where she has already promoted a lot of good, deny that there is even a *reason* to promote the greater good.[1] But is this plausible? Suppose that her blood contains a rare antibody, so that when she gives blood she ends up saving many hundreds of people's lives. It costs her next to nothing to donate—she doesn't find it unpleasant, or costly in financial or other terms. Here it would be unreasonable for her to refuse to help others in the future by citing how much she has already done.[2] One might suggest, alternatively, that she has done enough when she has taken on a certain amount of cost to help others in severe need.

[1] Kamm (1992, p. 356).

[2] Our example is not entirely fanciful. An Australian named James Harrison possesses blood with an antibody effective against rhesus disease (which causes pregnant mothers' blood cells to attack their foetus's blood cells), and whose blood donations have allegedly helped millions of people. However, Harrison himself has a strong aversion to both pain and the sight of blood; each blood plasma donation comes with some physical and psychological discomfort for him, so the costs to him of his efforts may not be so minimal to him as they are in our imagined case. Edwards (2015).

After all, many have supposed duties to assist to be limited by an agent's so-called "appeal to cost," so perhaps these duties are satisfied when the cost hits a level at which she can make such an appeal. But this simple solution is also inadequate. If a person donates 15 per cent of her income to save one person in need when she should have known that the effort would be in vain, because that person would be saved in advance via other means, she has squandered her resources without satisfying her duties to assist. But if satisfying these duties is not simply a matter either of success or of sacrifice, then what is it a matter of?

In this article, we attempt to make some headway in answering this question, which to our knowledge has been touched on but not systematically engaged with in the literatures on duties to assist and effective altruism. We will consider a number of factors of an agent's behaviour that might be thought to be either necessary or sufficient for her to have satisfied her duties to assist. We shall propose that whether a person has satisfied her duties to assist depends not on any single factor but on a complex interplay of several factors. These are the costs she takes on for this purpose, the connection (via the agent's beliefs and intentions) between the costs taken on and the outcomes to be achieved, the importance of the outcomes—various people helped in different ways—to be achieved, and the success of her efforts. A principal aim of effective altruism is to encourage people to pay greater attention to how efficient their expenditures are in addressing the needs of badly off people.[3] In the concluding section of this paper we explore whether we should go further, and incorporate a doctrine that inefficiency in expenditures can reduce or eliminate the degree to which such costs count towards satisfying duties to assist.[4]

1. Inputs: cost

What makes it seem unreasonable for a person to refuse to do more in the case of giving blood introduced above seems to be that, while she has done a lot of good, the agent has taken on precious little cost for this purpose (assuming, again, that she doesn't mind having her blood drawn). Taking on cost is not sufficient to satisfy a duty to assist, but it seems at least to be a necessary element for its satisfaction. A great deal of the literature on the duty to assist concerns just *how much* cost we

[3] See, for instance, MacAskill (2016, pp. 14–15).

[4] There might be such a requirement on other sources of duties too, such as duties that arise from being a beneficiary of injustice. We won't explore that possibility here. We recognize that there may be good reasons why the effective altruism movement might resist extending their concern with efficiency in this way.

are required to take on to help others in severe need.[5] Curiously, there has been relatively little discussion of precisely *which* costs are relevant for such calculations.[6] So we'll explore some options.

1.1 Utility

Perhaps the relevant cost is loss of utility, broadly understood. On this view, taking on utility loss to some threshold to help others in severe need is the cost element in determining whether these duties have been satisfied. This approach seems implausible. Consider a miser; he deplores spending money and above all giving it to charitable causes. It causes him great distress to make even very small financial contributions to charitable organizations. Has a wealthy miser satisfied his duties to assist once he makes some meagre contribution, simply because this costs him the right amount of utility? Surely not.[7] Nor does sacrificing utility seem a necessary condition for satisfying them. Consider a person who has always experienced strong and unconditional empathy with human suffering. This person decides early in life to pursue a career in medicine, and after her medical education is complete, spends much of her time volunteering with the International Medical Corps (IMC), working in conflict and disaster zones around the world, while working part-time to support herself. She enjoys her volunteering work more than the financially lucrative opportunities for full-time work in local practices that she could otherwise take up. She suffers no loss in utility in volunteering for IMC—she would find it tedious and unfulfilling to work full-time in ordinary medical practice—and yet seems a paradigm case of someone who has satisfied her duties to assist (indeed, may have far exceeded them).

[5] See for example Garrett Cullity's detailed analysis of more or less extreme demands that duties to assist can be interpreted as imposing on agents. Singer (1972) and Unger (1996) have famously argued that such duties impose extreme demands on us, while Cullity himself defends the view that duties to assist are only moderately demanding, though he notes that they still "demand more of us than many of us find comfortable." Cullity (2004, p. 3).

[6] Note that this issue parallels but is distinct from the discussion in the literature regarding the 'currency' of egalitarian justice or 'equality of what' debate: see Dworkin (1981a), (1981b), Cohen (1989), Sen (1980), Nussbaum (1992), Rawls (1971). That debate concerns whether individual advantage should be conceived in a theory of social justice in terms of utility, preference satisfaction, capabilities, social primary goods, or some admixture of these elements, and whether egalitarians should strive to achieve equality of one or another of these goods. The debate we engage with, on the other hand, concerns the kinds of costs that are relevant to satisfying duties to assist. Capabilities or utility, for example, may offer plausible approaches to assessing individual advantage in the context of a theory of social justice but be seriously flawed as accounts of the relevant cost for determining whether duties to assist have been satisfied.

[7] Our objection to utility as the appropriate metric for cost in assessing duties to assist has affinities with Dworkin's 'expensive tastes' criticism of welfare as the appropriate goal of egalitarian theories. "Equality of welfare seems to recommend that those with champagne tastes, who need more income simply to achieve the same level of welfare as those with less expensive tastes, should have more income on that account. But this seems counterintuitive." Dworkin (2000, p. 48).

1.2 Interests

Shelly Kagan maintains that the relevant 'cost' is an individual's loss of ability to promote her own interests, subjectively understood.[8] The relevant interests need not be selfish; an individual who happens to have an interest in volunteering at a local homeless shelter might pay a cost when she is asked to volunteer for a charity working on humanitarian relief for natural disasters instead, because the latter affects her ability to do the former.[9]

There are several problems with characterizing cost in this way for our purposes. First, it doesn't leave room for counting expenditures (e.g. of time, of money) as costs when they *don't* set back our interests. This seems counter-intuitive. Consider again our IMC volunteer. She passes up other opportunities because she finds the work with IMC exciting, challenging, and rewarding. She is in an intimate community with the other medical staff and volunteers. She feels good about her decision.

On Kagan's account, this person's activities wouldn't count towards fulfilling her duties to assist, because they cannot be characterized as a 'cost' to her, as he understands it: the relevant cost is a person's loss of ability to promote her own interests.[10] But in this case, it seems to be one of the person's interests to address the severe needs of those trapped in places that few others dare go. In taking up this project, she is simply pursuing her interests, and so has suffered no loss in her ability to promote them. Yet, as already noted, this seems a paradigm case of efforts that should count towards satisfying a duty to assist.[11]

This suggests that the costs that are relevant to duties to assist should be sensitive to expenditures of the relevant sorts *regardless* of how they interact with the interests of the assister. That is, our IMC worker's time and energy should be costs that count towards her satisfying her duties to assist. Indeed, to deny that undertaking such costs counts towards satisfying these duties seems to embrace a view of morality in which conduct isn't moral unless it is unpleasant or otherwise counter to the preferences or inclinations of the person engaging in it. This is not a very appealing view of morality.[12] One could perhaps argue that, although the IMC volunteer's conduct is morally praiseworthy, the fact that she incurs no

[8] Kagan (1991a, p. 233; see also 1991b). In a similar vein, Cullity refers to the costs imposed by duties to assist in terms of sacrifices of "sources of personal fulfillment" in our lives. Cullity (2004, p. 70).

[9] Kagan (1991a). [10] Kagan (1991a).

[11] In his recent book Singer makes a related point. He defines "effective altruism", and comments: "That definition says nothing about motives or about any sacrifice or cost to the effective altruist... [W]e should not think of effective altruism as requiring self-sacrifice, in the sense of something necessarily contrary to one's own interests. If doing the most you can for others means that you are also flourishing, then that is the best possible outcome for everyone" (Singer 2015, p. 5). See also Andreas Mogensen, Will MacAskill, and Toby Ord (2017).

[12] A view of this sort is often attributed to Kant, though many of his interpreters consider this to be a misreading of his view. For discussion see Herman (1981), and Baron (1984).

setback to her interests through her work means that this work should not count, or not count *as much* towards her satisfying her duties to assist. That is, we can praise her choices consistent with maintaining that she needs to do more in order to satisfy her duties to assist. But this implies that if she didn't do more, she would be criticizable for failure. That strikes us as counter-intuitive.

Kagan's view also implies that there would be large differences in what duties to assist require of different people who seem similarly situated in all morally relevant respects. Take a person who managed to internalize a positive disposition towards the expenditures she was making in service of those in need, so that these expenditures came to be aligned with her interests. The initial cost of overcoming the aversion would count as a loss of ability to pursue her own interests, but, once she had internalized new positive dispositions, those costs would be in line with her interests, and so not count towards discharging duties of assistance on Kagan's account. In that case, more could be asked of her. This would mean that she could be required to do a great deal more than another person who made no such efforts.[13] Generally we think that internalizing certain attitudes, values, and dispositions is a valuable means towards more ethical behaviour.[14] This gives us further reason to count expenditures of the relevant sorts towards satisfying duties to assist, regardless of how they affect the assister's interests.

1.3 Material costs

In discussing the utility view and Kagan's view focusing on interests, we've implicitly been alluding to other costs that agents can take on which do not directly relate to their interests, though they can certainly be relevant to their pursuit of those interests. But exactly what kinds of costs are these? Kagan himself suggests "money, time, effort, and life itself".[15] We'll say more about each of these in turn.

When organizations attempt to give a specific content to our duties to assist, they often frame them in terms of financial expenditure. For example, the organization Giving What We Can invites people to donate 10 per cent of their incomes, while in *The Life You Can Save* Peter Singer specifies a progressive scale of giving and invites people who earn more to give more.[16] Taking on monetary cost certainly seems relevant to satisfying duties to assist. Just how this input should figure in our assessment of whether someone has satisfied their positive duties is more difficult (we'll return to this issue below).

[13] Taken to an extreme, this could even create perverse incentives in people to not internalize a positive disposition towards certain charitable contributions.

[14] See, for example, discussion in Jamieson (2007).

[15] Kagan (1991a, p. 233; see also 1991b).

[16] See https://www.givingwhatwecan.org/pledge/ and Singer (2015, pp. 19–20).

Of course, all the money in the world would count for little, in terms of assistance, if there weren't people either willing to be paid to administer the assistance, or willing to do so unpaid. Money can buy material resources (materials to build houses and shelters, blankets and clothes, food and drink, medical supplies), and it can help people to deliver them. But it is not the whole story. Time and effort (or labour) are a crucial part of the story too, and taking on these costs too seem relevant to satisfying duties to assist.

What about physical costs? Some people would accept that there are extreme cases in which a person might be required to sacrifice her own life to save a significantly greater number of people. So if the stakes are high enough, there might be a duty of assistance to accept the loss of one's own life. (For example, imagine that a billionaire proposes to donate sufficient money to permanently end global hunger on the condition that he be allowed to murder you.) But setting these improbable cases aside, is it plausible that we can have duties to assist whose fulfilment requires the input of physical sacrifice?

If we can, then the satisfaction of duties to assist can also be measured, at least in part, by such sacrifices. And it seems sensible to discuss duties to assist in physical terms, counting towards their satisfaction, for example, the bruise, broken finger, or lost arm brought about in the course of a rescue or an intervention to prevent assault. In discussing the question of how much a person can be required to sacrifice in order to save a child, Barry and Øverland include being asked "to have your hair cut", "to suffer a kick in the leg", to "sacrifice a finger", to "lose a leg", to sacrifice "a hand, an arm, or a leg".[17] Singer discusses the donations of blood, bone marrow, and kidneys.[18]

Although these material costs we've been discussing are themselves objective, it seems that any plausible way of specifying *how much* of these costs agents must take on to assist others should take account of how the agents will be affected by such sacrifices. We noted that taking on monetary cost is relevant to satisfying duties to assist. However, determining how much particular monetary costs should count towards satisfying an agent's duty to assist is complicated by the fact that small amounts of money typically mean more to poorer people than to richer people. Intuitively, the poor person does more to satisfy their duty to assist through contributing $100 to poverty relief than does a very wealthy person. We shouldn't accommodate this by making assessments of costliness entirely subjective and dependent on the individual psychologies of those giving. A very wealthy miser may experience a small contribution as very onerous or find it motivationally difficult to provide it, but should we regard such aversions as relevant to his satisfaction of his duties?[19] We don't take such things into account to determine

[17] Barry and Øverland (2013, pp. 196–7). [18] Singer (2015, ch. 6).

[19] Our attitudes towards such cases may be different if we regard such aversions as entirely outside of the control of the agent. As Wolfgang Schwarz pointed out to us, if a person was "wired up" such

which particular rates of taxation are fair.[20] And this is not just because having a tax system that was tailored to the specificities of particular tax subjects within some income group would be impracticable, but because it would seem unfair to do so. The most plausible solution, in our view, is to appeal to (admittedly rough) shared understandings of how people should reasonably be affected by different material sacrifices. For example, many people would regard a poorer person's donation of 20 per cent of her income to be quite onerous, and a very rich person's donation of 20 per cent of her income to be not particularly onerous. This is true even if some particular rich person experiences the donation as a very serious imposition while a particular poor person does not. Our views about whether any given contribution to help others can reasonably be regarded as onerous are based partly on what we think most people do in fact find onerous.[21] But they are also based in part on our commitment to demanding that people cope with some of their personal idiosyncrasies when it comes to conforming to social standards for conduct.

We conclude, then, (*i*) that the 'cost' inputs should be regarded as plural and objective, including money, time, effort, and physical sacrifice, rather than subjective; but (*ii*) that how much these costs should count towards an agent's satisfaction of her duties should depend on common social understandings of how individuals variably situated should reasonably be affected by them.

2. Characteristics

So far, we've been focusing on the costs people take on to assist others in need. But what about what a person believes and intends about these expenditures? We might think that the state of an agent's mind is relevant to whether taking on some cost counts towards satisfying their duty to assist. One possibility would be that the agents must *intend* that the cost they take on be to help others in need. The relevant intentions might be understood restrictively or permissively. On the restrictive understanding, the costs an agent takes on must be for the primary reason of helping the people in need. The restrictive reading seems too strong. Consider a person whose primary motivation for contributing effort and resources to helping the poor is that doing so is an effective means of eliciting

that every time they made small contributions to help others they were caused to feel tremendous anguish and they were completely powerless to cultivate different dispositions, this (subjective) cost would seem relevant to what we could reasonably require them to do. But ordinarily we do not treat such aversions as hardwired into people in this way, even when we recognize that their upbringing and other features of their environment played a substantial role in the formation of their preferences and aspirations.

[20] Thanks to Laura Valentini for the example.

[21] For a related discussion see McElwee (2017).

esteem from others. He gives a very large proportion of his income to effective charities. Such a person's efforts seem to count towards the person's satisfying his duties to assist, even though we might be reluctant to praise his character. So too with the person who gives primarily to avoid a sense of moral guilt at doing nothing, rather than out of any genuine concern for the beneficiaries.

On the permissive understanding, all that is required is that agents intend to help others, even if this is not the primary reason for their action—the esteem-seeker and guilt-avoider intend to help those in need, even if this is only a side effect of their primary motivations. This seems largely correct, but needs one slight amendment if it is to avoid being too restrictive. Imagine a state that taxes its citizenry heavily to help the poor abroad. This should count towards their duties to assist being fulfilled. Yet it may be that some citizens are not aware of (or perhaps are not happy about) the fact that some of their resources are being used in this way. Of course, in this case there is still a collective agent (the state) to which the intention of assisting those in need might be attributed, or at least some individuals (other citizens and officials supporting the expenditures) who have the relevant intention. But that is not the same as the person who is taking on the cost—by way of her taxes—intending that her resources be used for this purpose.

This suggests that the duty to assist can be delegated in such a way that the requirement on intention falls on the agent the duty is delegated to, rather than the delegating agent. In those instances where individuals have delegated (voluntarily or not) their duties to assist out to the state, there is no requirement on the *individual* (although there will be on the state) to take on cost with the intention of assisting. But where individuals have not delegated duties to assist to their state, it is important that there is, in the background, some aim to assist. If a businessman makes an expensive investment from which he hopes to profit, but instead loses his money with the unintended and unforeseen consequence that some people in need are helped, this wouldn't seem to count towards his satisfying his duty to assist—it's just a bad investment that happened to have good consequences for people in need.

Our proposal, then, is that an agent's beliefs (or the beliefs of those acting on their behalf, in case their duties to assist have been delegated), first about the connection between the inputs and success, and second about the value of the assistance provided, are relevant to determining whether they have satisfied their duties to assist. We are not claiming that the agent's beliefs about connections between inputs and success must be *true*, only that they be *reasonable* (i.e. responsive to the readily available evidence). First, the agent must believe the expenditure to be *a* means to assistance. This is closely related to our discussion of intentions above; if the businessman lacks any awareness that his investment will assist people in need, then the fact that it happens to deliver benefits seems to be irrelevant to whether he's satisfied a duty to assist.

The proposed requirement to be responsive to the readily available evidence means that an agent must consider whether the recipient of assistance is likely to benefit from what she seeks to provide them with. Current practices are not always responsive to evidence in these ways. People who seek to assist others may fail to consult with the intended beneficiaries, and consequently may give them things they don't need or want, or even things that are counterproductive to their getting what they need and want.[22] When this happens, even agents that have taken on a lot of cost to help others may not count as having satisfied their duties to assist.

Suppose a person lacks a reasonable belief that her expenditures will connect to assistance, but has an intention to help. If her expenditures fail to secure assistance, it seems she will have failed to satisfy her duties to assist. But suppose that her expenditures *do* secure assistance. Will she then also have failed, or should success, even lucky success, count towards the satisfaction of duties to assist?

3. Success

So far, we've argued that the satisfaction of duties to assist consists in expenditures of money, time, effort, life, and limb, made with the right intentions and beliefs. But it seems to us that success should count too. In considering whether we can reasonably ask a person to do more, it seems clear that we should take account of their success. Someone who has secured a lot of assistance with the intention of helping may have done enough. If we're right about this, then satisfaction is disjunctive: one satisfies the duty to assist *either* by successfully providing assistance (with the intention of helping, but without a reasonable belief that the expenditure will actually help); or by failing to provide assistance while intending to help and having the reasonable belief that the expenditure will actually help. Should inefficiency in expenditures reduce or eliminate the degree to which such costs count towards satisfying duties to assist? Of course, expenditures can be more or less inefficient depending on the degree to which they fall short of maximally efficient expenditure. So the idea would be that at least *some* degree of efficiency is a necessary condition of some expenditure counting (or counting fully) towards the satisfaction of an agent's duty to assist. A requirement of efficiency is a requirement to not merely *assist*, but to assist in ways that make efficient use of one's expenditures.

One practical objection to any sort of efficiency requirement on giving is that people who succeed in assisting others—no matter how inefficiently—are still doing more than most people (most people do nothing), and telling them that

[22] For some examples, see MacAskill (2016), introduction and chapter 4.

they should be doing *even* more risks backlash—turning people off the idea of giving. As a matter of strategy, it should be those who don't assist at all, rather than those who assist inefficiently, that we should target. Our discussion here, however, focuses not on figuring out what we should *tell* people about what they ought to do when it comes to duties to assist; we're asking what they ought to do. That means exploring how duties to assist should be understood, even if it would be wiser to keep quiet about certain of their features for strategic reasons.[23] A theoretical objection might come from those who regard all assistance as supererogatory: to be commended, certainly, but not strictly required. Those holding such a view might argue that for that reason, *any* assistance is a good thing, and there's nothing to be said (apart from purely evaluative claims about what would have been better and worse states of affairs) about the different causes people choose, if they choose any causes at all, and the different means to pursuing those causes. Because assistance is supererogatory, on this view, there's no room to criticize those who do not provide it as *failing* in any duties, and there's certainly no room to criticize those who do provide it for failing to do something even better! It is questionable whether efficiency requirements are indeed out of place when it comes to supererogatory action. Pummer, for example, has argued that there are strong requirements of efficiency even in this case.[24] In any case, our discussion here is addressed to those who share our view that there are duties to assist, and thus also hold that a requirement of efficiency cannot be incoherent in this way.[25]

An efficiency requirement might be interpreted in three broadly different ways (we'll draw attention to many further complexities below). It might be interpreted in a fact-relative way, requiring that the expenditure of resources *actually* be efficient. Or it might be interpreted in a belief-relative way, requiring the agent to have acted efficiently relative to her beliefs. Or, finally, it might be interpreted in an evidence-relative way, requiring the agent to have acted efficiently relative to the evidence that she had or should have had available when making her choice.

Fact-relative efficiency doesn't seem a plausible requirement. Suppose that while a financial donation to the Against Malaria Foundation (AMF)—which distributes long-lasting insecticidal nets (LLINs) in developing countries—would ordinarily have been (and would be known to have been) an efficient means to assisting others, on one occasion it turns out to be very inefficient (because, say, so many people were donating to AMF when you gave that their servers crashed

[23] See Sachs (Chapter 9, this volume) for discussion.

[24] Pummer presents an interesting case—*Arm Donor*—in which we are invited to consider an agent who can intervene to prevent harm to others at the cost of an arm. He suggests that, even if a person's decision to intervene at this cost would be supererogatory, he must be efficient in preventing harm should he choose to intervene. If he can intervene at the cost of an arm to save one or a hundred strangers, but not both, he is morally required to save the hundred Pummer (2016, p. 83).

[25] See McMahan (2018) and Frick (2017) for critical discussion. Note that the debate about whether there are efficiency requirements when it comes to giving supererogatorily remains pertinent whether or not we affirm that there are genuine duties to assist.

without warning, and in restoring them the transaction went missing). In this case, you would have taken on cost *and* had the right intentions and beliefs. We think you would have done all that we might reasonably ask of you. It would be wrong not to count the costs you took on when considering whether we could reasonably ask more of you, despite your lack of success.

Belief- or evidence-relative efficiency do not appear to be plausible requirements either. Consider a person who doesn't choose what they believe will be efficient or doesn't choose what the available evidence suggests will be efficient, but nevertheless takes on cost with an aim of assisting those in need and chooses an option that turns out to be (fact-relative) efficient. We might criticize the person for failing to do their due diligence, but that is a separate matter from whether the costs they have taken on count towards satisfying their duty to assist. Would we say that just as much could be demanded of such a person to help others as could be demanded of a similarly well-off person who has not taken on any cost at all to assist others? This seems counter-intuitive. Our rejection of this requirement leaves open whether we would want to count inefficient expenditures as counting *to the same degree* as efficient expenditures—we'll return to this issue below.

So far, we've been considering the idea of an efficiency requirement quite generally. But there are different more precise ways any such purported requirement might be specified. On a first, minimalist understanding, this would be a requirement not to be grossly inefficient (not to choose *very* inefficient means of providing assistance); moderately, there might be a requirement to choose within a band of causes or courses of conduct of roughly equivalent efficiency (for example, to choose one of the ends generally thought to do a lot of good, but among which there is uncertainty or room for reasonable disagreement over exactly which is the best); and strongly, there might be a requirement to choose the *most efficient* means to providing assistance. An efficiency requirement might be applied only to the ends chosen, it might be applied only to the conduct pursuing those ends, or it might be applied to both.

For example, we might think that individuals have relatively broad discretion in choosing among candidate causes when trying to satisfy their duties to assist (e.g. they are free to choose animal rescue shelters over children's education charities), but are required to do what will best achieve the ends they choose.[26] Or we might think they do not have such freedom: they must choose which candidate duties to assist to take on by choosing the ends that will do the most good, all else being equal (e.g. if donating money to, or volunteering for, charities working against factory farming does more good than donating money to, or volunteering for, animal rescue shelters, then individuals should assist the former).[27] Finally,

[26] One worry about this proposal is that it is sensitive to how causes are individuated—we return to this point below.

[27] See discussion in Pummer (2016) and Singer (2015, ch. 13, esp. p. 138).

we might endorse both: all else being equal individuals must choose the most efficient means to the most important ends.[28]

Disagreement about whether individuals should have discretion regarding the ends to which they direct their efforts to assist connects to deep controversies in moral theory. We clearly cannot settle such controversies here, but it is worth considering further the forms that an efficiency requirement might take.

Note first that none of the arguments that might be offered in defence of allowing a person discretion in the ends they wish to promote justify a person's taking inefficient means to a given end once she has settled on that end. A person who takes the mitigation of child poverty in Africa as her end but chooses to give her money to an NGO that is much less efficient than other organizations in bringing about this end, for example, cannot appeal to any of these reasons to justify her choice. If there is a requirement of efficiency, then perhaps it applies more unequivocally to the choice of means rather than of ends? But there are some serious difficulties with a view that places efficiency requirements on means. First, determining whether someone has used inefficient means towards some end may not be straightforward. A person's ends can ordinarily be described in a more or less coarse-grained way. If Mischa sends resources to an NGO that is working in Bangladesh, her end could be described as that of helping poor people throughout the world, or it might instead be described as helping the poor in that region. The same means might be efficient with respect to helping the poor in that region, but inefficient with respect to helping poor people in the world at large, so long as it is possible to protect more poor people more cheaply in other parts of the world, e.g. in parts of Africa.

Perhaps this concern can be dealt with by saying that the relevant end is what really motivates the agent—what she actually cares about. Mischa seems to be the only person who can tell us which is the more apt description of the end that she is actually seeking to achieve through her efforts. However, there is an even more serious worry about such a view. It seems odd that, when Mischa's aim is helping the poor throughout the world, her contributions to the NGO she chooses count less towards fulfilling her duties to assist than if her end were instead trying to help the poor only in Bangladesh. If anything, we might regard the broader end as in some sense more praiseworthy, since it targets people in severe need independently of where they may live. In this case it also seems implausible that the value of the ends is somehow incommensurable.

[28] Singer (2015) discusses the value of donations to art galleries and museums compared to donations to interventions on mortality or morbidity. He argues that even if we don't take the line that no amount of enhanced aesthetic experience of gallery visitors can justify any amount of physical suffering (see esp. Scanlon (1998)), we can still compare visiting the gallery as it is (without the upgrades allowed by any bequest) and alleviating someone's suffering, against visiting the upgraded gallery and not alleviating someone's suffering. He concludes that "you'd have to be nuts" to choose the former. Singer (2015, p. 120).

One interesting upshot of committing to some efficiency requirement with respect to duties to assist is that it would give us greater scope to say something about responsibility. Imagine three different individuals: one chooses to donate money to a university that already has a hefty endowment; the next donates to the most effective NGO working for pay equity between men and women in Canada; and the last donates to the most effective charity working against the spread of malaria. The first is not efficiently promoting the good in either her chosen end or the means of pursuing it. Privately-funded tertiary education is comparatively low priority as a need which assistance might meet, and if a person's chosen end is tertiary education she should pick a university that is underfunded or otherwise struggling to survive. The second chooses an end that is only moderately important (because both men and women in Canada are very well-off compared to most of the rest of the world), but is efficient in her means of pursuing it. The third is arguably maximally efficient in both the end she chooses, and the means she takes to it.

We find intriguing the proposal that only the third has satisfied her duties to assist, although we do not have the space to defend that proposal here. (We don't take a position here on a more moderate version of this proposal, say, that only the second and third have satisfied their duties to assist.) Expenditures that would normally take an individual up to the satisfaction of her duties to assist—the point at which it would be unreasonable to ask her to do more—do not count as reaching that limit if they are inefficient to some degree. That gives us scope to assign further duties in such a case. Possibly the 'shortfall' between what was accomplished with the actual expenditures and what would have been accomplished with more efficient expenditures is still owed by the inefficient assister.

Singer discusses this kind of requirement, but his focus in that work is on describing the effective altruist movement rather than defending the claim that individuals are required to do the most good they can do.[29] Furthermore, he explicitly allows for understanding 'the most good' as the most good *you* can do (indexed to internal factors, taking a specific person with her talents and capacities). That makes it unlikely that he would go all the way to a strong requirement of efficiency, which looks to be focused more on external factors (how much good different means to the same ends produce, and how much good different ends produce relative to one another).

4. Conclusion

We have argued that there are three factors that are relevant in determining whether an agent has satisfied her duties to assist: inputs, characteristics, and

[29] Singer (2015).

success. We showed that the 'inputs' that can count towards satisfying such duties are plural, including money, time, effort, body parts, and even life itself. We argued that in terms of 'characteristics' there must be an intention to assist in the background (even if only as a side effect) of the actions undertaken, and a reasonable belief that the actions are a means to the end of assisting those in need. Actually assisting others could be sufficient for a person's satisfying her duty to assist (provided she has the relevant intentions). But we also concluded that it is not necessary, since a person who does what her evidence or reasonable beliefs tell her will provide assistance can count as satisfying her duties to assist even if it turns out that she has not succeeded in helping anyone.

We considered as an exception to this rule the person whose beliefs were formed in a particularly egregious way, noting that such a person may not count as satisfying her duties to assist even when she takes on substantial cost. Finally, in discussing 'success' we argued that those who take maximally efficient means to important ends (with the caveats just given for inputs and characteristics) will satisfy their duties to assist. However, those who choose unimportant ends, and particularly those who take highly inefficient means to whichever ends they have chosen, can thereby be candidates for having the costs they have taken on discounted, such that they come to have further duties to assist (to make up the shortfall between the assistance they did secure and the assistance they could have secured).[30]

References

Baron, Marcia. 1984. "The Alleged Moral Repugnance of Acting from Duty." *Journal of Philosophy* 81 (4): 197–220.

Barry, Christian. & Øverland, Gerhard. 2013. "How Much for the Child?" *Ethical Theory and Moral Practice* 16 (2013): 189–204.

Cohen, Gerald. "On the Currency of Egalitarian Justice." *Ethics* 99 (1989): 906–44.

Cullity, Garrett. 2004. *The Moral Demands of Affluence*. Oxford: Oxford University Press.

Dworkin, Ronald. 2000. *Sovereign Virtue. The Theory and Practice of Equality*. Cambridge: Harvard University Press.

[30] An earlier version of this paper was presented at the 'Ethics of Giving' conference at the University of St. Andrews, the 'Responding to Global Poverty' conference at the University of Oslo, and in seminars at the Australian National University, University of Edinburgh, and University of Adelaide. We are grateful to the audiences at those seminars for their critical comments, and especially to Hilary Greaves, Theron Pummer, RJ Leland, and Garrett Cullity for detailed written comments on earlier versions of this paper. Work on this essay was supported by a grant from the Australian Research Council.

Edwards, Ashton. 2015. 'Man with the "golden arm" has saved the life of 2 million babies." *Fox13Now*, 9 June (Accessed 8 February 2015). Available at https://www.npr.org/sections/thetwo-way/2018/05/14/611074956/australias-man-with-the-golden-arm-retires-after-saving-2-4-million-babies.

Frick, Johann. 7 April 2017. "Critical Précis of Theron Pummer's 'Whether and Where to Give.'" Available at http://peasoup.us/2017/04/philosophy-public-affairs-discussion-pea-soup-theron-pummers-whether-give-critical-precis-johann-frick/.

GiveWell. November 2014. *Against Malaria Foundation*. (Accessed 10 May 2015). Available at http://www.givewell.org/international/top-charities/AMF.

Herman, Barbara. 1981. "On the Value of Acting from the Motive of Duty." *Philosophical Review* 90 (3): 359–82.

Jamieson, Dale. 2007. "When Utilitarians Should Be Virtue Theorists." *Utilitas* 19 (2): 160–83.

Kagan, Shelly. 1991a. "The Appeal to Cost." In *The Limits of Morality*. Oxford: Oxford University Press.

Kagan, Shelly. 1991b. "Précis of the Limits of Morality." *Philosophy and Phenomenological Research* LI (4): 897–901.

Kamm, Frances. 1992. "Non-Consequentialism, the Person as an End-in-Itself, and the Significance of Status." *Philosophy & Public Affairs* 21 (4): 354–89.

MacAskill, William. 2014. "The cold, hard truth about the ice bucket challenge." *Quartz*, 14 August (Accessed on 10 October 2014). Available at http://qz.com/249649/the-cold-hard-truth-about-the-ice-bucket-challenge/.

MacAskill, William. 2016. Doing Good Better. London: Guardian Faber Publishing.

McElwee, Brian. 2017. "Demandingness Objections in Ethics." *The Philosophical Quarterly* 67 (266): 84–105.

McMahan, Jeff. 2018. "Doing Good and Doing the Best." In *The Ethics of Philanthropy: Philosophers' Perspectives on Philanthropy*, Paul Woodruff, ed. New York: Oxford University Press, Chapter 3.

Mogensen, Andreas, Will MacAskill, and Toby Ord. 2018. 'Giving Isn't Demanding'. In *The Ethics of Philanthropy: Philosophers' Perspectives on Philanthropy*, Paul Woodruff, ed. New York: Oxford University Press, Chapter 6.

Nussbaum, Martha. 1992. "Human Functioning and Social Justice. In Defense of Aristotelian Essentialism." *Political Theory* 20: 202–46.

Pummer, Theron. 2016. "Whether and Where to Give," *Philosophy & Public Affairs* 44 (1): 77–95.

Rawls, John. 1971. *A Theory of Justice*. Cambridge: Harvard University Press, rev. ed. 1999.

Sachs, Ben. "Demanding the Demanding", Chapter 9, this volume.

Scanlon, Thomas. 1998. *What We Owe To Each Other*. Cambridge: Harvard University Press.

Sen, Amartya. 1980. "Equality of What?" In *Tanner Lectures on Human Values*, Stanley McMurrin, ed. Cambridge: Cambridge University Press.

Singer, Peter. 1972. "Famine, Affluence and Morality." *Philosophy & Public Affairs* 1: 229–43.

Singer, Peter. 2015. *The Most Good You Can Do*. New Haven: Yale University Press.

Unger, Peter. 1996. *Living High and Letting Die: Our Illusion of Innocence*. New York: Oxford University Press.

11
Effective Altruism's Underspecification Problem

Travis Timmerman

1. Introduction

Whether any given act is supererogatory, obligatory, merely permissible, or impermissible depends upon the alternative acts available to the agent. But what exactly are the *relevant* alternative acts available to an agent? It turns out that this is a surprisingly difficult question to answer, yet it's one on which any complete normative ethical theory must take a stance. It's also one on which any effective altruist must take a stance. This may be unwelcome news for effective altruists since, as I will demonstrate, each of the dominant views in the literature generates verdicts that are *(i)* implausible in their own right and *(ii)* seemingly at odds with typical effective altruist commitments.

Considering a particular case will help make this issue less abstract:

> ***The Gig:*** Brandi has been invited by her friend, Chad, to attend his musical gig. Brandi can easily decide to attend the gig, and then decide at the gig to be supportive of Chad, which would be the best outcome. Unfortunately, Chad is a mediocre musician. Consequently, Brandi would not in fact decide to be supportive of Chad if she decided to attend his gig due to being irritated with Chad's performance—even though she *could* decide at the gig to be supportive. Since Chad would be deeply hurt, this would be the worst outcome. Brandi could alternatively decide not to attend Chad's gig, which would be better than the worst outcome, yet worse than the best outcome.[1]

To be sure, Brandi *can* decide to attend the gig, and once there, she *can* decide to be supportive of Chad. However, suppose that just isn't what Brandi *would* do if she were to attend. Here's the tricky philosophical question. Is Brandi morally obligated to accept or decline the invitation? Roughly, possibilists hold that Brandi is obligated to accept because accepting is part of the best series of acts she

[1] This example is drawn from Cohen and Timmerman (2016, p. 1).

can perform over the course of her life. By contrast, actualists hold that Brandi is obligated to decline because what would actually happen if Brandi declines is better than what would actually happen if she accepts.[2] So, unlike possibilists, actualists hold that facts about how an agent *would* freely act partly determine an agent's obligations.

What is recognizably today's actualist/possibilist debate can be traced back to Holly (Goldman) Smith's seminal paper, in which cases that are structurally identical to *The Gig* originated.[3] This paper helped illustrate that any plausible normative ethical theory has to take a stance on the scope of the options available to the agent. Since the deontic status of an act depends upon the relevant options available to the agent, a normative ethical theory will have to take a stance on what the relevant options are and, of course, that requires taking a stance on the actualist/possibilist debate.

As William MacAskill's contribution to this volume illustrates, the term *effective altruism* has been understood in different, yet related, ways. It may be understood as a normative claim that one should do the most good they can.[4] It may also be understood as a non-normative project, whereby one is committed to doing the most good they can with some or all of their expendable resources, irrespective of whether they believe they're obligated to act in this way.[5] In this volume, MacAskill defines it thusly as "the use of evidence and reason to figure out how to benefit others as much as possible, and the taking of action on that basis."[6]

In this chapter, I'll understand *effective altruism* broadly to include both the normative thesis and non-normative project conceptions. My general aim is to argue that any understanding of effective altruism (either as a normative thesis or as a non-normative project) that does not take a stance on the actualism/possibilism debate is woefully incomplete. I will be interested in what pursuing the effective altruist project amounts to for those committed to actualism or to possibilism and

[2] Given my case and the colloquial description of actualism and possibilism, this debate may appear to only present problems for maximizing consequentialist views. However, the issues raised by the actualism/possibilism debate apply to a wide range of normative ethical views. For instance, just with respect to consequentialism, this debate applies to satisficing consequentialist views, where the threshold for permissibility is determined by the goodness of the act relative to the agent's available act-alternatives. In order to determine the relative goodness of any given act, one must determine what the relevant act-alternatives are, and that requires taking a stance on the actualism/possibilism debate. More generally, this debate also applies to normative ethical views which hold that, all else being equal, one is obligated to maximize the good. Again, one would need to know which acts are the relevant options for the agent in order to determine which act-set the agent is obligated to perform in such cases. Since the actualism/possibilism debate concerns identifying the scope of acts that are *relevant options* for the agent, it seems to me that every normative ethical view must take a stance on the debate.

[3] Goldman (1976). [4] Singer (2016, p. vii). [5] Karnofsky (2013); MacAskill (2015).

[6] Effective altruism does not officially take a stance on the good or even whether people are morally obligated to maximize the good. So, effective altruism does not assume impartial consequentialism, even though some prominent effective altruists are utilitarian. Effective altruists may, and some do, adopt the evidential reason component of effective altruism, while remaining skeptical about the maximizing component.

how pursuing such a project maps onto the current practices and recommendations of those who currently self-identify as effective altruists. I will also argue that effective altruists should adopt my favored view, viz. hybridism, which avoids the independent problems to which actualism and possibilism are subject. I also argue that hybridism better coheres with each conception of effective altruism than its alternatives. Much of what I write applies to each existing conception of effective altruism. When that isn't the case, I will specify the particular conception I am invoking.

This chapter is structured as follows. In the next section, I will provide an overview of the actualism/possibilism debate and, in doing so, offer a brief defense of my positive view, viz. hybridism. After that, I illustrate how this debate bears directly on effective altruism literature. I then argue that effective altruism is subject to a dilemma. Effective altruists', at times, implicit actualist assumptions *(i)* commit them to conclusions seemingly antithetical to what typical effective altruists actually believe, as well as the spirit of the movement and *(ii)* undermine effective altruists' arguments against moral offsetting and giving to charities close to the heart. Yet, effective altruists', at times, implicit possibilist assumptions *(iii)* also commit them to conclusions seemingly antithetical to what typical effective altruists actually believe, as well as the spirit of the movement and *(iv)* undermine typical responses to demandingness worries for the normative conception of effective altruism.[7] I argue that the best way out of the dilemma is to accept hybridism.

2. Actualism, possibilism, and hybridism

Actualism and possibilism may be defined more precisely as follows:

> **Actualism:** At t an agent S morally ought to φ at t' iff (1) φ-ing at t' is an act-set under S's control at t, and (2) what would happen if S were to φ at t' is better than what would happen if S were to perform any incompatible maximally specific act-set under S's control at t.[8]

[7] For a defense of such a worry, see Timmerman (2015a).

[8] Unlike this formulation of actualism, early formulations did not build in a control condition. See Goldman (1976); Sobel (1976); Jackson and Pargetter (1986). These versions of actualism are subject to devastating problems. Most notably, they violate the principle of normative inheritance (Portmore forthcoming, ch. 4) and they generate conflicting obligations without saying which obligation takes priority Cohen and Timmerman (2016, pp. 11–12); Kiesewetter (2015, pp. 929–34); Portmore (2011, pp. 181–3). Subsequent versions of actualism built in a control condition, avoiding this problem. See, for instance, Goldman (1978, p. 202); Bykvist (2002, pp. 61–4); Jackson (2014). Douglas Portmore's (2011) and Jacob Ross's (2012) securitist views also count as versions of actualism for the purposes of this paper.

Possibilism: At *t* an agent *S* is obligated to φ at *t′* iff φ-ing at *t′* is part of the best act-set that *S* can perform from *t* to the last moment that *S* can possibly perform an act.

As *The Gig* suggests, possibilism is generally much more demanding of imperfect agents than actualism since possibilism requires agents to do the most good they can over the course of their entire life.[9] Actualism, however, doesn't require nearly as much from imperfect agents. This is because actualism allows agents to avoid incurring obligations to do good in certain cases in which the agent would freely choose not to bring about the good. In *The Gig*, for instance, at the time Brandi received the invitation, it is not under her control to both <attend the gig and be supportive of Chad>. Since she would freely choose *not* to be supportive of Chad if she chooses to attend the gig, Brandi avoids incurring an obligation to <attend the gig>. Possibilism, however, does not let Brandi off the hook simply because she is disposed to act wrongly. Possibilism, but not actualism, entails that unless an agent does the most good she can over the course of her entire life, she will have acted wrongly at some point in her life. In this respect, it's a more demanding view.

There are two standard objections to actualism in the literature. To help illustrate them, it will be beneficial to consider another case:

Selfish Sally: Sally has exactly $500 in her account and had planned to use it to purchase non-refundable non-transferable tickets to see a Bad Religion concert tomorrow. Unless Sally spends the $500 on herself today, she will face the following choice tomorrow: use the $500 to give to an effective charity, which would result in three innocent lives being saved, or purchase the concert ticket. It's not presently under Sally's control to both keep the money in her account today and use the money to save the three lives tomorrow. That is, she cannot ensure today that she uses the money to save the three lives tomorrow. However, it is presently under her control to keep the money in her account today. Moreover, if she does keep the money in her account today it would be under her control tomorrow to use the money to save the three lives. At that point, all she has to do to ensure that she saves the three lives is to intend to use the $500 to save the three lives. That is just not what she would do if she finds herself in that situation. Finally, Sally is aware of these facts and consequently decides to purchase the concert ticket for herself today rather than tomorrow.[10]

[9] There are exceptions, however. Actualism might require certain agents to make demanding sacrifices now (e.g. doing something unpleasant to develop a more altruistic character) in order to ensure that they do more good in the future. Possibilism, by contrast, wouldn't require such sacrifices. I thank Michelle Hutchinson for raising this issue. See Timmerman and Swenson (forthcoming) for discussion of other ways actualism can be more demanding than possibilism.

[10] This case is a modified version of a case given in Timmerman (2015b, pp. 1,516–17) and in Timmerman and Cohen (2016, p. 677).

Actualism entails that there is no time at which Sally has an obligation to save the three lives tomorrow. This is because actualism does not even regard saving the three lives as a relevant *option* for Sally in spite of the fact that actualists grant that this is something Sally *can* do. She can save the three lives by simply choosing to save the money today and, once tomorrow rolls around, choosing to use the money to save the three lives. The problem is that actualism seems to get Sally off the hook too easily. In other words, it's not demanding enough:

> **The Not Demanding Enough Objection:** Actualism permits an agent *S* to avoid incurring any moral obligation to φ, which S can easily fulfill, simply in virtue of *S*'s rotten moral character.[11]

To illustrate the second objection to actualism, suppose that if Sally purchases the concert tickets today, the deaths of the three people would be moderately painful, whereas if she purchases the concert tickets tomorrow their deaths would be extremely painful. According to actualism, then, Sally ought to purchase the concert tickets today, causing three people to suffer a moderately painful death. This is because, of all the acts presently under her control, purchasing the tickets today would result in the best outcome. Moreover, Sally would presumably be immune from moral criticism since, according to actualism, she fulfilled her moral obligations and, we can suppose, did so for the right reasons. This consequence of actualism, however, seems absurd to many to since (actualists and possibilists agree) Sally *can* ensure that none of the three people are harmed at all. Simply stated, actualism prescribes bad behavior:

> **The Bad Behavior Objection:** Actualism prescribes bad behavior, and acting on such prescriptions (according to actualism) presumably renders[12] an agent *S* immune from moral criticism, even when *S* can easily refrain from such behavior.[13]

2.1 Problems with possibilism

The aforementioned objections to actualism have led many to accept possibilism instead. However, possibilism is subject to at least one comparably difficult objection. As a result of ignoring facts about how agents would act in the future, possibilism generates action-guiding obligations that would result in the worst

[11] Jackson and Pargetter (1986, p. 240); Zimmerman (2006, p. 156); Portmore (2011, p. 207); Baker (2012, pp. 642–3); Timmerman (2015b, pp. 1,512–13).

[12] This is not strictly entailed by actualism, but it is entailed by actualism coupled with widely accepted axioms about moral blameworthiness.

[13] Wedgwood (2009); Ross (2013); Timmerman and Cohen (2016); Zimmerman (2017, p. 121).

possible outcome. To illustrate, suppose that Sally is offered a deal where if she purchases the concert ticket today, then the profits from the ticket would be used to save two lives. Sally still can, of course, use the money to save three lives tomorrow if she has the money at that time. However, if she purchases the concert tickets tomorrow, then no lives would be saved. Possibilism entails that Sally ought to forgo the opportunity to purchase the tickets today in order to save two lives, even though this would result in her purchasing the same tickets tomorrow and, consequently, failing to save anyone.[14] Possibilism prescribes this even though, no matter what Sally intends to do today, she would freely choose to *not* save the three lives tomorrow. This objection may be formulated more precisely as follows:

> **The Worst Outcome Objection:** Possibilism entails that an agent *S* can have an action-guiding obligation to φ even when φ-ing entails that *S* would perform an act-set that is deeply morally wrong and that is worse than the act-set *S* would perform if *S* were to ~φ.[15]

As these cases illustrate, while actualism and possibilism each enjoy some intuitive support, both generate intuitively incorrect verdicts in certain cases. I will now provide a prima facie defense of a hybrid view that, I believe, avoids the problems associated with actualism and possibilism.

2.2 Hybridism

Hybrid views posit two distinct moral "oughts", one actualist in nature and one possibilist in nature. These oughts are meant to jointly track the insights of both actualism and possibilism, yet be immune from the three aforementioned objections. Given space limitations, I cannot provide a full defense of any particular hybrid view here, so my goal is to make a prima facie case for hybridism. My more important goal is to illustrate how issues that arise in the effective altruism literature hinge on the actualism/possibilism debate in ethics. Although I am making a prima facie case for hybridism, different versions of the view have already been developed and fully defended in the literature.[16] In this section, I will focus on my favored version of hybridism, viz. *Single Obligation Hybridism* (SOH). In its simplest form, SOH posits a possibilist moral *obligation* that picks out the criterion of right and an actualist moral *ought* that functions as a sort of

[14] If this is not already intuitive, imagine that the stakes are much higher. We can suppose that there are a billion and one lives at stake and that Sally has the opportunity to save one billion of those lives if she purchases the ticket today.

[15] Goldman (1976, pp. 469–70); Woodard (2009, pp. 219–20); Portmore (2011, p. 211); Timmerman and Cohen (2016, p. 674).

[16] See Timmerman (2015b) and Timmerman and Cohen (2016).

decision procedure. The actualist moral ought is an action-guiding practical ought, not a moral obligation. Hybridist views take agents' shortcomings into its prescriptions, sometimes telling an agent to perform a wrong act now in order to prevent that person from performing an even worse act at a later time. SOH may be formulated more precisely as follows.[17]

Single Obligation Hybridism:

Possibilist Moral Obligation: At *t* an agent *S* has a possibilist moral obligation to φ at *t′* iff φ-ing at *t′* is part of the best series of acts that *S* can perform from *t* to the last moment that *S* can possibly perform an act.

Actualist Practical Ought: At t an agent S has most practical reason to φ at t′ iff φ-ing at t′ is under S's control at t and φ-ing at t′ is either (i) identical to the maximally-specific possibilist obligation that S has at t, (ii) a rationally permissible supererogatory act, or (iii) is the least rationally impermissible, all things considered, act-set presently under S's control at t. There is an act-set that satisfies (iii) iff no act-set presently under S's control at t satisfies conditions (i) or (ii).

The technical details of SOH are not centrally important for the purposes of this chapter. The most important elements of the view, for the purposes of this paper, may be understood by considering its applications in particular cases. Consider *Selfish Sally*. SOH entails that Sally has a possibilist moral obligation to refrain from purchasing the ticket today in order to use it to save the three lives tomorrow. This is because the possibilist obligation, which picks out the criterion of right, holds that agents are obligated to perform each act that is part of the best series of acts they can perform. The possibilist obligation can also serve to ground reactive attitudes. On plausible accounts of blameworthiness, Sally can be blameworthy to the extent she culpably fails to fulfill her possibilist obligations. Thus, SOH is immune from the *Not Demanding Enough Objection* and from the *Bad Behavior Objection*.

At the same time, SOH is immune from the *Worst Outcome Objection* because the actualist ought, not the possibilist obligation, is action-guiding. The actualist ought prescribes performing the act that would result in the best outcome *from among the set of acts presently under the agent's control*. Sometimes this is identical with the possibilist obligation and sometimes it isn't. This practical ought then serves the purpose of minimizing wrongdoing in light of one's present circumstances.

[17] I am using the term *obligation* narrowly as shorthand for *moral obligation* and the term *ought* broadly to refer to any claim about how one should act within any normative domain. So, a moral obligation is one type of moral ought, while a practical moral ought is another type of moral ought. We could also speak of what one prudentially ought to do, what one legally ought to do, and so on. This formulation of SOH is a simplified version of the one given in Timmerman and Cohen (2016, pp. 682–3). The simpler version of SOH suffices for the purposes of this paper, however, since none of my arguments hinge on the issues addressed in the more complex definition.

So, in *Selfish Sally*, SOH entails that Sally practically ought to forgo saving the three lives tomorrow in favor of saving the two lives today. Hybridism tells Sally to perform a wrong act now (i.e. saving two instead of three innocent lives) in order to prevent herself from performing an even worse act later (i.e. saving no lives). Stated over simplistically, hybridism tells effective altruists to act like actualists, even though they are obligated to act like possibilists. Now that I have made my prima facie case for hybridism, I'll turn to the implications of this debate for effective altruism.

3. *A dilemma: effective altruists' contradictory assumptions*

The actualism/possibilism debate has, until now, been completely overlooked in the effective altruism literature. However, a number of people who self-identify as effective altruists implicitly appeal to actualist or possibilist considerations in their work. I'll use the term *effective altruist* to refer to someone who believes that they ought to be doing the most good they can either because they endorse effective altruism as a normative thesis or because they have adopted effective altruism as a non-normative project. So, as I am using the term, any effective altruist believes that they ought, in some sense, to be doing the most good they can. Those who accept the normative thesis believe they are *morally obligated* to do the most good they can.

Those who have only adopted effective altruism as a non-normative project believe they ought, qua effective altruist, to do the most good they can. This ought is not referring to a moral obligation. Such effective altruists have adopted the project of doing the most good they can because they believe such a project to be worthy of pursuit, likely in virtue of the fact that they perceive it as morally good (even supererogatory). In order to successfully achieve the aim of their project, they need to do the most good they can. So, the ought in question is one that picks out a necessary means to achieve a (morally important) aim. Analogously, someone who takes on the project of being vegan because they believe it to be a (non-obligatory) project worthy of pursuit ought, in this sense, not to consume animal products. Someone who takes on the project of writing a scientifically informed op-ed about vaccines ought, in this sense, to learn the relevant science. In short, this ought doesn't refer to a moral obligation; it refers to a necessary means of achieving one's goal.

Here's the problem. Effective altruists implicitly appeal to actualism when warding off concerns that effective altruism is too demanding, too impractical, or too out of sync with the "real world".[18] Yet, they also implicitly appeal to

[18] One charitable way of understanding this last criticism is that effective altruism is too close to ideal theory when it should be focused on non-ideal theory.

possibilism when warding off concerns that effective altruism licenses bad behavior or lets some agents off the hook too easily. Since actualism and possibilism are defined in terms of moral obligations, and since they make incompatible claims about which possible outcomes are relevant options for the agent, they are contradictory. Thus, effective altruists cannot consistently appeal to both in their theorizing.

3.1 Effective altruists' implicit actualist assumptions

Two prominent effective altruists, Peter Singer and William MacAskill, frequently implicitly appeal to actualism in their work on effective altruism and specifically do so when trying to assuage concerns about the demandingness of being an effective altruist.[19] The demandingness concerns mainly arise for effective altruism understood as a normative thesis (which is how Singer understands it), rather than understood as a non-normative project (which is how MacAskill understands it).[20] Understood solely as a non-normative project, effective altruism is demanding only insofar as one voluntarily takes on sacrificial projects to maximize the good. These conceptions do not entail that one is morally obligated to do the most good they can, and so are less demanding in this respect.[21]

In *The Most Good You Can Do*, Singer discusses the lives of a number of actual effective altruists,[22] all of whom keep some "modest level of comfort and convenience" even if it's possible for them to do more good by giving up these luxuries.[23] Singer appears to endorse this strategy because choosing to live without this level of comfort and convenience is likely to be "counterproductive".[24] When discussing the sacrifices one must make to be an effective altruist, Singer adds that "if you find yourself doing something that makes you bitter, it's time to reconsider."[25] He then rhetorically asks whether it would really be best if you chose to do

[19] In a personal correspondence, when presented with each view, Peter Singer endorsed actualism.

[20] See Sachs's contribution to this volume for a discussion of whether confronting people with arguments for demanding moral requirements would be counterproductive (Chapter 9). Sachs argues that there is "no solid basis" for believing that it would be.

[21] In his contribution to this volume, MacAskill cites a number of effective altruist surveys, which reveal that 65.4 percent of respondents accept utilitarianism or some other form of consequentialism, and so a substantial percentage of effective altruists likely endorse the normative thesis that one is obligated to do the most good they can. However, 70 percent thought that the definition of effective altruism should be non-normative, and so endorse the non-normative project conception for the purposes of the movement.

[22] None of these supposedly exemplary effective altruists live up to the demands of a possibilist effective altruism. But, from Singer's descriptions, they seem to generally live up to the demands of an actualist effective altruism, which is to say that they make choices that will result in them doing the most good *holding fixed the facts about how they would act if they make any given choice*. This is some defeasible evidence that committed effective altruists are disposed toward accepting actualism.

[23] Singer (2016, p. 28). [24] Singer (2016, p. 29).

[25] Singer (2016, p. 29).

something that made you bitter. Singer's suggestion appears to be that you ought to avoid such choices because they would result in you doing less good as an effective altruist than if you made choices that prevented you from being bitter. This general advice is given after considering an effective altruist named Julia who decided to have a child in spite of the fact that this would reduce the amount of overall good Julia could do over the course of her life.[26]

Singer raises similar considerations later in the text when discussing the demandingness of taking a high-paying job one doesn't find intrinsically valuable in order to earn to give. He recognizes that earning to give is "not for everyone" and cautions against it for people who won't be enthusiastic about "making profits for their employer" even if doing so is necessary for one to do the most good they can over the course of their life.[27] Such considerations are echoed by MacAskill in *Doing Good Better*. In the section on what choices prospective effective altruists should make when picking a career, he advises people to pick careers that make them happy, justifying this prescription by pointing out that "if you're not happy at work, you'll be less productive and more likely to burn out, resulting in less impact in the long term."[28] In another paper, MacAskill also considers the possibility that taking a high-paying job will result in one becoming "corrupted by one's colleagues" as a result of having to socialize with people who hold anti-effective altruist values.[29] He proceeds to suggest ways to mitigate this, and other, risks. MacAskill nevertheless grants that such considerations need to be taken into account by prospective effective altruists.[30] He even factors these considerations into the expected value of the choices one makes, which implicitly assumes actualism over possibilism. Similar considerations are raised throughout the chapter on effective altruist career choices. In the concluding chapter, MacAskill advises his readers to set up a recurring donation at a charity for actualist reasons.[31]

Singer's actualist assumptions even predate effective altruism. In *The Life You Can Save*, Singer argues that failing to help family members in need "would be going too much against the grain of human nature."[32] He then suggests that people "take care of their families in an entirely sufficient way on much less than they are now spending" and donate the money they have left over to those living

[26] An exact parallel between Singer's and MacAskill's actualist response to effective altruists may be found in Peter Railton's (1984). In that paper, Railton addresses demandingness worries for consequentialism by implicitly assuming actualism. Along the same lines, Singer and Katarzyna de Lazari-Radek briefly mention, and seem to endorse, Frank Jackson's decision-theoretic consequentialism (1991), which itself assumes actualism. See Singer and de Lazari-Radek (2014, pp. 326–7). Another, not mutually exclusive, possibility is that Singer's actualist assumptions are rooted in his commitment to esoteric morality. See his and de Lazari-Radek's (2010). Singer's remarks in his (2016b, §2) supports this hypothesis. See also Skelton (2016, pp. 141–2).

[27] Singer (2016, p. 47). [28] MacAskill (2015, p. 149). [29] MacAskill (2014, p. 281).

[30] MacAskill (2014, p. 281). [31] MacAskill (2015, p. 197). [32] Singer (2009, p. 40).

in extreme poverty.[33] Actualist considerations even appear to be at the heart of Singer's "Realistic Approach" to effective giving,[34] which sets standards based on what *would* (not what *could*) result in the highest total giving for most individuals (Singer 2009: 154).[35]

3.2 The problem with accepting actualism and being an effective altruist

Although appeals to actualism may help mitigate demandingness worries, actualism also seems to permit actions seemingly antithetical to the commitments of effective altruism understood as a normative claim and as a non-normative project. For instance, actualism entails that Sally is obligated to frivolously spend money on concert tickets today instead of saving three lives tomorrow, but surely Sally fails to do the most good she can by making such a choice. While it's true that, with respect to her alternatives today, choosing to <purchase the concert ticket> would result in more good than choosing to <keep the money in her account>, it's also true that Sally can do more good by choosing to <keep the money in her account> today and then choosing to <donate that money to an effective charity> tomorrow. Actualists and possibilists agree that Sally *can* <keep the money in her account and donate that money to an effective charity>. So, actualists and possibilists agree about which acts agents can, and cannot, perform. Their disagreement concerns the relationship between agent's free actions and their moral obligations. In this case, they disagree about whether Sally is obligated to <keep the money in her account> given that she would then freely decide <not to donate that money to an effective charity>. Consider another example.

> **Partying Pete:** Pete is contemplating gambling away his millions of dollars over a weekend in Vegas. In doing so, he'll bring some pleasure to himself and friends. Regardless of his intentions today, if Pete does not choose to spend his money in Vegas this weekend, he'll later decide to spend it on blood diamonds for himself, although he could, at the later time, decide to donate any money he has to an effective charity.

Actualism entails that Pete is obligated to spend his millions partying in Vegas. But surely Pete does not even come close to doing the most good he can by gambling away his millions. After all, actualists and possibilists agree that Pete *can* forgo a

[33] Singer (2009, p. 40). [34] See, in particular, Chapter 10 of Singer's (2009).

[35] Singer also makes remarks along these lines in his (2017, p. 161). Although Singer's remarks seem to assume actualism, they may also just be the product of his two-level utilitarian view. Similar remarks are made in his (2011, p. 213).

Vegas trip and then donate his money to an effective charity. Yet, actualists deny that Pete has an obligation to forgo gambling away his millions in Vegas. Effective altruists who accept actualism inherit the *Not Demanding Enough* and the *Bad Behavior* objections. This is a problem for those who accept effective altruism as a normative thesis because Pete doesn't seem to come remotely close to doing the most good he can. Yet, if actualism is true, then Pete would be acting in accordance with the normative thesis. This is a problem for those who accept effective altruism as a non-normative project because Pete doesn't seem to be acting in accordance with the project of doing the most good he can. Yet, if actualism identifies the relevant options, then Pete gambling away his millions is perfectly in line with the effective altruism project. This strikes me as highly implausible. These considerations provide good reason for effective altruists to reject actualism and yet, in turn, threaten to undermine effective altruists' response to demandingness worries.

3.3 Effective altruists' implicit possibilist assumptions

In response to such worries, effective altruists may be inclined to accept possibilism. In fact, in other contexts, effective altruists even implicitly assume possibilism in response to worries that effective altruism is too permissive. Ethical offsetting is one such example. Ethical offsetting is "the practice of undoing harms caused by one's activities through donations or other acts of altruism".[36] Carbon offsetting is an instance of ethical offsetting. A more unconventional example would be personally killing and skinning animals to make a fur coat for oneself, but then donating to non-human animal charities to "cancel out" the number of non-human animal deaths one causes. Killing animals to make a fur coat, however, seems to be in tension with effective altruism understood either as a normative thesis or as a non-normative project. One can do more good by getting others to give up fur, while also giving up fur themselves. In objecting to ethical offsetting on these grounds, effective altruists have implicitly assumed possibilism.[37]

Effective altruists have repeatedly argued that people should not simply give to charities that are "close to their heart" because doing so is often radically ineffective.[38] MacAskill has forcefully argued that one should not let their affinity with a charity (including concern for particular recipients of the charity) even

[36] Zabel (2016).

[37] See, for example, (Zabel 2016, §2). Interestingly, while possibilism seems to be implicitly assumed in Section 2, actualist considerations are appealed to in the "Caveats' section". This suggests that both considerations resonate among prospective effective altruists and provides additional reason to accept hybridism.

[38] Singer (2009, ch. 4–7); Singer (2016, §4); MacAskill (2016, ch. 3–5).

partly determine one's choices about where to give.[39] Doing so would be favoring the less important needs of a group of people over the more important needs of another group on the morally irrelevant basis that you happen to know members of one group. Criticisms of the ineffectiveness of using a "close to the heart" heuristic strike me as apt, yet they do implicitly assume possibilism. After all, giving to charities that are "close to the heart" may do more to ensure that one remains sufficiently motivated to give in the future, resulting in them doing more good in the long run than if they now chose to give to an effective charity only to later succumb to *akrasia*.[40]

While anyone working on the ethics of charity or ethical offsetting will have to take a stance on the actualism/possibilism debate, these issues are of special concern for effective altruists. This is because these issues highlight the dilemma effective altruists face.

3.4 The Problem with accepting possibilism and being an effective altruist

Accepting possibilism would have some radical implications for effective altruism. Possibilism combined with the conception of effective altruism as a normative thesis entails that one's present obligations require them to perform the acts that would let them do the most good they can over the course of their entire life independent of considerations about how they would freely act in the future. This may mean that such effective altruists are obligated to forgo donating anything now in favor of investing all their money in order to donate as much as possible on their deathbed even if, on their deathbed, they would choose to donate nothing. It also renders irrelevant the seemingly practical considerations MacAskill and Singer raise about whether one should decide to "earn to give".[41] Most notably, considerations about whether one *would* suffer from "burnout" if they take a labor-intensive job that leaves little room for a social life and considerations about whether one *would* become "corrupted" by their co-workers and cease to give to charity are irrelevant to how one is obligated to act if possibilism is true. More generally, any effective altruist who accepts possibilism is committed to the claim that people should completely ignore their motivational structure when

[39] MacAskill (2015, pp. 41–2). See also (Pummer 2016) for a compelling argument that if one is going to choose to give to charity, they are obligated to give to one that would do the most good even when it would be permissible for them to have not donated at all.

[40] For a discussion of charities' retention strategies and their effects on donor retention rates, see Singer (2009, ch. 4) and Singer (2017, pp. 175–8). See also Schervish and Havens (1997), especially their discussion of the *frameworks of consciousness* motivating factors (p. 241). See also Green and Webb (2008) and Sargeant and Woodliffe (2008). This issue has also been discussed in detail on effective altruist blogs. See, for instance, http://lesswrong.com/lw/6z/purchase_fuzzies_and_utilons_separately/.

[41] MacAskill (2015, ch. 9); Singer (2016, ch. 4).

determining how to act, sometimes resulting in one foreseeably bringing about the worst possible outcome. This seems antithetical to effective altruism understood as a normative thesis because it requires people to act in ways they know will not only result in them acting wrongly, but also result in the least (not the most) amount of good. This seems antithetical to effective altruism understood as a non-normative project because someone committed to doing the most good shouldn't make choices they know will result in the least amount of good.

Both actualism and possibilism generate commitments seemingly antithetical to each type of effective altruism. Moreover, combining actualism with effective altruism (understood as a normative thesis or as a non-normative project) undermines typical effective altruist responses to ethical offsetting and to donating to charities close to the heart. On the other hand, combining possibilism with effective altruism (understood as a normative thesis) undermines effective altruists' standard response to demandingness worries. Effective altruists are thus faced with a dilemma. I will now argue that the best way out of the dilemma is to accept hybridism.

4. Hybridism

Hybridism retains the benefits of both actualism and possibilism, yet is immune from each of the aforementioned problems. Unlike actualism and possibilism, it's also consistent with the spirit of each type of effective altruism. Recall that hybridism posits a possibilist moral obligation. So, it avoids the *Bad Behavior* and *Not Demanding Enough* objections because it requires agents, such as *Selfish Sally* and *Partying Pete*, to do the best they can throughout their life. At the same time, hybridism avoids the *Worst Outcome Objection* because it posits an actualist practical ought. This component of hybridism is uniquely important for effective altruism understood as a normative thesis because it can address demandingness worries at the practical level.[42] Hybridism allows that the considerations raised by Singer and MacAskill discussed in Section 3 *are* considerations that one should take into account when deciding how to act. Although, crucially, they are considerations that do not affect one's obligations, but rather, the practical choices one should make in light of their own moral shortcomings.

The ramifications of a hybridism for issues of special concern to effective altruists are worth reviewing. Someone prone to *akrasia* may have extra reason to donate to charities that utilize effective marketing tactics, have high donor retention rates, and are close to one's heart. Contrary to the standard effective altruist suggestion then, people often practically ought to give to suboptimal

[42] It's possible that MacAskill and Singer are primarily concerned about addressing demandingness worries at the practical level anyway.

charities. Similarly, ethical offsetting may frequently be what one practically ought to do, even if it's immoral. One ought to ethically offset (or donate to suboptimal charities) when, of all the acts one can presently ensure she performs, ethical offsetting (or giving to suboptimal charities) would result in the least amount of badness. Adopting hybridism should lead to a more nuanced understanding, and perhaps greater acceptance of, these practices in the effective altruism community.

5. Conclusion

This paper served two goals. First, I explored the implications of the different viable answers to the actualist/possibilist debate for effective altruism. Interestingly, prominent effective altruists seem disposed to endorse the most popular answer (i.e. actualism), which entails that effective altruism is much less demanding than some of its critics believe.[43] Yet, there are good reasons to believe that actualism is both false and antithetical to effective altruism, understood either as a normative thesis or a non-normative project. Rejecting actualism, however, undermines common responses effective altruists give to demandingness objections. To make matters worse, there are good reasons to believe that possibilism is also false and antithetical to effective altruism, understood either as a normative thesis or a non-normative project. Rejecting possibilism, however, undermines common arguments effective altruists make against moral offsetting and giving to charities close to the heart. This is the dilemma effective altruists face. Second, I sketched my own positive solution on behalf of effective altruism. Effective altruists can escape this dilemma by adopting hybridism, or so I've argued.[44]

References

Baker, Derek. 2012. "Knowing Yourself—and Giving Up on Your Own Agency in the Process." *Australasian Journal of Philosophy* 90 (4): 641–56.

Bykvist, Krister. 2002. "Alternative Actions and the Spirit of Consequentialism." *Philosophical Studies* 107 (1): 45–68.

[43] See, e.g. Nakul Krishna's (2016), Amia Srinivasan's (2015), and Colin McGinn's (1999). Jeff McMahan reviews, and rebuts, a number of criticisms of effective altruism in his (2016).

[44] For helpful comments and discussion, I would like to thank Christian Barry, Amy Berg, Donald Bruckner, Alexander Dietz, Karl Ekendahl, Dan Fogal, Johann Frick, Jens Johansson, Michelle Hutchinson, Eden Lin, Theron Pummer, Ketan Ramakrishnan, Olle Risberg, Simon Rosenqvist, Ben Sachs, Peter Singer, Preston Werner, and audiences at the University of St. Andrews, Uppsala University, and the 2018 Philosophy, Politics, and Economics Conference. I owe a special thanks to Hilary Greaves, who provided incredibly detailed and insightful written comments on multiple drafts of this paper, which significantly improved the final product. Work on this paper was supported by a grant from the National Endowment for the Humanities and from Seton Hall University's URC summer grant.

Cohen, Yishai, and Travis Timmerman. 2016. "Actualism Has Control Issues." *Journal of Ethics and Social Philosophy* 10 (3): 1–19.

Goldman, Holly S. 1976. "Dated Rightness and Moral Imperfection." *The Philosophical Review*, 85 (4): 449–87.

Goldman, Holly S. 1978. "Doing the Best One Can." In *Value and Morals: Essays in Honor of William Frankena, Charles Stevenson, and Richard Brandt*, Alvin Goldman, ed. Dordrecht: D. Reidel.

Green, Corliss, and Deborah Webb. 2008. "Factors Influencing Monetary Donations to Charitable Organizations." *Journal of Nonprofit and Public Sector Marketing* 5 (3): 19–40.

Jackson, Frank, and Robert Pargetter. 1986. "Ought, Options, and Actualism." *The Philosophical Review* 95 (2): 233–55.

Jackson, Frank. 1991. "Decision-Theoretic Consequentialism and the Nearest and Dearest Objection." *Ethics* 101 (3): 461–82.

Jackson, Frank. 2014. "Procrastinate Revisited." *Pacific Philosophical Quarterly* 95 (4): 634–47.

Karnofsky, Holden. 2013. "Effective Altruism." *The GiveWell Blog*, 13 August (Accessed 11 June 2018). Available at https://blog.givewell.org/2013/08/13/effective-altruism/.

Kiesewetter, Benjamin. 2015. "Instrumental Normativity: In Defense of the Transmission Principle." *Ethics* 125 (4): 921–46.

Krishna, Nakul. 2016. "Add Your Own Egg." *Examined Life* (Accessed 23 June 2017). Available at http://thepointmag.com/2016/examined-life/add-your-own-egg.

MacAskill, William. 2014. "Replaceability, Career Choice, and Making a Difference." *Ethical Theory and Moral Practice* 17 (2): 269–83.

MacAskill, William. 2015. *Doing Good Better*. New York: Penguin Random House.

MacAskill, William. 2016. "Banking: The Ethical Career Choice." In *Philosophers Take on the World*, D. Edmonds, ed. New York: Oxford University Press.

MacAskill, William. Forthcoming. "The Definition of Effective Altruism." In *Effective Altruism: Philosophical Issues*, Hilary Greaves and Theron Pummer, eds. New York: Oxford University Press.

McGinn, Colin. 1999. "Our Duties to Animals and the Poor." In *Singer and His Critics*, D. Jamieson, ed. Oxford: Blackwell.

McMahan, Jeff. 2016. "Philosophical Critiques of Effective Altruism." *The Philosopher's Magazine* 73: 92–9.

Portmore, Douglas. 2011. *Commonsense Consequentialism: Wherein Morality Meets Rationality*. New York: Oxford University Press.

Portmore, Douglas. Forthcoming. *Opting for the Best*. New York: Oxford University Press.

Pummer, Theron. 2016. "Whether and Where to Give." *Philosophy and Public Affairs* 44 (1): 77–95.

Railton, Peter. 1984. "Alienation, Consequentialism, and the Demands of Morality." *Philosophy and Public Affairs* 13 (2): 134–71.

Ross, Jacob. 2012. "Actualism, Possibilism, and Beyond." In *Oxford Studies in Normative Ethics*, Mark Timmons, ed. New York: Oxford University Press.

Sachs, Ben. Forthcoming. "Demanding the Demanding." In *Effective Altruism: Philosophical Issues*, Hilary Greaves and Theron Pummer, eds. New York: Oxford University Press.

Sargeant, Adrian, and Lucy Woodliffe. 2008. "Building Donor Loyalty: The Antecedents and Role of Commitment in the Context of Charity Giving." *Journal of Nonprofit and Public Sector Marketing* 18: 47–8.

Schervish, Paul G., and John Havens. 1997. "Social Participation and Charitable Giving: A Multivariate Analysis." *Voluntas* 8 (3): 235–60.

Singer, Peter. 2009. *The Life You Can Save*. New York: Random House.

Singer, Peter, and Katarzyna de Lazari-Radek. 2010. "Secrecy in Consequentialism: A Defence of Esoteric Morality." *Ratio* 23 (1): 34–58.

Singer, Peter. 2011. *Practical Ethics*. New York: Cambridge University Press.

Singer, Peter, and Katarzyna de Lazari-Radek. 2014. *The Point of View of the Universe: Sidgwick and Contemporary Ethics*. New York: Oxford University Press.

Singer, Peter. 2016. "The Most Good You Can Do: A Response to the Commentaries." *Journal of Global Ethics* 12 (2): 161–9.

Singer, Peter. 2017. *Ethics in the Real World*. New York: Princeton University Press.

Skelton, Anthony. 2016. "The Ethical Principles of Effective Altruism." *Journal of Global Ethics* 12 (2): 137–46.

Sobel, Jordan Howard. 1976. "Utilitarianism and Past and Future Mistakes." *Noûs* 10 (2): 195–219.

Srinivasan, Amia. 2015. "Stop the Robot Apocalypse." *London Review of Books* 37 (18): 3–6.

Timmerman, Travis. 2015a. "Sometimes There is Nothing Wrong with Letting a Child Drown." *Analysis* 75 (2): 204–12.

Timmerman, Travis. 2015b. "Does Scrupulous Securitism Stand-Up to Scrutiny? Two Problems for Moral Securitism and How We Might Fix Them." *Philosophical Studies* 172 (6): 1,509–28.

Timmerman, Travis, and Yishai Cohen. 2016. "Moral Obligations: Actualist, Possibilist, or Hybridist?" *Australasian Journal of Philosophy* 94 (4): 672–86.

Timmerman, Travis, and Philip Swenson. Forthcoming. "How to be an Actualist and Blame People." In *Oxford Studies in Agency and Responsibility, Vol. 6*, David Shoemaker, ed. New York: Oxford University Press.

Wedgwood, Ralph. 2009. "Against Actualism." *PEA Soup*, 11 September (Accessed 20 May 2017). Available at peasoup.typepad.com/peasoup/2009/09/against-actualism.html.

Woodard, Christopher. 2009. "What's Wrong with Possibilism." *Analysis* 69 (2): 219–26.

Zabel, Claire. 2016. "Ethical Offsetting is Antithetical to Effective Altruism." *Effective Altruism Forum*, 5 January (Accessed 20 May 2017). Available at http://effective-altruism.com/ea/ry/ethical_offsetting_is_antithetical_to_ea/.

Zimmerman, Michael. 1996. *The Concept of Moral Obligation*. New York: Cambridge University Press.

Zimmerman, Michael. 2006. "The Relevant Risks to Wrongdoing." In *The Good, the Right, Life and Death: Essays in Honor of Fred Feldman*, Kris McDaniel, Jason Raibley, Richard Feldman, and Mark Zimmerman, eds. Burlington: Ashgate Publishing Co.

Zimmerman, Michael. 2017. "Prospective Possibilism." *The Journal of Ethics* 21 (2): 117–50.

12

The Hidden Zero Problem

Effective Altruism and Barriers to Marginal Impact

Mark Budolfson and Dean Spears

1. The hidden zero problem: An initial illustration

Suppose for the sake of argument that practitioners of effective altruism (EA) are completely correct about the amount of good done by their top charities. Is there is any further reason to worry that giving to these charities is not an effective way of doing good?

It turns out that there is, and a real-world illustration of the worry is based on the fact that several billionaires closely follow the recommendations of EA, and can credibly commit to "top up" the revenues of many of the charities that EA recommends, in order to ensure that those charities meet operating budget targets. These facts are readily knowable based on public information (see references later in this section). In some previous years, because the amount of plausible shortfall in all of the top-ranked EA charities *combined* was only several tens of millions of dollars per year, and because this group of billionaires had the capacity to top up such charities to erase *much more* than that level of shortfall and arguably seemed to commit to making sure that no real funding needs went unmet, during that time the expectation associated with donations to these leading EA charities of, say, a magnitude of $1,000 was arguably that no difference was made to the operations of the charity, and slightly less money was transferred from the billionaires to those charities.[1] If so, the expected effect of a donation to an EA recommended charity during this time period, even assuming the charities did just as much good as EA advisors claimed, would have been merely to transfer money to a billionaire in the United States, and accomplish nothing for the global poor.

In recent years, this situation has likely changed in connection with at least one and perhaps more leading EA charities, which may now have much more capacity to scale up operations quickly, as discussed near the end of this section. But an important philosophical point remains, namely that this example of how donations by normal people could have zero positive effect illustrates what we call the

[1] Here we bracket the possibility that the expectation could zero because it is knowable that e.g. donations less than or equal to $1,000 amount to insignificant digits in all of the relevant decision-making by charity organizations, billionaires, and others—compare Budolfson (2018).

hidden zero problem, which is that the marginal effect of an action often depends on a hidden parameter that is ignored in widespread EA analyses of efficacy, where that parameter might realistically have the value of zero in a way that ensures that individual actions are not efficacious. In the billionaires example, the hidden parameter is the marginal effect of a donation on the operating budget of a charity; the phenomena of billionaires topping up charities to predetermined targets illustrates how such a parameter could be zero even if all of the other parameters that EA evaluators track actually have the positive values that EA proponents claim—and if such a parameter is zero, then the marginal effect of a donation can be zero regardless of how positive the other parameters are the EA proponents track.

In the next section, we articulate this hidden zero problem more formally, and in later sections we provide a number of additional important examples of this problem for EA. We emphasize that there is no argument here that top-rated EA charities should not exist or should pursue other activities. We are instead focused narrowly on the question of what the expected effect is of an individual's donation, and what an ordinary individual donor has reason to do. In the rest of this section, we consider the dynamics of the particular billionaires example that we introduced above in more detail.

The possibility of billionaires standing ready to top up top-rated charities is occasionally acknowledged by EAs, but is then quickly dismissed as not relevant to reality.[2] The only commentator we know who has taken the issue seriously is Iason Gabriel. However, Gabriel believes that the billionaires example is not ultimately a big deal on the grounds that if individual donations do in fact reduce the amount that billionaires donate to top-rated EA charities, then that simply means that those billionaires will then donate the money saved to the next best charities instead—thereby ensuring that an individual's donation does have some significant positive marginal effect, albeit slightly less than the effect EA proponents claim.[3]

However, it is an empirical claim that billionaires have invested the same amount in other slightly less effective charities instead. Unfortunately, that claim appears false in light of publicly available information that shows that in the past, EA-directed billionaires have for principled reasons not been willing to redirect excess money to charities "further down the list". In what follows, we detail the publicly available evidence for this, which suggests that the billionaires problem may well have created a hidden zero in the recent past, even if the situation has now evolved.

The importance of the problem becomes clear from a careful study of what might be called the recent "pivot toward billionaires in EA", in which billionaires now dominate the funding for top EA charities, together with the fact that there

[2] Compare MacAskill (2015, p. 119).
[3] Gabriel (2016) introduces the billionaires problem to the literature.

are only a handful of top ranked EA charities, many of which have a surprisingly low limit (by the organization's own account) to the resources it can absorb and genuinely turn into welfare gains. The leading example of the pivot toward billionaires is provided by Good Ventures, a foundation run by billionaires Cari Tuna and Facebook co-founder Dustin Moskovitz, which in the recent past, by its own claims, had so much money to invest that it could not find nearly enough opportunities to invest its vast resources consistent with the EA criteria it endorses as a constraint on making donations. In light of this, until recently it is possible that it reliably filled any *genuine* need for resources that could be converted into welfare gains by top EA charities.[4] (Throughout we understand "top-rated EA charities" to be the top charities recommended by the EA evaluator GiveWell.org.)

To understand in detail the way the pivot toward billionaires may have undermined the marginal effect of individual donations in previous years, it is important to see that Good Ventures *alone* represented over *two thirds* of all money moved to EA charities in 2015, as tracked by EA advisor givingwhatwecan.org.[5] Beyond this, the most important facts here (reported by Good Ventures, GiveWell, and others) are that:

(a) Good Ventures represents *only one* among a growing number of EA-focused "billionaires".[6]
(b) Good Ventures now funds and collaborates with the dominant EA advisor GiveWell in investment and strategic decision-making, and so Good Ventures makes its decisions in a way that perfectly tracks the dominant EA consensus.[7]
(c) Good Ventures *alone* has so much money that, by their own lights in several previous years they have been able *by themselves* to easily meet all of the funding needs of *all* of the charities that are deemed to be sufficiently effective to be worthy of investment on EA grounds, while still not being able to spend *nearly* as much money as they would like because they judge

[4] For more detail, a good place to start is two blog posts from GiveWell, Karnofsky (2015b), and Hassenfeld and Rosenberg (2015), and one blog post from Good Ventures, Karnofsky (2015a). A slightly older but important discussion superseded by the preceding is Karnofsky (2014).

[5] MacAskill (2016).

[6] For example, the Effective Altruism Global 2015 conference was advertised as "the largest ever convening of thought leaders, entrepreneurs, billionaires, CEOs, investors, and scientists, and more who are applying reason and data to tackle the world's biggest challenges", with a raffle competition to "win a ticket to EA Global (Effective Altruism Global) featuring Elon Musk". (Josh Jacobson, "Announcing the Doing Good Better Giveaway", Effective Altruism Forum, online at http://effective-altruism.com/ea/kn/announcing_the_doing_good_better_giveaway, accessed 8 April 2016 (same access date for other citations below unless context makes clear otherwise.)

[7] For example, a post on the Good Ventures website by Holden Karnofsky, at the time the director of both GiveWell and the Open Philanthropy Project, begins by stating that "Throughout the post, 'we' refers to GiveWell and Good Ventures, who work as partners on the Open Philanthropy Project", Karnofsky (2015a). As a result, we here sometimes use "GiveWell" to refer to what are, on paper, two organizations, GiveWell and the Open Philanthropy Project.

that after their investments there are no more good EA opportunities for them to invest in.[8]

(d) In some previous years, arguably Good Ventures committed to meeting all the funding needs of the top-ranked EA charities that were essentially connected to those charities' actual activities of doing good.[9]

Given these publicly available facts, in some previous years it is arguable that one should have expected that among charities that are judged by EA to be top charities, any would-be shortfall in donations that would have any actual important impact on the operations of that charity would have been offset by funding from Good Ventures *alone*—which is, again, only one among a growing number of deep pockets that are closely following EA advice.

Further, contrary to the argument that the billionaires example is not a big deal, in the past Good Ventures has reported that it does not redirect excess money to projects "further down the list". On the contrary, Good Ventures—like many in the EA community—has explicitly endorsed the strategy of not redirecting money to charities further down the list, because it operates on the explicit principle that the next charities down the list are not worth giving to, and instead money is better saved or invested in other strategic initiatives—and those investments still leave Good Ventures in a position where it is unable to spend as much money as it would like.[10]

A further possibility is that billionaires might save the money that they do not donate today with the intention to donate to another high-quality charity later. However, even in a case where this is true, and even assuming inflation adjusted dollar-for-dollar substitution to later giving, this would not neutralize the billionaires example, because the effectiveness would still be substantially less than EA evaluations suggest for a number of reasons: the future investment is by hypothesis less effective (since otherwise the billionaire would donate now); wellbeing is improving quickly in poor countries, which may be expected to reduce the value of EA opportunities in the future; the marginal product of EA activities may be

[8] From the Good Ventures blog: "Good Ventures hopes to give away several billion dollars over the coming decades, which—when accounting for likely investment returns—would imply hundreds of millions of dollars per year in grants for an extended period of time at peak giving. In 2014, Good Ventures gave ~$15 million to GiveWell's top charities and an additional ~$8 million based on Open Philanthropy Project recommendations. In other words, their current level of giving is nowhere near where they hope it will eventually be" Karnofsky (2015a).

[9] For both of these aspects of their strategy, see Karnofsky (2015b). It is important to note that only a part of what GiveWell calls "room for funding" represents a need for funds that have an important impact on those charities actual activities of doing good—for discussion of this, see Hassenfeld and Rosenberg (2015).

[10] See Tuna (2015) announcing Good Ventures grants, which tracked the recommendations given to it by Hassenfeld and Rosenberg (2015) to focus on funding on only the top-rated EA charities, following the advice that it is better to save resources for future investments than invest in charities that are not top ranked.

expected to decline as they become well-known and the world becomes richer with more altruism dollars to invest; the billionaire might not actually donate in the future for many reasons including death, decreased control over assets, new taxes or economic loss, or for any other reason.

In light of these considerations, together with other publicly available facts about the decision-making strategy of Good Ventures and other billionaires, we believe that in some previous years ordinary donations to top EA charities may not have done much good. If the donations of ordinary individuals accomplished anything, it may have been to reduce the amount that billionaires give to EA causes, increasing the bank account balances of these billionaires or their foundations. Thus, the billionaires example appears to be a significant problem: individual donations to top-rated EA charities may well have done no good for this reason at some times in the recent history of EA, and in fact may have done harm insofar as one agrees that a transfer from ordinary people to billionaires is harm—especially problematic if those ordinary people are misled about the nature of the transfer they are making.[11]

At the same time, these empirical dynamics are in flux, and the billionaires example could no longer be a problem if there is a change in capital allocation dispositions by billionaires, or if there is a large increase in the capacity of top charities to turn additional capital into wellbeing. For example, GiveWell indicates that starting in 2017 the charity GiveDirectly increased its capacity to turn capital into wellbeing, in a way that could arguably make the billionaires problem not as relevant to that specific charity (even if it remained relevant to other top EA charities).[12]

In what follows we set aside the specifics of the billionaires example, partly because the underlying empirical facts are unstable, for reasons just noted. Instead, we focus on explaining why there are likely to be many other hidden zero problems for EA elsewhere that arise from very different sources that we identify below, where those different sources are also more timeless and empirically stable than the billionaires problem. Thus, the billionaires problem provides a compelling

[11] For one way of developing a fairness-based objection to effective altruism on this sort of grounds, see Gabriel (under review).

[12] See the section on 'room for funding' in GiveWell's 2017 evaluation of GiveDirectly: https://www.givewell.org/charities/give-directly/january-2017-version#Roomformorefunding. Proponents of EA generally tend to put a more optimistic spin on room for funding and interaction with large donations; for recent discussion see: https://app.effectivealtruism.org/funds/why. A more pessimistic view is that room for funding estimates do not necessarily exclude amounts that EA evaluators know will be filled by Good Ventures or other billionaires, and beyond that, any gaps that remain by EAs' own lights also do not have nearly as high marginal product as the gaps they recommend the billionaires fill, partly because remaining gaps are based not on actual immediate need for funding for activities, but rather on increasingly speculative estimates of how strategic and capacity-building decisions in the further future might shake out differently if they have extra dollars now above and beyond what they actually have the capacity to use now—e.g. see http://blog.givewell.org/2015/11/18/our-updated-top-charities-for-giving-season-2015.

and easy-to-understand initial illustration of a more fundamental and more timeless worry about the efficacy of EA donations, which is our focus in the remainder of the paper.

2. Analyzing the nature of the hidden zero problem, and the correct fundamental equation for EA vs. equations actually used in EA evaluation of charities

In this section, we articulate a fundamental analysis of the marginal effect of donations, which provides a more formal conceptualization of the hidden zero problem that was illustrated by the billionaires problem above. This analysis more clearly explains why donations that score very well on the existing metrics endorsed by EA might still have zero marginal effect (or net negative effects). By clearly distinguishing a number of distinct factors that are often ignored by EA, the equation also helps to clarify the logical space of factors relevant to the evaluation of charitable investments, as well as the logical space of objections to the effectiveness of specific charities.

Here is the equation we take to summarize the dynamics relevant to the marginal effect of a donation to a specific charity C to the lives saved by C:

$$\left(\frac{\Delta \textit{Lives Saved by C}}{\Delta \textit{Donation to C}}\right)=\left(\frac{\Delta \textit{Lives Saved by C}}{\Delta \textit{Activity by C}}\right)*\left(\frac{\Delta \textit{Activity by C}}{\Delta \textit{Budget of C}}\right)*\left(\frac{\Delta \textit{Budget of C}}{\Delta \textit{Donation to C}}\right)\cdots$$

$$\left(\text{Correct EA}\right)$$

The hidden zero problem arises from the possibility that one or more of the terms on the right-hand side could be zero, which would imply that the marginal effect of a donation (the left-hand side) to the lives saved by that charity is also zero regardless of how large the other terms are. More generally, the problem is one of "hidden elasticities": EA evaluations are generally blind to the fact that some terms in this equation are even relevant to a correct analysis of marginal impact—i.e. the right-most term. The ellipsis at the end indicates that in specific instances a complete equation will require a further multiplicative step each time the activity is passed along to another person or task along the chain from altruistic donor to final beneficiary. The billionaires problem illustrates how the expected change in budget per change in donation by ordinary non-billionaires could be zero, and how such a hidden zero could exist even if we assume that EA practitioners are entirely correct about the amount of good done by the charities they recommend. (Here and in what follows, for ease of exposition we use "lives saved" as intuitive shorthand for what ultimately makes for better or worse outcomes, so as to bracket the independently controversial issue of what should be valued and how.)

A further complication is that the equation above will not be fully correct insofar as there are spillovers from your donation to *C* onto the activities of other charities, and spillovers beyond *C* onto anything else that affects outcomes. To capture all those, one would have to calculate the change in good done due to everything other than *C* for a change in donation to *C*, and add those effects as in the right-most term here:

$$\left(\frac{\Delta Lives\ Saved}{\Delta Donation\ to\ C}\right) = \left(\frac{\Delta Lives\ Saved\ by\ C}{\Delta Donation\ to\ C}\right) + \left(\frac{\Delta Lives\ Saved\ other\ than\ by\ C}{\Delta Donations\ to\ C}\right)$$
$$(\text{Marginal Effect of a Donation})$$

For example, Gabriel's reply to the billionaires problem can be understood as arguing that the right-most term added here is importantly positive because of the spillover of your donation to *C* onto the additional lives saved by the next best charities down the line. We've presented some reasons above for doubting that this specific spillover has the magnitude Gabriel assumes. More importantly, in the next section we'll cite arguments from Angus Deaton that the right-most term here is generally negative because of unintended side effects of charities beyond the lives they are directly focused on improving.[13]

In the rest of this section, we contrast the earlier equation Correct EA with a number of different equations that are often used in actual EA evaluations. This helps clarify why the dynamics behind the hidden zero problem matter, and why structuring analyses more intentionally on Correct EA can improve the accuracy of EA evaluations and EA thinking. In later sections, we provide more stable sources of hidden zero problems for EA beyond the billionaires problem, and we identify a number of different fundamental mechanisms that lead to these problems.

To begin, it is worth noting that there are bad methods of charity evaluation that should not be mistaken for EA evaluation. At the top of the list are evaluators such as Charity Navigator that base evaluations primarily on metrics such as percentage of budget spent on administrative expenses, which is inappropriate as any sort of measure of doing good. To see why this is inappropriate, consider a charity that does active harm with every dollar donated, but also spends a very low percentage of its budget on administrative expenses. This "charity" will be ranked very highly based on the percentage of its budget spend on administrative expenses. Now compare this to a second charity that must spend a higher percentage of its budget on administrative expenses, because this is necessary for it to operate in a domain where it then is able to do enormous net good per dollar with the rest of its budget. Obviously, the second charity would be engaged

[13] See factor (c) below.

in more effective altruism than the first, even though the first would score better on the inappropriate metric of percentage of budget spend on administrative expenses.[14]

With this in mind, a first pass at a genuine metric for evaluating charities on effective altruist grounds, we might consider the following:

$$\left(\frac{\Delta Lives\ Saved}{\Delta Donation}\right)=\left(\frac{Total\ Lives\ Saved}{Total\ Budget}\right) \tag{EA1}$$

Equation EA1 could then be used to estimate the average cost per unit of good associated with different charities, which might then be used, in a particularly crude form of EA analysis.

A more detailed analysis might add an additional term that allows such an analysis to be more readily connected to empirical studies:

$$\left(\frac{\Delta Lives\ Saved}{\Delta Donation}\right)=\left(\frac{Total\ Activity}{Total\ Budget}\right)*\left(\frac{Total\ Lives\ Saved}{Total\ Activity}\right) \tag{EA2}$$

Using this equation EA2, the term Total Lives Saved/Total Activity might be investigated with RCTs and the like, and the term Total Activity/Total Budget can be estimated in a straightforward way.

To see the problem with equations EA1 and EA2, which might be called "average effect metrics", we need only note that marginal effect is not the same thing as average effect—where in connection with EA, we are interested in marginal effect, namely, the actual difference that would be made by additional investment in a charity.

At its current best, EA analyses sometimes rely on a more sophisticated equation than EA1 and EA2, where this more sophisticated equation does not simply equate the marginal effect of additional charity with the average effect. In particular, GiveWell and other leaders in current best practices for EA evaluation can be understood as aiming to use the following more sophisticated marginalist metric:

$$\left(\frac{\Delta Lives\ Saved}{\Delta Donation}\right)=\left(\frac{\Delta Lives\ Saved}{\Delta Activity}\right)*\left(\frac{\Delta Activity}{\Delta Budget}\right) \tag{EA3}$$

In this equation, the (marginal) effect of a donation is understood as the change in lives saved per change in activity (at the margin) (e.g. marginal lives saved per additional bed nets distributed) multiplied by the change in activity per change in

[14] Singer (2015); MacAskill (2015).

budget (at the margin). This equation is on the right track because it invokes actual elasticity terms (i.e. terms that quantify the percentage change in one variable that will result from a change in another) on the right-hand side of the sort relevant to marginal effects, which is an improvement over the explicitly averagist effect metrics of EA1 and EA2.[15]

However, even if one assumes for the sake of argument that EA is using EA3 and is entirely correct about the terms on its right-hand side, and is thus entirely correct about the good done by its top-rated charities, the hidden zero problem is that it could still be dubious that *donations* to those charities would do any good, because of the possibility that the term Δ *budget*/Δ *donation* could still be zero (i.e. that zero might be the correct value of that term in Correct EA above). Furthermore, EA evaluators' methods often invoke estimations and reasoning about the other elasticities in EA3 that make their actual method better represented by equation EA2 above. This is true, for example, as EA evaluators often rely on average effect metrics such as the total activity of an organization divided by its total budget as a proxy for the marginal effect of additional lives saved per additional budget. And note that despite frequent discussions of *crowdedness*, *tractability*, and *impact* by EA evaluators, those notions do not play much of a role in the actual spreadsheets where evaluations are performed—and even if they were incorporated into the spreadsheet fully, they would not remove the hidden zero worry that e.g. Δ *budget*/Δ *donation* could be zero. Finally, notions of *crowdedness*, *tractability*, and *impact* are in any event highly imperfect proxies for the marginalist notions they are intended to track, as one of us argues in another paper.[16] To verify that we are not being uncharitable or misunderstanding EA analyses, the reader can compare these claims to the actual spreadsheets used by GiveWell and other EA sources in charity evaluations.[17]

Having now analyzed the nature of the hidden zero problem and, more fundamentally, the marginal effect of donations and the problem of "hidden elasticities", in the remainder of this chapter we examine two of the elasticities in the right-hand side of the Correct EA equation in more detail. We highlight empirically stable mechanisms identified by economics and other disciplines that provide reason to worry that Δ Lives Saved/Δ Activity and Δ Budget/Δ Donation could be hidden zeros (or worse). We consider these in turn.

[15] For an introduction to the methods of leading EA evaluators, see: MacAskill (2015), https://www.givewell.org/how-we-work/criteria, https://www.givingwhatwecan.org/research/methodology, and http://www.openphilanthropy.org/research/our-process. Of particular interest are GiveWell's explicit cost-effectiveness calculations in spreadsheets available at: http://www.givewell.org/international/technical/criteria/cost-effectiveness/cost-effectiveness-models. The reader can judge the extent to which these EA evaluators are using methods more akin to EA1, EA2, EA3, or Correct EA—we submit that their methods are often closest to EA2. For more on the ethical dimension of the argument, see Singer 1972, Singer 2009, Lichtenberg 2013, Singer 2015, and Budolfson under review b.

[16] Budolfson (under review a).

[17] Givewell 2015 and Budolfson (under review a).

3. Arguments that Δ Lives Saved/Δ Activity could be a hidden zero or worse: Evidence that RCTs may not be representative of future results and other empirical considerations

Among the evidence that the EA community cites, randomized controlled trials (RCTs) are of central importance and are often cited by EA as the "gold standard" of evidence.[18] However, Nobel Laureate Angus Deaton, Nancy Cartwright, and others have offered a critique of conclusions about effectiveness that depend on the kind of quick reliance on RCTs that is common in the EA community.[19]

The core of the critique is that there is a large inferential gap between the RCTs that EA depends on, and the conclusions EA draws from them. The basic objection is that when EA concludes on the basis of an RCT that an intervention would be highly effective if scaled up and deployed widely, the following facts (*a*) and (*b*) generally prevent that conclusion from being supported by the evidence:

(*a*) We don't have reason to think the intervention is going to work even when scaled up within the location of the RCT, partly because the equilibrium that results from a very large number of such interventions might have very different properties from the one that emerges from a handful of such interventions in an RCT (this is one way RCTs, like other causally well-identified empirical studies, often lack external validity—in this case, by lacking generalizability to additional interventions in the same context).

(*b*) We don't have reason to think that such an intervention would have similar positive effects elsewhere (as opposed to negative effects) (this is another way RCTs often lack external validity—in this case, lack of generalizability to interventions in different contexts—i.e. it may not be generalizable to other populations/locations).

What works in one village might not work in a neighboring village, and it certainly might not work in another region where people have very different customs and societies, and where there are empirically different background facts. Instead, the intervention could do harm. For example, a program that is verified with an RCT to promote latrine use (rather than open defecation) in largely-Muslim Bangladesh could discourage latrine use in a Hindu part of neighboring India, just a few miles away.[20]

In this way, the truth in some cases could be worse than a hidden zero—instead, deploying the intervention could do net harm rather than merely no good, consistent with the internal validity of the RCT that is used by EA to conclude that it

[18] https://blog.givewell.org/2012/08/23/how-we-evaluate-a-study
[19] Cartwright and Hardie (2012); Deaton and Cartwright (2017).
[20] Coffey and Spears (2017).

would do good. In other words, (a) and (*b*) draw attention to ways in which Δ Lives Saved/Δ Activity could be a hidden zero or worse—or at least close to zero in a way that undermines EA evaluators' conclusions—consistent with RCT results such as those cited in connection with leading EA charities. For real-world examples, see debates about whether EA recommendations of deworming charities have been based on flawed inferences from RCTs,[21] whether EA recommendations on cash transfers have been based on flawed RCTs that ignored their longer-term negative side effects,[22] whether evidence-based policy recommendations on sanitation are based on flawed inferences from RCTs,[23] and others. To be sure, the problems of internal and external validity are well-understood (although not overcome) by the best econometric practitioners of the development economics literature. The current point is that limits to external validity and the barriers to generalization may not be explicit in any particular study, and that they are ordinarily overlooked in the actual practice of EA evaluations.[24]

Deaton also argues that an additional important factor operates through politics and institutional development:

> (*c*) we have reason to expect large-scale deployment of EA interventions to have negative side effects beyond (*a*) and (*b*) that cannot practically be measured by RCTs.

For example, Deaton believes that even public health interventions that genuinely save lives tend to have longer-term negative consequences by preventing the evolution of public health institutions and other stepping stones to good governance and self-sufficiency within the society that receives the EA treatment. Investments by charities also tend to unintentionally benefit powerful oppressors in society, who are often the main forces standing in the way of social progress. In this way, even the best large-scale interventions tend to retard an entire society's escape from deprivation, as these are the key factors for escape. If the cost of delaying an entire society's escape from deprivation in such a way were quantified, Deaton seems to believe that we should expect the harm done to outweigh the lives saved even by the most promising EA interventions.[25]

On the basis of all of these considerations, Deaton generally opposes the recommendations of EA evaluators, which are based on what he sees as overly quick inferences from RCTs—as Deaton puts it, "If it were so simple, the world would already be a much better place. Development is neither a financial nor a

[21] Humphreys (2015); Berger (2015).

[22] Haushofer and Shapiro (2018); Ozler (2018); compare the earlier short-run results in Haushofer and Shapiro (2016).

[23] Hammer and Spears (2016); Coffey and Spears (2018).

[24] Cartwright and Hardie (2012), Deaton and Cartwright (2017), Bates and Glennerster (2017).

[25] Deaton (2013).

technical problem but a political problem, and the aid industry often makes the politics worse."[26] Instead, he joins many other leading economists in arguing that the best bet to help the global poor is to try to change international policies that handicap their growth and equitable development, particularly agricultural and trade policies.[27]

A full empirical test of Deaton's conclusions is beyond the state of econometric science and the data available. So, we do not take a position here on Deaton's conclusions about what truly effective altruism would require. Here we merely note that Deaton, Cartwright, and others' objections to the use of RCTs identify timeless sources for potential hidden zeros or worse in the face of even well-conducted RCTs that EA evaluations take as the "gold standard" of evidence.[28]

4. Arguments that Δ Budget/Δ Donation could be a hidden zero: Principal-agent problems and other empirical considerations

Are there empirically stable reasons why Δ Budget/Δ Donation could be a hidden zero? In this section we draw on theoretical and empirical literature from economics to show that it is realistic that this could be a hidden zero even in a situation where an organization's budget is known not to be topped up to funding targets due to the incentives that fundraisers generally have.

Specifically, here we identify a novel mechanism for donation crowd-out: the principal-agent problem of an organization's fundraising. Principal-agent problems arise when principals (e.g. directors of an organization) can only imperfectly monitor the efforts of agents (e.g. employees, contractors)—which is almost always the case in an actual organization. Because agents often have different goals than principals, in these cases it is likely, other things being equal, that agents will be motivated to act in their own best interests, contrary to the goals of the organization that are defined by its principals.

In any sufficiently large development organization, to be a candidate for EA's attention, a managerial *principal* who is responsible for the overall direction of the organization is likely to cooperate with *agents* in the organization of multiple types: at least two types are program implementation agents and fundraising agents. It is a special property of international charities, unlike many businesses, that implementation and revenue-collecting agents can be different people, perhaps located on different continents, and never encountering one another in person.[29]

[26] Deaton (2015). [27] See Stiglitz (2003).

[28] For additional discussion, see Budolfson and Spears under review.

[29] Contrast this with the case of a retail business that is paid precisely when it provides a service to its customer, so fundraising and service provision are necessarily linked.

In international development, the principal-agent challenges for implementation agents are well-known and well-studied.[30] Indeed, because implementation principal-agent relationships are often a part of the program design being evaluated as a part of a development project, the EA movement explicitly considers these relationships in selecting projects and they are at the heart of the public advocacy by proponents of evidence-based development policy.[31]

In contrast, the *fundraising* principal-agent problem receives little attention in the development economics literature, and almost no attention in the EA literature. However, agency problems may be at least as important in fundraising. In many charities, fundraising is done by dedicated staff who report to organization principals. Fundraisers are in some way incentivized to successfully raise funds. This incentive could take various forms:

- **Fixed target.** Fundraisers are paid a salary that is independent of the amount of money they raise, except that they are fired if they do not raise enough funds in a specific period.
- **Flexible target.** Fundraisers are paid a fixed salary, and the probability of being fired is decreasing in the amount of funds they raise.
- **Sharecropping.** Fundraisers "sharecrop" with the charity, keeping a fixed percentage of the funds they raise.
- **Billionaire's charade.** A billionaire has promised to ensure the fundraising operation meets the principal's target budget; the fundraising continues merely to save the billionaire some money and to preserve the appearance of a normal charity.

The consequences of the principal-agent arrangement for effective altruists depend on its details. For example, in the sharecropping case, the elasticity of the organization's budget with respect to a donation is less than one by the amount of the sharecropping. In the fixed target case the elasticity could approach zero: if effort is costly, then (abstracting away from risk aversion) fundraising agents would always collect precisely their target, and a surprise donation would be entirely captured by the fundraiser in the form of reduced effort, with no extra money passed on to the organization.[32] This would imply that in the fixed target case the marginal benefit of a donation in terms of lives saved is zero, no matter how effective the organization's program is at its development goals, just as in the billionaire's charade case.

[30] Chaudhury et al. (2006); see also World Bank (2004). [31] Banerjee and Duflo (2011).

[32] See the paper by James Snowden (Chapter 5 in this volume) for a perspective on risk aversion and effective altruism.

An existing but young empirical literature has estimated the value of Δ Budget/Δ Donation for a number of different kinds of charities and other entities. Naturally, like any set of empirical studies, this literature contains research of varying persuasiveness and immediacy of application to the elasticities that EA evaluators need to know. The table below presents a set of estimates from the literature of the effect of revenue (of various sources available for empirical study) on organizations' budgets:

Source	Method	Elasticity
Andreoni et al (2014)	effect of UK government grants, matching on charity score	depends on size; >1 for smallest
Kingma (1989)	effect of government grants on donations to US public radio	0.865
Heutel (2014)	effect of private donations on US government grants	small, but evidence inconclusive
Andreoni and Payne (2011)	effect of government grants; panel data on US charities	0.25
Andreoni and Payne (2012)	effect of government grants; panel data on Canadian charities	0 (or negative)

This is not an exhaustive list, nor do we necessarily endorse the empirical methods of these papers. In particular, one inapplicability of many of the studies in the table is that they focus on government grants, rather than small private donations, because large grants are particularly amenable to the techniques of causal identification. These estimates may or may not generalize well to EA evaluation; assessing such generalizability would be an important goal of further investigation.

Despite those limitations, we believe three conclusions are clear from the table:

- Some estimated elasticities are much below 1 (where 1 would imply that an extra donation translates into an increase in the organization's budget exactly dollar-for-dollar); these studies therefore give evidence that the problem we highlight could be a large practical concern.
- The estimated elasticities vary radically across studies; these studies do not give us confidence that the elasticity is in fact any particular number.
- Some studies present evidence that the elasticity varies across organizations; this is theoretically expected, and suggests that EA evaluations need organization-specific estimates.

In particular, the empirical literature includes estimates of *zero*. In cases where this is true, the additional effect of a donation would be zero—no matter how effective an organization's programs are and no matter how rigorous and generalizable the evidence of a program's effectiveness is—because the donation would have no effect on the budget or extent of the program implemented. This is not a mere theoretical possibility: it is quantitatively suggested by at least some of the empirical estimates in the literature. If these estimates should be considered wrong or inapplicable, it is important to understand why.[33]

5. Conclusion

EA evaluators point to many facts that seem to suggest opportunities for ordinary people to improve the lives of the world's poorest. But whether these are actual opportunities to improve lives depends on factors highlighted by the Correct EA equation above that have not previously been considered in EA analysis. If any one of the terms in that equation is a hidden zero, then the product is zero, and an altruistic gift is likely not effective. By examining two links in the chain of elasticities within the equation in detail (namely, the change in lives saved that results from change in activity, and the change in organizational budget that results from a change in donations) we have seen that theoretical and empirical literature from economics and other disciplines gives reason to be concerned that, in many cases of practical relevance, some of these terms are in fact hidden zeros, or worse. As a result, even if one agrees with the facts highlighted by existing EA evaluations, there is room to worry that donations to those charities might still do no good or even be harmful on balance.

In sum, the equations above describe the marginal effect of donations, and highlight neglected factors that are relevant to correct consequentialist analysis.[34]

[33] In addition to the references in the table, see also Andreoni and Payne 2003, Duncan 2004, Bernheim 1986, and Warr 1982. Since we first presented this paper, EA evaluators have introduced a crude estimate of the impact of EA funding on the revenues of EA charities and other charities. This is a positive step in the direction of capturing some of these dynamics; however, it is aimed at only one small class of potential hidden zeros, and does not attempt to quantify a large range of others, such as unintended negative side effects of the sort discussed by Deaton, or the interactions within EA funding discussed in the first section in connection with the pivot toward billionaires. Furthermore, even within the class at which it is aimed, it currently tends to be based on judgmental estimates of the relevant effects, rather than empirically quantified estimates. Nonetheless, it is a model of how EA estimates can be improved in practice. See https://blog.givewell.org/2018/02/13/revisiting-leverage/.

[34] Thanks to Elizabeth Ashford, Anne Barnhill, Alexander Berger, David Boonin, Luc Bovens, Emily Clough, Sarah Conly, Jonathan Courtney, Diane Coffey, David Faraci, Seb Farquhar, Iason Gabriel, Hilary Greaves, Michelle Hutchinson, Alison Jaggar, Peter Jaworski, Will MacAskill, Sarah McGrath, Theron Pummer, Rob Reich, Ben Sachs, James Snowden, Daniel Wodak, and audiences at Bowling Green, the London School of Economics, the University of St. Andrews conference on the philosophical foundations of effective altruism, the Georgetown Business school workshop on methodology in applied ethics, and students in Princeton's Introduction to Moral Philosophy course taught by Sarah McGrath.

References

Andreoni, James, and Abigail Payne. 2003. "Do government grants to private charities crowd out giving or fund-raising?" *American Economic Review* 93 (30): 792–812.

Andreoni, James, and Abigail Payne. 2011. "Is crowding out due entirely to fundraising? Evidence from a panel of charities." *Journal of Public Economics* 95 (5): 334–43.

Andreoni, James, and Abigail Payne. 2012. "Crowding-out charitable contributions in Canada: New knowledge from the north." Working Paper No. w17635. *National Bureau of Economic Research.*

Andreoni, James, Abigail Payne, and Sarah Smith. 2014. "Do grants to charities crowd out other income? Evidence from the UK." *Journal of Public Economics* 114: 75–86.

Banerjee, Abhijit. and Esther Duflo. 2011. *Poor Economics: A Radical Rethinking of the Way to Fight Global Poverty.* PublicAffairs.

Bates, Mary Anne, and Rachel Glennerster. 2017. "The Generalizability Puzzle". *Stanford Social Innovation Review*, Summer: 50–4.

Berger, Alexander. 2015. "New Deworming Reanalyses and the Cochrane Review." Givewell Blog. Available at http://blog.givewell.org/2015/07/24/new-deworming-reanalyses-and-cochrane-review.

Bernheim, Douglas. 1986. "On the Voluntary and Involuntary Provision of Public Goods." *American Economic Review* 76 (4): 789–93.

Budolfson, Mark. Under review a. "Utilitarian Virtues of Boring Low-Hanging Fruit, Even When Investing Many Millions."

Budolfson, Mark. Under review b. "Global Ethics and the Problem with Singer and Unger's Ethical Argument for an Extreme Duty to Provide Aid."

Budolfson, Mark. 2018. "The Inefficacy Objection to Consequentialism, and the Problem with the Expected Consequences Response." *Philosophical Studies* 176 (7): 1711–24.

Budolfson, Mark, and Dean Spears. Under review. "Mapping the Empirical Objections to Effective Altruism."

Cartwright, Nancy, and Jeremy Hardie. 2012. *Evidence-Based Policy: A Practical Guide to Doing it Better.* Oxford: Oxford University Press.

Chaudhury, Nazmul, et al. 2006. "Missing in Action: Teacher and Health Worker Absence in Developing Countries." *The Journal of Economic Perspectives* 20 (1): 91–116.

Coffey, Diane, and Dean Spears. 2017. *Where India Goes: Abandoned Toilets, Stunted Development and the Costs of Caste.* HarperCollins.

Coffey, Diane, and Dean Spears. 2018. "Implications of WASH Benefits Trials for Water and Sanitation." *Lancet Global Health* 6: 615.

Deaton, Angus. 2015. "Response to Effective Altruism." *Boston Review.* Available at http://bostonreview.net/forum/peter-singer-logic-effective-altruism.

Deaton, Angus. 2013. *The Great Escape.* Princeton University Press.

Deaton, Angus, and Nancy Cartwright. 2017. "Understanding and Misunderstanding Randomized Controlled Trials." *Social Science & Medicine* 210: 2–21.

Duncan, Brian. 2004. A Theory of Impact Philanthropy. *Journal of Public Economics* 88 (9–10): 2,159–80.

Gabriel, Iason. Under review. "Is Effective Altruism Fair to Small Donors?" 2016a typescript.

Gabriel, Iason. 2016. "Effective Altruism and its Critics." *Journal of Applied Philosophy* 34 (4). Page references are to the "online first" edition.

GiveWell.org. 2015. Spreadsheet Methodology. Available at http://www.givewell.org/files/DWDA%202009/Interventions/GiveWell_cost-effectiveness_analysis_2015.xlsx.

Hammer, Jeffrey, and Dean Spears. 2016. "Village Sanitation and Child Health: Effects and External Validity in a Randomized Field Experiment in Rural India." *Journal of Health Economics* 48: 135–48.

Hassenfeld, Elie, and Josh Rosenberg. 2015. "Our Updated Top Charities for Giving Season 2015." Givewell Blog. Available at http://blog.givewell.org/2015/11/18/our-updated-top-charities-for-giving-season-2015.

Haushofer, Johannes, and Jeremy Shapiro. 2016. "The Short-Term Impact of Unconditional Cash Transfers to the Poor: Experimental Evidence from Kenya." *Quarterly Journal of Economics* 131 (4): 1,973–2,042.

Haushofer, Johannes, and Jeremy Shapiro. 2018. "The Long-Term Impact of Unconditional Cash Transfers: Experimental Evidence from Kenya." Working paper. Available at http://jeremypshapiro.com/papers/Haushofer_Shapiro_UCT2_2018-01-30_paper_only.pdf.

Heutel, Garth. 2014. "Crowding Out and Crowding in of Private Donations and Government Grants." *Public Finance Review* 42 (2): 143–75.

Karnofsky, Holden. 2015a. Should the Open Philanthropy Project be Recommending More/Larger Grants? Good Ventures. Available at http://www.goodventures.org/research-and-ideas/blog/should-the-open-philanthropy-project-be-recommending-more-larger-grants.

Karnofsky, Holden. 2015b. "Good Ventures and Giving Now vs. Later." GiveWell Blog. Available at http://blog.givewell.org/2015/11/25/good-ventures-and-giving-now-vs-later.

Karnofsky, Holden. 2014. "Donor Coordination and the 'Giver's Dilemma.'" GiveWell Blog. Available at http://blog.givewell.org/2014/12/02/donor-coordination-and-the-givers-dilemma.

Kingma, Bruce. 1989. "An Accurate Measurement of the Crowd-Out Effect, Income Effect, and Price Effect for Charitable Contributions." *Journal of Political Economy* 97 (5): 1,197–207.

Humphreys, Macartan. 2015. "What Has Been Learned from the Deworming Replications: A Nonpartisan View." Columbia. Available at http://www.columbia.edu/~mh2245/w/worms.html.

Lichtenberg, Judith. 2013. *Distant Strangers: Ethics, Psychology, and Global Poverty.* Cambridge University Press.

MacAskill, William. 2015. *Doing Good Better*. Guardian Faber.

MacAskill, William. 2016. Presentation at Yale University. 6 May 2016.

Ozler, Berk. 2018. "GiveDirectly: Three-Year Impacts, Explained." World Bank Blog. Available at http://blogs.worldbank.org/impactevaluations/givedirectly-three-year-impacts-explained.

Singer, Peter. 1972. "Famine, Affluence, and Morality." *Philosophy & Public Affairs* 1 (3): 229–43.

Singer, Peter. 2009. *The Life You Can Save*. Random House.

Singer, Peter. 2015. *The Most Good You Can Do*. Yale University Press.

Stiglitz, Joseph. 2003. *Globalization and its discontents*. Norton.

Tuna, Cari. 2015. "Our Grants to GiveWell's 2015 Recommended Charities." Available at http://www.goodventures.org/research-and-ideas/blog/our-grants-to-givewells-2015-recommended-charities.

Warr, Peter. 1982. "Pareto Optimal Redistribution and Private Charity." *Journal of Public Economics* 19 (1): 131–8.

World Bank. 2004. *World Development Report: Making Services Work for Poor People*. World Bank.

13

Beyond Individualism

Stephanie Collins

Introduction

In this chapter, I argue that group contexts pose two problems for individuals who are engaged in the project of using evidence and reason to benefit others as much as possible—the project, roughly speaking, that Will MacAskill identifies with effective altruism.[1] The first problem is that collective agents—as well as individual ones—can engage in morally worthy projects and (more importantly) can bear moral duties. When a collective bears a moral duty, the collective's members have 'membership duties'. For citizens of powerful democratic states, membership duties threaten to be numerous, varied, and weighty. They may leave little space for the project of benefiting others as much as possible. The second problem is that individuals who aim to benefit others as much as possible have reasons to signal their willingness to coordinate. These reasons imply that the actions an individual ought to take are likely not actions that ensure the marginal difference the individual makes is as high as possible. The combined result of these two problems is that the project of individually and marginally benefiting others as much as possible might reasonably take a back seat in an individual's day-to-day reasoning about what they morally ought to do.

Membership duties

Some groups can—and can have duties to—engage in morally worthy projects. I will call such groups 'collectives'. Roughly, a collective is a group of individuals with a group-level moral decision-making procedure—a procedure that can take in reasons (including moral reasons), deliberate upon them, and output decisions and instructions for enacting those decisions—that is 'operationally distinct' from the procedures held respectively by members. Its procedure is operationally distinct in that (*i*) the reasons it takes in differ from the reasons any of its members take in when deciding for themselves and (*ii*) its method for processing those reasons is

[1] MacAskill (Chapter 1, this volume).

different from the method of any one member when deciding for themselves.[2] As an example, a collective might take the moral beliefs of *all* members and process these using a *majoritarian* method, thereby using a distinctively group-level set of inputs, and deliberative procedure, to arrive at the moral beliefs of the collective. Members are unlikely to use these inputs, processed in this way, when deliberating upon the moral beliefs they will hold themselves.

This can lead to distinctively collective-level moral agency—and, thereby, distinctively collective-level actions and duties—in the following way. When a collective operates its procedure over time, it acquires various beliefs (including moral beliefs), preferences, intentions, and so on. The collective then faces rational pressure to maintain coherence amongst these. Responding to this pressure, the collective might come to hold a moral belief that few—or even none—of its members holds.[3] This belief might rationally compel the collective to decide to do something right or wrong—again, even if no individuals agree with, or control for, this collective decision.[4] When a collective decides to act (including performing actions that are right or wrong), it will distribute roles to members jointly sufficient for enacting the decision. When members act within and because of their roles to successfully enact the decision, these actions by members are actions of the collective.[5] In this way, collectives can perform actions—including committing wrongs and producing goods—that are ontologically distinct from the actions of the aggregate of their members.[6]

To be clear, the idea here is not that we must posit collective actions and duties because sometimes individuals 'make no difference' or 'make an imperceptible difference' to a group-level outcome. For the vast majority of collectives' actions, members will make some small difference to what the collective does—even if just by ensuring that the collective's action occurs in one specific way rather than another. To illustrate, when I give a lecture, this partly constitutes the university's action of providing lectures. But my individual action *does* make a difference to the exact way in which my university provides lectures—I can ensure the university provides (at least some) lectures that are interactive, or not, for example. So individual members can make perceptible differences to collectives' actions, and yet those actions can be distinctively collective: my university's action of providing lectures was the result of an intention produced by a decision-making procedure that is distinct from the procedure of any of its members. This is what makes it a collective's action. Conversely, there are cases in which individuals (seem to) make *no* difference to an outcome in which they are (broadly speaking) involved, yet there is no group-level decision-making procedure, and so no collective agent,

[2] Collins (under contract, ch. 6); French (1984); Rovane (1998); List and Pettit (2011).
[3] Rovane (1998); List and Pettit (2011). [4] Pettit (2007). [5] French (1984).
[6] For discussion of this ontological distinctness, see List and Spiekermann (2013).

and so no collective actions or duties.[7] What I will say about membership duties has no bearing on the latter cases (though what I will say in the next section—on coordination—will).

That is: a group is a collective agent if and only if it has a rational group-level decision-making procedure. Sometimes members make a difference to the collective's actions; sometimes they do not; in either case, the existence of a group-level decision-making procedure is what determines that there exists a collective agent with its own actions and duties. The collective is not independent or free-floating; it is physically constituted by members.[8] But *if* there is a group-level decision-making procedure that has distributed roles to members sufficient for enacting the group's decision, then the control over that outcome is wielded by the collective itself.[9]

Much more could be said about these issues. For now, I will assume that collectives—and their projects and actions, and their duties to engage in projects and perform actions—are entities in our moral universe. And I will assume that collectives can have the full complement of moral duties: duties to keep promises, to avoid causing harm, to return benefits received from injustice, to rectify past harms, to help those particular others whose needs most depend on their actions, and so on.[10] Most of these duties have the following features: they entail claim-rights, they are dischargeable (rather than 'imperfect'), they are enforceable, and they are derived from 'the right' as constraints on action, rather than derived from 'the good' as the goal of action. On many ethical theories, these features give these duties priority over the project of benefiting others-at-large as much as possible. I will not assume that that priority is absolute—but I will assume that it exists.

Finally, I will assume that many powerful groups in our world—states, multinational corporations, intergovernmental organizations, and so on—are collectives that bear this range of duties. When we consider such powerful collectives, it is clear that their duties are weighty. After all, their promises tend to be backed by more formal commitments; they have a dangerously high propensity to cause harm; any benefits they have received from injustice tend to be large; their ability to assist those in need runs deep; and the harms they have caused tend to be devastating. And they interact with more persons than most individuals do, simply due to the scale of their operations. So, powerful collectives' duties tend to be weightier (in virtue of more fully satisfying various scalar duty-generating criteria), and more numerous (in virtue of the collective's interacting with more persons), than the analogous duties held by individuals.

[7] Such cases are described by Parfit (1984, ch. 3); Kagan (2011).

[8] Richie (2013); Hess (2018). [9] Strand (2012).

[10] On collectives' abilities to bear this range of duties, see Collins and Lawford-Smith (2016).

This is stark when considering states. Because states' power is so pervasive, they acquire numerous duties. These duties have various grounds: the extreme harms states have caused via their imposition of oppression, colonialism, and present-day trade policies; the huge benefits they have received via the same impositions; the weighty promises they have made via treaties; and (in the case of affluent states) their strong ability to assist those whose need depends on their actions. These features of states are the grounds of duties—held by the state—that are owed to whichever specific entities (individual or collective) the state has harmed, or has benefited from the plight of, or has made promises to, or has the ability to assist, or so on. Additionally, states have final authority over a territory. This produces an unusual kind of duty: a duty owed to occupants of that territory, to use democratic procedures to create, enforce, and apply just laws within that territory, where these laws bestow benefits (most abstractly, rights) upon the territory's occupants. Arguably, this duty is grounded in the state's being in a unique position to confer these benefits upon those within its territory, in virtue of its having final de facto authority over that territory.

What do all these duties—held by states—imply for states' members? A lot. Although collectives are ontologically distinct from their members, this is in roughly the way a solar system is ontologically distinct from the planets that constitute it.[11] There is not the collective, over there, with its duties, and the members, over here, with their duties.[12] Some facts about the whole have implications for the constituent parts, even though the whole has properties that the parts do not. In particular, I have argued elsewhere that if a collective has a duty to see to it that *X*, then:

(1) Each member has a duty to use their role, as appropriate, to put inputs into the group's decision-making procedure with a view to it being the case that (the procedure distributes roles to members in a way that): if enough members used their roles with a view to seeing to it that *X*,[13] then that would be sufficient for *X* in a high proportion of likely futures. These are '*X*-sufficient' roles.

(2) Once *X*-sufficient roles are distributed, then each member has a duty to use their role, as appropriate, with a view to seeing to it that *X*.[14]

[11] Hess (2018, p. 41) uses this analogy.

[12] Such stark separateness is implied by Jeff McMahan when he asserts that 'I am neither a community nor a state. I can determine only what I do, not what my community or state will do' McMahan (2016, p. 97). His first sentence is true; his second is false: I'll go on to suggest that McMahan's actions within-and-because-of his role in a collective determine (via constituting) *aspects* of actions of that collective, even if the collective acts differently at the overall level.

[13] I return below to cases in which members know that *X* will not in fact happen.

[14] Collins (2017, 40–3).

When a member 'uses their role with a view to seeing to it that *X*', they act *within* (i.e. consistently with) and *because of* their role so as to increase the likelihood of *X*. Importantly, (*1*) and (*2*) might mean using the more fundamental aspects of one's role (e.g. one's right to free speech) to challenge other, less fundamental, aspects of one's role (e.g. that one pays taxes that serve unjust purposes). That is: a member's actions in discharging her membership duties are active and contestatory, not passive and obedient. Of course, in some collectives, one's role might not include any scope for pushing the collective towards distributing other roles. In such a collective, the most one can do is to use one's role—that is, act consistently with and because of one's role—with a view to seeing to it that *X*. If a member's role positively excludes actions (role-distributing or otherwise) with a view to *X*, then the 'as appropriate' clause is not met, and the member does her membership duty simply by checking that there is nothing she can do towards *X* within her role. (She might then have a duty to act upon the collective 'from the outside'—but this would not be a *membership* duty, i.e. a duty held qua member that contributes towards the collective's fulfilment of *its* duty.)

Call (*1*) and (*2*) 'membership duties'. In a state, *X* might be 'creating, enforcing, and applying just laws', 'apologising for wrongs done to the indigenous population', 'negotiating with other states to close international tax loopholes', 'increasing and redirecting the foreign aid budget', and so on. If an individual is a member of a state, and if that state has such a duty, then the individual has a membership duty.[15]

What does this imply for the project of benefiting others as much as possible? It implies that our duties as members of powerful collectives (most conspicuously, states) threaten to consume the time, energy, and money that we might have spent on that project.[16] States' duties—particularly their duties grounded in past wrongdoing—are weighty, varied, and numerous. So—I will now suggest—citizens' membership duties are likewise weighty, varied, and numerous. This is so, I will suggest, *even if* a citizen's doing her membership duty will make a tiny difference, in expectation, to whether her state ends up 'seeing to it that *X*' in some realization or other. (Though, to reiterate, my point is not that members make *no* difference, in expectation, to whether—or certainly to in what realization—collectives do their duties. It is just that such difference-making is not a necessary condition on membership duties.)

To see the weight of membership duties, consider a member of a democratic state. She does her membership duty by voting for a morally good election

[15] I assume liberal-democratic citizens are members of states in the relevant sense. On this, see Collins and Lawford-Smith (ms).

[16] Using a different framework, Ashford (2018) argues that we should *both* act as members of powerful collectives *and* use some resources to benefit others as much as we marginally, individually, and directly can with those resources. As stated above, I am assuming that directed, dischargeable, enforceable, constraint-based duties—including where those duties are held by collectives—are more important than projects directed at benefiting others-at-large.

candidate—and using her right to free speech to encourage her compatriots to do the same—despite the overwhelming evidence that the candidate's evil rival will win. Her collective's duty is 'seeing to it that a morally good candidate is elected' and she has acted within and because of her role with a view to that, by way of voting and campaigning. When we consider merely the expected difference her action will make to whether the collective does its duty in some realization or other, the value of her action looks low indeed.[17]

But her action should not be assessed solely on the basis of its expected difference-making. The *content* of her duty is to act so as to make *X* more likely, but that duty's *strength* is not determined simply by the expected difference her action will make to *X*. Instead, the strength of her duty is also partly determined (and increased) by the fact that it is a pro tanto duty-fulfilling feature *of the state* to have constituent parts that do their membership duties, regardless of the likelihood that those membership duties will lead to the state doing its overall duty.

This might sound strange, so let me draw an analogy between a state and an individual moral agent. I assume an individual's attitudes towards others can have intrinsic moral value. Yet sometimes an individual has the right attitudes, without performing the right action that accords with those attitudes. The classic example of such an individual is Huckleberry Finn in Mark Twain's novel *The Adventures of Huckleberry Finn*.[18] Huck respects his friend Jim, who is a slave. Huck has real human sympathy for Jim. Yet, at various points in the novel, Huck acts contrary to this respect and sympathy. This is because he also views Jim as an object and the rightful property of his former owner. Whatever else we say about Huck, the following is true: Huck is morally right in a way (he has respect and sympathy for Jim) *and* Huck is morally wrong in a way (Huck views Jim as an object). Overall, the 'right aspects' get put aside, and 'wrong aspects' lead Huck to do wrong (at least at several points in the novel). His right attitudes are overridden (and sometimes disregarded) in his deliberations. In certain of his actions, his rightful attitudes are not reflected at all. But even as he does moral wrong, we want to approve those overridden or disregarded aspects of him that are morally right—that is, we want to approve his attitudes of respect and sympathy, and judge them to have value, *even though* they have made no difference to what Huck does.

My suggestion is that we view the *members* of a collective analogously to the *aspects* of an individual.[19] That is: a member who does her membership duty performs an action that constitutes a 'right aspect' of her collective, regardless of whether her doing her membership duty is disregarded at the level of her collective's deliberations, and even if it is not reflected in what her collective does overall. When a member acts within and because of her role with a view to her collective

[17] Gelman, Silver, and Edlin (2012).
[18] Twain (1884); for philosophical discussion, Bennett (1974); Arpaly (2002).
[19] I expand on this, and on the Huck Finn analogy, in Collins (2018).

doing its duty, this is a right aspect of the collective. This is just as it is a right aspect *of Huck* that he has respectful and sympathetic attitudes to Jim, regardless of what he does overall. Of course, that aspect would have *even more* value if it were (or had higher expectation of being) efficacious at the level of what Huck does overall. But such causal efficacy does not exhaust the value of Huck's attitude: that attitude is still of value even once it has become fully determined that it will not affect Huck's actions. I hope this is obvious in the case of Huck. If I am right that collective agents and individual agents should be viewed analogously in these matters, then it is also true of a collective such as a state. A member doing their membership duty is like Huck having respectful and sympathetic attitudes: morally right, even if inefficacious.

How, then, is a membership duty's importance to be assessed? The importance of a given membership duty is a function of two things: first, its expected efficacy at inducing the collective to discharge its overall duty; second, the importance of that overall collective duty (which will, in turn, be partially a function of what type of duty it is: to repair harm done, return benefits received, keep promises, etc.). The second of these reflects the value of an entity's having aspects (in the collective case, members) that accord with its duty, even if that entity will not do its duty overall. The bigger and more politically significant a collective is, the more weighty, stringent, and demanding its duties will be. So, the more weighty, stringent, and demanding the relevant membership duties will be (holding expected efficacy constant).[20]

My claim is not that membership duties *always* override an individual's non-membership duties—including the duty to engage in the project of benefiting others as much as possible. If much good—or much right—can be done by ignoring one's membership duties, then that might be what an individual all-things-considered ought to do.[21] But if the collective is socially and politically significant—if it is, for example, a state or multinational corporation—then one's membership duty will be weighty enough to *compete* with the good one can do on one's own. By 'compete', I mean that the membership duty and the duty to do good must be balanced against one another in one's deliberations about what to do on a particular occasion, and that neither should be persistently favoured across many occasions. A more precise statement of the relative values would fail to do justice to the distinct (perhaps incommensurable) nature of the values. Suffice to say, sometimes, you ought to take to the streets to voice your views qua citizen (even if this

[20] This conception of what collectives' duties imply for members' duties is similar to Woodard's (2011) proposal, but my argument relies on collective agency (and its similarities to individual agency) in a way Woodard rejects. The role of collective agency in generating reasons for members to unilaterally do their parts is likewise not considered by Dietz (2016, pp. 971–5), who therefore concludes (in my terminology) that membership duties exist only if the collective will do its overall duty if I do my membership duty.

[21] Berkey (2018).

will not change your state's behaviour), or take to the picket line to voice your views qua employee (even if your employer will not listen)—because these are the membership duties that are entailed by your state's or employer's duties that it owes to specifiable entities—rather than spending that time benefiting others-at-large as much as possible.

Coordination duties

There is a second problem that group contexts pose for individuals who are engaged in the project of benefiting others as much as possible. This second problem is internal to that project: that is, whereas membership duties suggested we have reasons to do something other than pursue that project, the present problem persists if one assumes that the project should be pursued. The problem is best introduced via a simple example, depicted below.[22]

	Hunt stags	Hunt rabbits
Hunt stags	5, 5 (10)	0, 3 (3)
Hunt rabbits	3, 0 (3)	3, 3 (6)

In the example, two individuals are out hunting. Each can choose to hunt either stags or rabbits. It will take two of them to kill a stag, but each can kill a few rabbits on their own. So, if each chooses to hunt stags, then each will receive five units of wellbeing. Each individual who hunts rabbits will receive three units of wellbeing. If one of them hunts stags on their own, then that individual will receive no wellbeing. The total value produced by the two agents together appears in parentheses in the matrix. I will assume both aim to benefit others as much as possible, and both weigh others' wellbeing equally to their own. So this total value is what they each care about.

There are two Nash equilibria: two situations in which neither has a reason to change their strategy once they learn the other's strategy (assuming that the other will not change their strategy). These are, first, the situation in which both hunt stags and, second, that in which both hunt rabbits. So what you should do depends on what you think the other will do: if you think the other will hunt stags, you should hunt stags; if you think the other will hunt rabbits, you should hunt rabbits. This is not helpful if you have no beliefs about what the other person

[22] The example derives from Rousseau (2004, pp. 29–30); it is discussed extensively by Skyrms (2001). A similar example is discussed by Dietz (2019) in the context of effective altruism, but Dietz posits group reasons to solve the problem—as we shall see, my solution rejects group-level reasons in groups that are not agents.

will do—especially if you know that the other person is rational and has no beliefs about your potential actions (in which case, they will get stuck with the same two conditionals).[23]

Of course, we usually have beliefs about what other people will do. And if your credence that the other person will choose to hunt stags is higher than about 0.41, then your choosing to hunt stags will maximize expected goodness.[24] And it might seem that your credence that the other person will choose to hunt stags will definitely be higher than 0.41, because, as Parfit puts it, 'the unique best outcome is clearly salient. It is the obvious place to meet.'[25] So, Parfit thinks, people will naturally have a high enough credence that the other person will choose to hunt stags. So each will reason their way into hunting stags, via aiming to maximize expected value.

Unfortunately, it is sometimes reasonable for each individual to have a high credence that the other will hunt rabbits. In this case, expected value theory will tell each to hunt rabbits. And yet, there is an intuitive sense in which something has gone wrong in such a case: they should have coordinated on hunting stags. Lest this sound like something that would never happen, consider how the stag hunt is analogous to the real-life project of helping others as much as possible. Roughly, we might replace 'hunt stags' with 'pursue systemic change' (as discussed by Gabriel and McElwee[26]) and replace 'hunt rabbits' with 'pursue marginal change'.[27] All those who are concerned to help others could act with a view to systemic changes in international institutions—pushing their states and intergovernmental organizations for reform of international processes, norms, and laws. Alternatively, each could donate some percentage of their income to charities that are seeking to make incremental improvements to the lives of the world's worst-off. If all pursued incremental improvements, then this would do some good. But it is plausible that this would not do as much good as if all acted responsively to one another with a view to systemic change. Finally, there is the outcome where some act responsively to one another with a view to systemic change, and some contribute to incremental improvements. Here, the efforts of the systemic changers will be futile—and the efforts of the incremental improvers will do some good, but less than half the good that would have been done if all had engaged in systemic change. If an individual reasonably has a high credence that others will pursue incremental change, then that individual should also pursue

[23] Bacharach (2006, p. 44); Gold and Sugden (2007); Tuomela (2013, ch. 7).

[24] I thank Hilary Greaves for pressing this.

[25] Parfit (1988, p. 13).

[26] Gabriel and McElwee (Chapter 7, this volume).

[27] I am not the first to suggest an analogy between the stag hunt and the project of helping others as much as possible. Benjamin Todd (2016) has worried that those within the effective altruism social movement might end up 'hunting rabbits' via piecemeal interventions, instead of pursuing 'large scale changes'. But Todd finds this unlikely, since '[s]tag hunt situations arise rarely in real life, because if both groups communicate, then they'll both go for stag.' The problem of communication is the one I highlight below.

incremental change. And yet, something has intuitively gone wrong—the world has fallen short of an attainable ideal—if all those who want to help others as much as possible pursue incremental change, as a result of them each reasonably having a high credence that the others will do likewise.

So what should each do?[28] A natural answer is that they should communicate with the others, so that everyone comes to believe that everyone else will pursue systemic change, so that everyone can reason their own way into doing likewise. This answer is not available in the usual set-up of the stag hunt, where it is assumed the players cannot communicate. But it does seem available in the real-world case of individuals who are concerned to help others as much as possible. This is roughly the answer of Donald Regan's 'cooperative utilitarianism'. In brief, according to Regan, each individual should take the following five steps:

(1) Be willing to take part in the joint attempt to produce the best possible consequences by coordinating with whoever is willing to coordinate, whoever they turn out to be (where it could be that you are the only one);
(2) Determine who else is a 'cooperator', i.e. such that they: (*a*) have taken step (*1*); and (*b*) have correctly identified who else has taken step (*1*);
(3) Ascertain what the behaviour will be of the non-cooperators (i.e. those who do not meet conditions (*a*) and (*b*));
(4) Identify the best pattern of behaviour for yourself and the other cooperators, given the behaviour of the non-cooperators that was ascertained at step (*3*);
(5) Do your part in the pattern identified at (*4*).[29]

This gives the following nice result: if you believe others will pursue incremental change no matter what, then you should not identify them as cooperators; if you are willing to pursue systemic change, then others should identify you as a cooperator. So, what each should do depends on which others have been identified as cooperators.

The pressing problem is how to identify cooperators—and how to get others to identify you as a cooperator. Regan does not solve this problem, saying it 'simply does not matter, in theory. (In practice, of course, it may matter a great deal).'[30]

[28] Dietz (2016) argues that in cases like this, *the group* should pursue systemic change (hunt stags) even while *the individuals* should pursue marginal change. Parfit (1988, pp. 7–9) suggests likewise. I am sceptical that non-collective groups can bear reasons (see Collins (ms, chs 2–3) for arguments that they cannot bear duties). And the group I'm concerned with in this section—namely, that constituted by all people who are concerned to benefit others as much as possible—is not a collective agent. I also don't think this solution captures what's intuitively gone wrong. So I am cutting straight to the question of what each hunter should do, where this doesn't derive from what the group should do.

[29] This paraphrases Regan (1980, pp. 135–6); Regan's full formulation is at (1980, pp. 157–8), but the additional details don't deal with the communicative issue I highlight below.

[30] Regan (1980, p. 152).

But this does not mean philosophers can safely ignore the problem. After all, the line between theory and practice here is vague: it is unclear exactly in what sense the issue of communication is merely practical, even though the coordination problem as a whole is theoretical. One could say that the 'theoretical solution' is easy: the solution is 'converge on hunting stags; everything else is merely practical.' But presumably this would not satisfy Regan qua theoretical solution. So it is unclear why he rests content with not exploring the communicative issue.[31] And even if the problem of communication is purely practical, we should consider how to solve it.

Parfit also does not solve the communication problem. He gives three conditions that are jointly sufficient for an individual obligation to cooperate on the optimal outcome:

> When (*1*) the members of some group would make the outcome better if enough of them acted in some way, and (*2*) they would make the outcome best if all of them acted in this way, and (*3*) each of them both knows these facts and believes that enough of them will act in this way, then (*4*) each of them ought to act in this way.[32]

The question is how we can come to have the knowledge and beliefs in Parfit's condition (*3*). When we find ourselves in situations like the stag hunt, we need to form the right beliefs about others—and, crucially, help others to form the right beliefs about us—before any of us can even satisfy the precondition (of having a belief that the others will cooperate) on having an obligation to act for the best overall outcome, let alone satisfy the obligation itself.

The problem is that those who are trying to benefit others as much as possible are a diverse bunch. The bunch includes trade unionists, activists, advocacy organizations, and those involved in local and national politics—as well as 'incremental changers', that is, those who contribute to incremental change and who advocate that others should do the same. This raises the question of how, and whether, incremental changers are sending signals that encourage other potential cooperators to view incremental changers as cooperators or as non-cooperators; as stag hunters or as rabbit hunters. Numerous potential parties to systemic change are more likely to perceive incremental changers as *not* willing to take part in the joint attempt to help others as much as possible by coordinating with whoever is willing to coordinate. Simply put, if one flagrantly hunts rabbits, then one is probably not signalling willingness to hunt stags.[33] This is particularly—but not

[31] Parfit agrees, describing Regan's theory as a 'partial failure' due to its failure to 'wholly explain how the agents manage to cooperate'(Parfit (1988, p. 6)).

[32] Parfit (1984, pp. 78–9).

[33] Thus it's inadequate to say, as Peter Singer does, that 'effective altruists are already organizing together. Charities are themselves a form of coordination, enabling thousands of donors to work together for a common goal, and beyond that, the effective altruism movement has several

only—so if one is pursuing incremental change through such anti-systemic-change methods as earning-to-give while working in a job that perpetuates the very system that systemic change would overhaul. This is hunting rabbits in a way that scares away stags.[34]

To this, an incremental changer might object there is little consensus over which precise systemic change to pursue, how to pursue it, or how to signal that one is a cooperator. In the terms of the analogy: there is no agreement on where the stags are, how to hunt them, or how to let fellow hunters know that you would like to hunt them. Even if we concede this, it is no reason to give up on hunting stags. After all, the numbers in the matrix are net gains, so they already reflect the costs of various way of finding stags, planning the hunt, signalling willingness, and so on—where the costs of these diverse and numerous means are weighted by the probability that those means will be successful if the agent in question attempts to take them. The objector is effectively contending that 'pursuing systemic change' (where this includes the value of the pursuit, not just the value of the change once realized) would not be as valuable (relative to marginal change) as the analogy suggests. Such an objector would then need to turn to the arguments of Gabriel and McElwee, which I will refrain from reproducing.[35]

A second objection to the stag hunt analogy is that—in the case of systemic change—hunting rabbits is a good way to hunt stags. For example, by funding anti-malarial bed nets, one improves people's health. When people have good health, they are more able to cooperate for systemic change. Thus, incremental change boosts the prospects for systemic change. This is sometimes called a 'flow-through effect': the benefits 'flow through' the direct recipients (bed net users) to indirect recipients (those whose rights are protected by the system that bed-net-users later campaign for).[36] It is as if you are nursing a sick hunter by feeding them rabbits. This makes the sick hunter able to hunt stags in future. However, at the same time, the nurse is giving the sick hunter reason to identify the nurse as a rabbit hunter. This gives the sick hunter reason to be a rabbit-hunter themselves when the time comes, because (to reiterate) if everyone is hunting rabbits, then the best thing to do is to hunt rabbits.

How, then, does one signal one's willingness to coordinate for systemic change? This is an empirical question, but the general answer is obvious: act directly upon the systems that need changing. This can be done via protests and demonstrations,

"meta-charities" like The Life You Can Save, Giving What We Can and the Centre for Effective Altruism, which are doing their best to expand the movement or assess which charities are the most effective, and get more people involved in giving to effective charities' Singer (2016, p. 168). That is, 'effectives altruists' (by which, from context, I suspect Singer means incremental changers) are engaging in coordinated mass rabbit hunting.

---

[34] Earning-to-give in harmful jobs is advised against by, for example, the charity 80,000 Hours, but not for the reasons I give here (Todd (2017)).

[35] Gabriel and McElwee (Chapter 7, this volume).

[36] Karnofsky (2013).

membership and activism within political parties, involvement in trade unionism, and voting—alongside giving to those organizations that directly press for systemic change (advocacy organizations being prime examples).[37] Ethical consumption—buying fair trade products, eating vegan, and so on—can also be understood as signalling one's willingness to work with others to pursue systemic change.[38] Signalling willingness will often mean acting for causes that others are already acting for, that is, causes that are not neglected by others. It might also mean acting for causes that do not seem tractable when considering just the marginal effect of one's own individual contribution.

Importantly, such signalling cannot be done by simply making a *one-off* public declaration. One cannot simply post on social media 'I'll push for systemic change if you all do!', and then turn around to pursue marginal change until others post likewise. For one's signal to be convincing, and for it be communicated to those beyond one's immediate circle, it is better if the signal is persistent, consistent, and insistent. Of course, if one persistently, consistently, and insistently posts about one's willingness on social media, then this may well do part of the trick. But even ongoing declarations of that kind will only get the signal across to a small audience—at least for those of us whose social media circle consists mostly of people we already know.

That said, in theory, one can signal one's willingness to cooperate for systemic change while also pursuing (some types of) marginal change. One can be a conscientious citizen, consumer, union member, Amnesty International donor, *and* donor to charities that make incremental improvements in people's lives. However, by focusing our immediate efforts on the project of marginally and individually benefiting others as much as possible, we run two risks: first, distracting ourselves from the importance of signalling for systemic change (since each of us has only so much time, energy, and money); second, signalling that we are opposed to cooperation for systemic change—especially if we pursue incremental change in a vocal way.

Conclusion

The two problems I have explored combine to suggest that the project of ensuring that oneself—as a marginal individual—benefits others as much as possible might reasonably be crowded out of a person's practical reasoning.

First, as members of states (and other collectives), we have duties to act within and because of our roles in the collective with a view to the collective responding to

[37] These suggestions are in the spirit of Srinivasan (2015) and Herzog (2016), though my argument for them differs from both.
[38] Lawford-Smith (2015).

the duties that apply to it. The duties that apply to collectives are not just duties to benefit others-at-large as much as possible, but are also duties not to do harm, to repay for harms done, to keep promises, and so on. Individuals' 'membership duties' gather weight not just from the member's expected effect on the collective's overall actions, but also from the fact that an individual's fulfilling their membership duty constitutes a right aspect of their collective. Second, an individual should not act so that they (as an individual) benefit others as much as possible, if this would distract them from—and send the wrong signals about—the greater change that a coordinated group could produce.

This suggests that political action is more important than might be implied by the simple idea of acting, as a marginal individual, to benefit others as much as possible. It suggests that we should attend to causes that are not neglected by others, and that might not be tractable by individual action. If effective altruism is a project in which one uses 'evidence and reason to figure out how to benefit others as much as possible, and [takes]...action on that basis',[39] then we may need to revise the project before committing to it. Perhaps we should engage in the project of (*1*) using evidence and reason to figure out to which others we have duties—where those duties might arise via our membership in collective agents—and (*2*) taking initial steps towards working together with others to ensure that we and others are responsive to those duties.

Acknowledgements

For helpful comments, I thank Brian Berkey, Hilary Greaves, Lisa Herzog, Brian McElwee, Avia Pasternak, Theron Pummer, Christian Wendelborn, and audiences at the 2016 meeting of the Association for Social and Political Philosophy (LSE) and a 2016 workshop on Effective Altruism (Oxford).

References

Arpaly, Nomy. 2002. *Unprincipled Virtue: An Inquiry into Moral Agency*. Oxford: Oxford University Press.

Ashford, Elizabeth. 2018. "Severe Poverty as an Unjust Emergency." In *The Ethics of Giving: Philosophers' Perspectives on Philanthropy*, Paul Woodruff, ed. Oxford: Oxford University Press, Ch. 4.

Bacharach, Michael. 2006. *Beyond Individual Choice: Teams and Frames in Game Theory*. Princeton: Princeton University Press.

Bennett, Jonathan. 1974. "The Conscience of Huckleberry Finn." *Philosophy* 49 (188): 123–34.

[39] MacAskill (Chapter 7, this volume).

Berkey, Brian. 2018. "The Institutional Critique of Effective Altruism." *Utilitas* 30 (2): 143–71.

Collins, Stephanie. 2018. "Who Does Wrong When an Organisation Does Wrong?" In *Collectivity: Ontology, Ethics, and Social Justice*, Kemdy M. Hess, Violetta Igneski, and Tracy Isaacs, eds. London and New York: Rowman and Littlefield, Ch. 9.

Collins, Stephanie. 2017. "Duties of Group Agents and Group Members." *Journal of Social Philosophy* 48 (1): 38–57.

Collins, Stephanie, and Holly Lawford-Smith. 2016. "Collectives' Duties and Individuals' Duties: A Parity Argument." *Canadian Journal of Philosophy* 46 (1): 38–58.

Collins, Stephanie. Under contract. *Group Duties: Their Existence and Their Implications for Individuals*. Oxford: Oxford University Press.

Collins, Stephanie and Holly Lawford-Smith. ms. "We the People."

Dietz, Alexander. 2016. "What We Together Ought to Do." *Ethics* 126 (4): 955–82.

Dietz, Alexander. 2019. "Effective Altruism and Collective Obligations." *Utilitas* 31 (1): 106–15.

French, Peter. 1984. *Collective and Corporate Responsibility*. New York: Columbia University Press.

Gabriel, Iason and Brian McElwee. Chapter 7, this volume.

Gelman, Andrew, Nate Silver, and Aaron Edlin. 2012. "What is the Probability that Your Vote Will Make a Difference?" *Economic Inquiry* 50 (2): 321–6.

Gold, Natalie and Robert Sugden. 2007. "Collective Intentions and Team Agency." *Journal of Philosophy* 104 (3): 109–37.

Herzog, Lisa. 2016. "Can 'Effective Altruism' Really Change the World?" *OpenDemocracy*. Available at https://www.opendemocracy.net/transformation/lisa-herzog/can-effective-altruism-really-change-world#.

Hess, Kendy M. 2018. "The Peculiar Unity of Corporate Agents." In *Collectivity: Ontology, Ethics, and Social Justice*, Kemdy M. Hess, Violetta Igneski, and Tracy Isaacs, eds. London and New York: Rowman and Littlefield, Ch. 2.

Kagan, Shelly. 2011. "Do I Make a Difference?" *Philosophy and Public Affairs* 39 (2): 105–41.

Karnofsky, Holden. 2013. "Flow-through Effects." *The GiveWell Blog*, 15 May. Available at https://blog.givewell.org/2013/05/15/flow-through-effects/.

Lawford-Smith, Holly. 2015. "Unethical Consumption and Obligations to Signal." *Ethics and International Affairs* 29 (3): 315–30.

List, Christian, and Philip Pettit. 2011. *Group Agency: The Possibility, Design, and Status of Corporate Agents*. Oxford: Oxford University Press.

List, Christian, and Kai Spiekermann. 2013. "Methodological Individualism and Holism in Political Science: A Reconciliation." *American Political Science Review* 107 (4): 629–43.

McMahan, Jeff. 2016. "Philosophical Critiques of Effective Altruism." *The Philosopher's Magazine* 73: 92–9.

Parfit, Derek. 1984. *Reasons and Persons.* Oxford: Oxford University Press.

Parfit, Derek. 1988. "What We Together Do." ms.

Pettit, Philip. 2007. "Responsibility Incorporated." *Ethics* 117 (2): 171–201.

Regan, Donald. 1980. *Utilitarianism and Cooperation.* Oxford: Oxford University Press.

Richie, Katherine. 2013. "What Are Groups?" *Philosophical Studies* 166 (2): 257–72.

Rousseau, Jean-Jacques. 2004. *Discourse on the Origin of Inequality.* Dover thrift edition, edited by Greg Boroson. New York: Dover Publications.

Rovane, Carol. 1998. *The Bounds of Agency: An Essay in Revisionary Metaphysics.* Princeton: Princeton University Press.

Singer, Peter. 2016. "The Most Good You Can Do: A Response to the Commentaries." *Journal of Global Ethics* 12 (2): 161–9.

Skyrms, Brian. 2001. "The Stag Hunt." *Proceedings and Addresses of the American Philosophical Association* 75 (2): 31–41.

Srinivasan, Amia. 2015. "Stop the Robot Apocalypse." *London Review of Books* 37: 3–6. Available at http://www.lrb.co.uk/v37/n18/amia-srinivasan/stop-therobot-apocalypse.

Strand, Anders. 2012. "Group Agency, Responsibility, and Control." *Philosophy of the Social Sciences* 43 (2): 201–24.

Todd, Benjamin. 2017. "Is It Ever Okay to Take a Harmful Job in Order to Do More Good? An In-depth Analysis." Available at https://80000hours.org/articles/harmful-career/.

Todd, Benjamin. 2016. "The Value of Coordination." 80,000 Hours, 8 February. Available at https://80000hours.org/2016/02/the-value-of-coordination/.

Tuomela, Raimo. 2013. *Social Ontology: Collective Intentionality and Group Agents.* Oxford: Oxford University Press.

Twain, Mark. 1884 (2012). *The Adventures of Huckleberry Finn.* London: Vintage.

Woodard, Christopher. 2011. *Reasons, Patterns, and Cooperation.* New York: Routledge.

14
Overriding Virtue

Richard Yetter Chappell

I take beneficence to be impartial: directing us to help others as best we can, no matter whether those others be near to us or far away. I don't mean to imply by this that impartial beneficence is the *only* morally relevant norm, such that we may never do anything *but* help others as best we can. Rather, the claim is just that, *within the domain of beneficence*, impartial maximizing is correct: the reasons of beneficence favour saving a distant many over a nearby few, all else equal. Many consequentialists will of course take impartial beneficence to be all there is to morality. But it is important to stress that one needn't be a consequentialist to find *this aspect* of consequentialist thought highly appealing. Impartial beneficence could be supplemented by any number of other norms, e.g. constraints that rule out utilitarian sacrifice or rights violations even when done "for the greater good". I also leave open that the demands of beneficence may be subject to limitations, to ensure that agents have significant leeway to pursue their own projects no matter how many others need their aid. (But I do assume that beneficence is a *significant*, non-trivial component of morality.)

Impartial beneficence, thus understood, seems an important component of a broadly cosmopolitan moral outlook. But it fits uneasily with common sentimentalist intuitions about moral virtue. For example, we typically think that a good person must be sensitive to those around them. We expect the good person to be motivated by moral emotions, such as sympathy and empathy, which are most easily engaged by those who are nearby or otherwise salient.[1] But the most objectively pressing moral needs tend not to be found on our doorsteps. Impartial beneficence may thus direct us to override our natural moral sentiments in pursuit of the greater good. Is *doing* (the most) good thereby in tension with *being* a good person? The challenge may be amplified by considering the popular adage, "charity begins at home." We may well look askance at a moral point of view that seems to uphold Dickens's Mrs. Jellyby, with her neglected family and "telescopic philanthropy"—able to "see nothing nearer than Africa"[2]—as a paragon of virtue. There would at least seem something a bit morally awkward or uncomfortable about ignoring the homeless on our doorstep so as to instead donate a greater amount to global poverty relief.

[1] Slote (2007). [2] Dickens (1853, ch. 4).

On the other hand, it would seem excessively complacent to just assume that our evolved psychologies and emotional dispositions are entirely above reproach. It isn't as though we could plausibly hold that needy individuals who are salient to us are thereby objectively more deserving of aid, or that those who are out of sight thereby deserve to be neglected.[3] This may be taken to suggest that the traditional conception of virtue requires modification, and that true benevolence may at times require us to override or redirect our natural sympathies. Or so I will argue in this paper. The challenge is to develop a conception of moral virtue that fits with a modern cosmopolitan moral outlook, without thereby valorizing the neglectful, callous character of Mrs. Jellyby.

1. Sentimentalism and its limits

Slote (2007) advocates a form of sentimentalist virtue ethics that grounds our obligations in considerations of whether our actions "reflect or exhibit or express an absence (or lack) of fully developed empathic concern for (or caring about) others".[4] A crucial fact about normal human empathy is that it is engaged "more deeply or forcefully" by "immediate" or salient needs than by "need known only by description".[5] As a result, on Slote's view we will often have stronger moral reasons to address local or immediate needs than we do to address needs that are geographically or temporally distant.

A theoretical concern with this approach is that our moral sentiments cannot be above criticism. We should not accept racism or sexism *even if* it turned out, empirically, that natural human empathy was more strongly and readily engaged by members of one's own race or gender. (Indeed, in-group biases are sadly far from being merely hypothetical.) Even if we grant the optimistic assumption that such biases are not endemic to human empathy, the mere *possibility* of such problematic natural biases suffices to establish that our natural moral sentiments are in principle open to moral challenge.

In addressing such concerns, Slote at one point wrote: "The ethics of empathy may here be hostage to future biological and psychological research, but I don't think that takes away from its *promise* as a way of understanding and justifying (a certain view of) morality."[6] On the contrary, if we *know* that there is a possible situation in which sentimentalism is *not* the correct moral theory, then we can

[3] Unger (1996) similarly argues that many common intuitions about aid are heavily influenced by morally irrelevant considerations of "conspicuousness". For a contrasting view, see Kamm (1999).

[4] Slote (2007, p. 31).

[5] Slote (2007, pp. 23–4). Though it's worth flagging that Slote depends upon the further, less obvious, assumption that this must remain true of *fully developed* human sympathy.

[6] Slote (2007, p. 36). However, Slote tells me that he no longer considers sentimentalism to be contingent in this way.

ask ourselves what the *correct* moral theory in that situation would be. And once equipped with that correct possible moral theory—one that provides an independent justification for rejecting racist and sexist sentiments even when sentimentalism cannot—then we may wonder what we need sentimentalism for. What is stopping that counterfactually correct moral theory from also being the correct moral theory in the actual world?

Sentimentalism does seem to do well at capturing common moral intuitions, however. Consider a classic case where sentimentalism diverges from more "coldly" rationalistic approaches to ethics: Some miners are trapped in a mineshaft, and the cost of rescuing them would empty a budget that would otherwise be invested in safety mechanisms to prevent such calamities recurring in future. We are to suppose that we cannot both rescue the current miners and protect future ones, and that a greater number of future miners will die if we fail to invest in the safety mechanisms (they will not themselves be rescuable when future disasters strike). Slote notes that we "typically feel morally impelled to help the [present] miners rather than (at that point) expend an equivalent amount to install safety devices in the mines that will save a greater number of lives in the long run."[7] Endorsing this sentiment, he suggests that anyone with the opposite preference "shows a certain deficiency in empathy" and that as a result "we think of him or her as less compassionate and as acting less well than someone who would choose to save the presently trapped miners."[8]

This seems to me to be a case where our natural moral sentiments lead us astray. Important though our sentiments may be, it seems deeply misguided and self-indulgent—a kind of moral fetishism—to elevate their moral importance above that of human lives or considerations of rational desirability. This verdict may be supported by appeal to the "veil of ignorance" heuristic.[9] To ensure a fair and unbiased moral verdict, consider what would be rationally chosen by self-interested agents (who lack any potentially distorting moral assumptions) who are temporarily deprived of any knowledge of their own identities or locations in time, space, or society. When thinking of each person in society as an equally likely candidate for being "themselves", and noting the greater number of future miner lives at stake in the decision than present ones, it seems that the prudent agent would be rationally compelled to prefer that we save the greater number, i.e. install the safety devices rather than rescue the presently trapped miners (assuming, again, that for some reason it is impossible to do both). This is the social policy that has the greatest expected value for agents, given that they do not know which individual they will turn out to be. So, given that preventative measures are (*ex hypothesi*) more effective than post hoc remedies, given a forced choice between the two options we—rationally and morally—must prefer the

[7] Slote (2007, pp. 25–6). [8] Slote (2007, p. 27).
[9] Harsanyi (1953); cf. Rawls (1971).

former.[10] In sum: When lives and emotions come into conflict, we must prioritize others' lives as being more important.

We should reject Slote's sentimentalism as insufficiently critical of our given moral emotions. Nonetheless, I think it important to bear in mind the insights to be gained from Slote's work, especially regarding the connection between natural moral sentiments and common *intuitions* about what it takes to be a good person. When impartial beneficence prescribes actions or policies that promote the greatest good at the cost of proximate needs that more easily engage our natural empathy, there is a risk that such prescriptions may appear callous or lacking in compassion. Advocates of impartial beneficence may thus find cause to reflect carefully on how their prescriptions relate to virtues of character, especially compassion.

2. Benevolence and abstract sympathy

Benevolence, or generalized well-wishing, is the virtue most naturally associated with impartial beneficence. The benevolent agent wants things to go as well as possible for people (and other sentient beings) overall, whoever and wherever they may be. Stable possession of benevolent desires is surely a genuine virtue: Not only is such a character trait of significant instrumental value in tending to produce good (value-promoting) actions, it also instantiates a kind of *intrinsic* appropriateness in that it reflects the agent's *orientation towards the good*.[11]

This conception of benevolence finds voice within Bertrand Russell's account of abstract sympathy as the most fully developed form of sympathy:

> There is a purely physical sympathy: a very young child will cry because a brother or sister is crying. This, I suppose, affords the basis for the further developments. The two enlargements that are needed are: first, to feel sympathy even when the sufferer is not an object of special affection; secondly, to feel it when the suffering is merely known to be occurring, not sensibly present. The second of these enlargements depends largely upon intelligence. It may only go so far as sympathy with suffering which is portrayed vividly and touchingly, as in a good novel; it may, on the other hand, go so far as to enable a man to be moved emotionally by statistics. This capacity for abstract sympathy is as rare as it is important.[12]

The possibility of such abstract sympathy undermines the charge that it is necessarily "callous" to maximize net welfare at the cost of more proximate interests. On the contrary, such impartially benevolent preferences may instead reveal a deeper wellspring of emotional concern for others than is found in the merely

[10] But cf. N. Daniels (2015); See also Mogensen (Chapter 15, this volume).
[11] Hurka (2001). [12] Russell (1926/2003, p. 48).

ordinarily (concretely) sympathetic. Indeed, we should surely expect that the compassion of the ideally virtuous agent would extend more broadly than our own flawed and imperfect compassion manages to do. Insofar as moral perfection is thought to involve a kind of universal love, it is very natural to conceive of the ideally virtuous agent as one who would feel the moral-emotional pull of others' needs just as strongly even when they are distant from the agent herself. And it would certainly not be callous or lacking in compassion when such an ideally virtuous agent acted upon her expansive sense of compassion to protect a greater number of people despite their lack of proximity (just as there is nothing callous about saving the nearby many over the nearby few).

Of course, we are not ideally virtuous agents. Even many of us who are moved by moral reasons to prefer saving the greater number may nonetheless find that this verdict conflicts with our strongest sympathetic impulses (which remain tethered to more proximate, salient needs). This raises interesting questions about how to evaluate our characters when we choose to save the distant many over the nearby few. Is this a virtuous choice, since it is done for good moral reasons and in recognition that this is what the ideally virtuous agent would do? Or is it disreputably callous, as we are in fact overriding our strongest sympathetic impulses, and letting harm come to those we see most vividly, merely for the sake of some "greater good" that we do not fully (i.e. emotionally) comprehend? To answer this question, consider the following character trait:

Abstract benevolence: The disposition to allow abstract, globally-oriented moral reasons to override or redirect one's natural inclination to prioritize the most salient needs one faces, when this is necessary to address more objectively pressing needs.

I propose that abstract benevolence is a neglected virtue, specific to imperfect agents like ourselves, that serves to moderate the biasing effect of ordinary sympathy. It helps us to better meet the impartial demands of an appropriately cosmopolitan moral code, whilst recognizing the centrality of locally oriented moral emotions like sympathy to our moral lives.

3. Overridden or redirected sympathy?

If we accept abstract benevolence as a modern-day virtue, we must address the question of how to resolve the tension it creates with the traditional virtue of sympathy. For although my above account specifies that globally oriented moral concerns should win out over more limited, merely locally oriented ones, it leaves open how this is to be achieved. One possibility is that the full force of one's felt sympathy remains unchanged, and optimal action is instead secured by buttressing one's motivational strength of will for acting contrarily to this felt emotion. This would be for abstract benevolence to involve *overriding* one's ordinary sympathy. Alternatively, one could conceive of this new virtue as involving the *redirection* of one's sympathetic impulses towards the promotion of the greater good, leaving no residual tension between one's moral emotions and motivations at all.

This theoretical choice will determine the answer to a simple yet vexing question: How should we feel about passing by the local soup kitchen or homeless shelter, en route to donate to a more cost-effective developing-world charity? Should our ordinary sympathy still be activated, but simply overridden by the recognition that distant others are in even greater need, thus leaving us feeling *torn*? Or should our sympathetic impulses be *wholeheartedly* redirected toward the greatest needs?[13]

Wholehearted redirection may be more pleasant for the agent themselves, but I take that to be the wrong sort of reason for identifying something as a virtue. (We are not asking what character traits are most instrumentally beneficial, but rather which have the kind of intrinsic appropriateness that renders them fit to be considered virtues.) Some theorists, drawn to the idea of a *unity of the virtues*, may think it important to avoid internal tension or conflicting moral emotions or impulses within the virtuous agent.[14] But I see no good reason to deny that virtuous agents may feel conflicted. After all, if virtues consist in a kind of orientation toward the good, and goods can conflict (as well we know), then it stands to reason that virtuous motivations may likewise conflict. Indeed, a single virtue—such as generosity—may simultaneously pull us in conflicting directions.

So, absent some further argument of which I am unaware, the case for redirection seems weak. By contrast, I think there are compelling reasons to favour the conception of abstract benevolence as merely *motivationally overriding* our sympathetic impulses, which persist in their emotional force nonetheless. For the resulting emotional conflict better reflects the moral facts on the ground, where there are genuinely conflicting interests at stake.

It is fitting to have distinct intrinsic desires for each intrinsic good, and so—as I've argued elsewhere—the separateness of persons calls on us to separately value (desire) each person's wellbeing.[15] As a result, if forced to choose just one of two innocent lives to save, you should feel *ambivalent* rather than *indifferent* about the

[13] While I raise this question within the non-ideal context of an agent who needs abstract benevolence to make up for their biased sympathy, it's worth flagging that similar questions arise even in the ideal case of the agent capable of fully-fledged sympathy for the distant many. Should they still feel sympathy for the nearby few (just overridden this time by their greater sympathy for the many, rather than by their rational appreciation of the reasons to prioritize the many)? I think the answer to this question will also be "yes", for the same reasons as discussed below.

[14] Though the more plausible view in this vicinity is just that one cannot possess a subset of virtues (to their fullest or most ideal extent) in isolation from other virtues: to be even partly ideally virtuous requires a practical intelligence that entails all the virtues. This is compatible with external circumstances forcing "painful choices" upon the agent. See Annas (2011, ch. 5–6).

[15] Chappell (2015).

choice, as you should have separate (equally strong) desires pulling you in opposite directions. More generally, when facing trade-offs between the interests of different people, you should feel at least somewhat torn, even if it's clear which option does the most good (and hence is most worth choosing). The lesser interest is merely *outweighed*, not *cancelled*. So it is appropriate for the normative force of the lesser interest to continue to exert some emotional and motivational pressure on a moral agent (even if it is, as it should be, ultimately outweighed by greater forces pulling in the other direction). This in turn helps to explain the intuitive appropriateness of *pro tanto* regret: the thwarted lesser interest creates a "moral remainder" that leaves the virtuous agent feeling less than fully satisfied by their choice, despite recognizing that it would have been even worse to favour the lesser interest at the cost of the greater.

This is all in striking contrast to cases where the trade-off is between two merely instrumental goods (to the same final end). Offered a choice between two £20 bills, it would be bizarre to feel torn or ambivalent about the decision. It is a matter of indifference, because the bills do not matter in themselves, but are mere financial instruments—a purpose served equally well by either bill. In short: money is fungible.

In similar fashion, one's interest in some financial investment may be wholly redirected (without remainder or regret) if a better investment opportunity comes along. But I trust that most readers will share my sense that it would be a mistake for us to regard individual people and their interests as wholly fungible in the way that money is. Don't get me wrong: difficult decisions must be made when interests conflict, and they must be made judiciously (carefully weighing the interests at stake and opting for the option that is best on net, rather than ignoring such details and merely flipping a coin). My point is just that an accurate understanding of the moral landscape requires us to acknowledge that these decisions *are* difficult—even when the math involved is not—because those whose interests have been overridden still deserve our sympathy.

We thus find that moral agents should feel torn about passing by the local soup kitchen or homeless shelter even when they do so in order to do more good elsewhere.[16] Doing the most good is the right decision, but when trade-offs are involved it should not be an entirely comfortable decision. We may not be in a position to adequately help everyone, but we can at least show them the respect of recognizing the "moral remainder" that their loss has injected into the situation. To fail to do so would arguably constitute a lack of adequate respect for their

[16] Though I don't mean to suggest that the degree of *pro tanto* regrettability is what explains the *weight* of the felt conflict. For example, it will naturally feel more difficult to override especially salient needs than it would be to make a similarly regrettable trade-off where none of the competing needs were so salient (e.g. between competing global charities). As cognitively limited agents, we cannot always regret every regrettable thing; our emotional responses are instead heavily influenced by factors such as salience. See Chappell & Yetter-Chappell (2015).

value as separate persons, and so would reveal a flaw of moral character, even if the agent's actions were impeccably value-promoting.

4. Beneficence and special obligations

One may doubt whether the sketched solution is adequate to the problem we began with. Suppose that Mrs. Jellyby felt terribly about neglecting her children—is that enough to get her off the hook, morally speaking? If not, we must think that the problem with Mrs. Jellyby is not anything so subtle (or abstract) as merely neglecting the separateness of persons. Her problem, we are apt to think, is that she is neglecting *her children*, to whom she owes a special responsibility of care. In other words: it's not *philanthropy* she's doing wrong, we're apt to think, but rather *parenthood*.

Because of this, the case of Mrs. Jellyby turns out not to be such a good analogy to the trade-offs prescribed by impartial beneficence (whose advocates do not, after all, generally recommend that people neglect their own families). Here it is worth repeating the point that one need not be a utilitarian to embrace impartial beneficence. The latter norm remains neutral on the most controversial aspects of utilitarianism—its rejection of special obligations, moral options, and moral side constraints—and merely directs us to maximize the good insofar as this violates no prior moral duties. It applies most straightforwardly when choosing between strangers to whom we have no special obligations; more complicated cases require supplementation by one's broader moral commitments.[17] (Might we have a special duty of care to others—even strangers—in our local communities, or to whom we stand in the relation of co-citizen? I am dubious of such extended partiality, but suppose for sake of argument that I am wrong about this. This still does not challenge the impartiality of beneficence. It merely presents one more special obligation that must be satisfied before we can turn our attention to the demands of beneficence proper.)

So, defenders of special obligations will not regard the moves made in the previous section sufficient to justify neglecting one's loved ones for the greater good. But that's fine, because this paper does not seek to defend such actions. The relevant question is instead whether there is something wrong (or unvirtuous) about an impartial approach specifically *to philanthropy*: after satisfying all applicable special obligations, is it necessarily callous or unduly neglectful for us to pass over the interests of strangers close to home in seeking out the most cost-effective global philanthropic opportunities? Here I think the response sketched in the previous

[17] One possible basis for such special obligations—Slote's sentimentalism—was rejected earlier in the paper. But other possible bases remain. For example, I take the arguments of this paper to be compatible with the sort of "objective" (non-sentimentalist) view of partiality found in Parfit (2011, ch. 6).

section is successful. That is, while it might be problematically callous to feel unmoved by the interests of salient others in need, there is nothing wrong or uncompassionate about exemplifying the virtue of abstract benevolence in a way that overrides (rather than cancels) the motivational force of one's local sympathy. Here the agent is fully moved by the needs of those nearby. They are just moved all the more strongly by the greater needs of others, no matter that those others are far away.[18]

References

Annas, Julia. 2011. *Intelligent Virtue*. Oxford: Oxford University Press.

Chappell, Richard Yetter. 2015. "Valuc Receptacles." *Noûs* 49 (2): 322–32.

Chappell, Richard, Y., and Helen Yetter-Chappell. 2015. "Virtue and Salience." *Australasian Journal of Philosophy* 94 (3): 449–63.

Daniels, Norman. 2015. "Can There be Moral Force to Favoring an Identified over a Statistical Life?' In *Identified versus Statistical Lives: An Interdisciplinary Perspective*, Glenn Cohen, Norman Daniels, and Nir Eyal, eds. New York: Oxford Scholarship Online.

Dickens, Charles. 1853. *Bleak House*. Available at http://www.online-literature.com/dickens/bleakhouse/5/.

Harsanyi, John C. 1953. "Cardinal Utility in Welfare Economics and in the Theory of Risk-taking." *Journal of Political Economy* 61 (5): 434–5.

Hurka, Thomas. 2001. *Virtue, Vice, and Value*. Oxford: Oxford University Press.

Kamm, Frances. 1999. "Famine Ethics: The Problem of Distance in Morality and Singer's Ethical theory." In *Singer and His Critics* edited by Dale Jamieson. Oxford: Blackwell, pp. 174–203.

Mogensen, A. 'The Callousness Objection'. Chapter 15, this volume.

Parfit, Derek. 2011. *On What Matters*. vol. 1. Oxford: Oxford University Press.

Rawls, John. 1971. *A Theory of Justice*. Cambridge, MA: Harvard University Press.

Russell, Bertrand. 1926/2003. *On Education*. Oxford: Routledge.

Slote, Michael. 2007. *The Ethics of Care and Empathy*. New York: Routledge.

Unger, Peter. 1996. *Living High and Letting Die*. New York: Oxford University Press.

[18] Thanks to Hilary Greaves, Theron Pummer, and Helen Yetter-Chappell for helpful comments.

15
The Callousness Objection

Andreas Mogensen

1.

A number of philosophers have been led to embrace a stringent conception of the demands of beneficence by reflecting on a famous thought-experiment proposed by Peter Singer:

> *Shallow Pond*: You are walking past a shallow pond in which a small child is drowning. You can save the child without any danger to yourself, but wading into the pond will muddy your clothes and shoes. If you don't save the child, she will die.[1]

Just about everyone agrees that you are obligated to save the child. As described above, the cost of doing so may seem very low. But we can imagine that the clothes and shoes you are wearing are very expensive and will be damaged beyond repair. Perhaps they are rented clothes that you must pay to replace. Even if the resultant financial loss is imagined to run into the hundreds of dollars, few would agree that this can justify you in allowing the child to die. Others have imagined variations on *Shallow Pond* that drive the cost up even higher. Woollard notes that "the agent is intuitively required to save the child from drowning... even if the agent thereby misses an important meeting, losing £10,000, or misses an interview for his or her dream job."[2]

Granting that you are sometimes morally obligated to shoulder very significant burdens to save the life of an unknown and imperilled child, how far does this extend? In particular, what should we make of the following case?

Donation: You know that by donating a certain amount to the Against Malaria Foundation[3] to fund the distribution of long-lasting insecticide-treated bed nets in Malawi, one fewer child will die from malaria.

[1] Singer (1972).

[2] Woollard (2015, p. 157). For even higher costs, see the *Bob's Bugatti* case in Unger (1996, pp. 135–6). For doubts about the significance of this case, see Barry and Øverland (2016); Woollard (2015, p. 157).

[3] GiveWell (2018) estimates that the cost to the Against Malaria Foundation of saving the life of a child under five is $4,471–$4,491. Since not all benefits derived from distributing nets involve saving

Assuming that the amount required to save a life in *Donation* is not greater than the amount we feel you ought to be willing to bear to save the life in *Shallow Pond* and its variants, is our obligation to save a life in *Donation* any weaker?

Many find it hard to identify any morally significant difference between these cases. Although we naturally expect people to be less motivated to save a life in *Donation*, it's tempting to suppose that this simply reflects various psychological biases,[4] such as a greater tendency to be moved by more salient needs.[5] Some philosophers—most notably, Singer and Unger—therefore endorse *The Equivalence Principle*: Our obligation to save a life in *Donation* is at least as strong as our obligation to save a life in *Shallow Pond*.[6]

If the *Equivalence Principle* is true, it would seem to follow that morality is extraordinarily demanding and that most of us do not give nearly enough. It may seem that we ought to keep on making very great economic sacrifices in order to save additional lives through donations, proceeding until the point at which we either cannot save any more individuals, or at which the cost of doing so is so great as to excuse a person in walking past a child drowning in a shallow pond.[7]

Of course, many philosophers contest the *Equivalence Principle*, appealing to one or more factors that supposedly differentiate *Shallow Pond* from *Donation*, such as the physical proximity of the child,[8] the fact that you are the only person in a position to help,[9] the existence of a unique emergency situation that is unlikely to be repeated,[10] or the presence of some particular, identifiable child who needs your help.[11] In my view, philosophers including Arneson, Ashford, Cullity, Singer, and Unger have successfully cast doubt on these attempts to differentiate *Shallow Pond* from *Donation* so as to undermine the *Equivalence Principle*.[12] What I want to consider in this chapter is an objection to the *Equivalence Principle* that is more indirect, but arguably more powerful. It does not attempt to specify the key difference between *Shallow Pond* and *Donation*, but rather attempts to show that there *must* be such a difference, because we are otherwise committed to morally repugnant conclusions.

Here is the objection. Suppose the *Equivalence Principle* is true. Then in those variants of *Shallow Pond* where saving the child is significantly costly, you ought *not* to save the child, contrary to our intuitions. Why not? Because in failing to save the child and foregoing the economic cost, you can save a greater number of

young lives, they estimate the cost per outcome *as good as* averting the death of a child under five to be in the range \$757–\$3,197.

[4] Singer (2009, pp. 45–62). [5] Unger (1996, pp. 75–82).
[6] Singer (1972, 1993); Unger (1996).
[7] However, see Cullity (2004) for a sustained critique of this line of reasoning.
[8] Kamm (2000); Miller (2004); Woollard (2015). [9] Cohen (1981); Murphy (2000).
[10] Schmidtz (2000). [11] Gomberg (2002); Hare (2012); Smith (1990).
[12] Arneson (2004, 2009); Ashford (2000, 2003); Cullity (2004); Singer (1972, 1993, 2009); and Unger (1996).

lives through donations.[13] You ought to save a greater number of lives rather than a smaller number, all else being equal. Assuming the *Equivalence Principle*, it would then seem to follow that you ought to let the child right in front of you drown and donate what you save in refusing to save her. Intuitively, this is repugnant.[14] Therefore, we should reject the supposition that all else *is* equal in respect of saving a child drowning in the shallow pond and saving a child through donations.

Call this the *Callousness Objection*. To my knowledge, it has not received very much discussion.[15] It is pressed most forcefully by Gomberg, and is discussed by Murphy, Cullity, Appiah, and Woollard.[16] I suspect that people underestimate the force of the *Callousness Objection* by supposing that proponents of the *Equivalence Principle* will happily bite the bullet and dismiss any contrary intuition out of hand.

Whatever the reasons for its neglect, this chapter will focus on evaluating the *Callousness Objection*. I consider three different ways in which someone otherwise attracted to the *Equivalence Principle* might respond to the objection. The first is the dismissive, bullet-biting response noted above. The second appeals to the difference between act-evaluation and character-evaluation. Finally, I consider the *Ecumenical Solution*, which draws on Parfit's suggestion that we should distinguish between two different senses in which one obligation can be stronger than another: a *cost-requiring* sense and a *conflict-of-duty* sense.[17] A recent theory of the moral significance of the distinction between identified and statistical lives due to Frick will be used to explore the *Ecumenical Solution*, albeit with inconclusive results.[18]

2.

As noted in the previous section, it may seem obvious what proponents of the *Equivalence Principle* would say in response to the *Callousness Objection*: they should bite the bullet and dismiss our intuition as mistaken. Having persuaded themselves of the *Equivalence Principle*, philosophers like Singer and Unger are already committed to the idea that our moral intuitions radically underestimate

[13] Thus, consider the variant proposed by Woollard in which saving the child means missing out on £10,000. By the current exchange rate, this is $13,143.2. Assuming we accept the estimated cost in footnote 3, £10,000 is therefore nearly the same as is required to save three under-fives in expectation.

[14] If you are able to save a much greater number of lives, leaving the one to drown might well seem permissible. The argument presented here is supposed to show that if the *Equivalence Principle* is true then it ought to be permissible to leave the one to drown provided that you are able to save *any* greater number of lives through donations.

[15] It was first put to me in conversation by Nicola Mastroddi, to whom it occurred spontaneously.

[16] Gomberg (2002); Murphy (2000, p. 129); Cullity (2004, pp. 200–1); Appiah (2006, pp. 160–1); and Woollard (2015, pp. 132, 142–3, 155–6); Fried (1969) discusses similar issues, though not in relation to questions about the demands of beneficence. See also Chappell (2016).

[17] Parfit (2017). [18] Frick (2015a, 2105b).

the strength of our obligations to distant needy strangers. It should hardly surprise them if our intuitions misfire again when the opportunity to save a greater number of distant strangers via donations is put in competition with the opportunity to save a child drowning right in front of you. The view that we should save the distant strangers may be thought no more counterintuitive than the thought that failing to save a life via donations is as wrong as failing to rescue the child from the pond. If we had fully internalized that idea, we might expect that we would not be moved at all by the *Callousness Objection*.

I think that biting the bullet in this way is costlier than it initially seems, and I will present three arguments supporting that verdict.

The first two objections hinge on the following observation. According to the *Callousness Objection*, if the *Equivalence Principle* is true, then our intuitions about *Shallow Pond* and its variants are not to be trusted, because they tell us that you ought to save the child at significant financial cost, whereas you ought instead to let the child drown, since this allows saving more lives. Although the opportunity to save a life via donations is not stated in the description of *Shallow Pond*, adding in this detail simply makes clear what would in fact be possible. Asking us to simply dismiss our intuition about this "new" variant of *Shallow Pond* therefore seems to call into doubt our intuitions about the variants of this case that we have otherwise considered, given that they strike our intuitions as overwhelmingly similar.[19] Simply dismissing these intuitions as untrustworthy is problematic for proponents of the *Equivalence Principle*, as they need them to play at least two important roles.

The first is in deriving a highly demanding conception of the requirements of beneficence from the *Equivalence Principle*. Of itself, the *Equivalence Principle* tells us only that the moral requirement to save a life in *Donation* is at least a strong as that in *Shallow Pond*. To arrive at the conclusion that the morality of beneficence is highly demanding, we need to know that the requirement to save a life in *Shallow Pond* is very strong. To arrive at that conclusion, it seems we have to consult our intuitions about *Shallow Pond*.

Singer may reply that this rests on a misunderstanding of his methodology. As he explains: "the drowning child analogy is best seen as an *ad hominem*, and not as a way of grounding the argument for a demanding view of our obligations to the poor. The point of the analogy is to force people to recognize an inconsistency

[19] Singer and/or Unger could respond by describing a variant of *Shallow Pond*, where the possibility of saving distant strangers is explicitly ruled out, insisting that this case isn't relevantly similar to the others, since it contains no moral factors of a kind that we systematically neglect, thereby allowing us to view our intuitions about *this* particular scenario as reliable. However, reliability is a property not of *token* intuitions, but of *types* (compare Conee and Feldman (1998)). It's not clear exactly how to type intuitions, but it seems notable that the different variants of *Shallow Pond* that we've considered strike our intuitions so similarly. They do not *feel* relevantly different. I think this gives us good grounds for supposing that these intuitions manifest a similar underlying mode of response, and should therefore be considered reliable or unreliable *as a class*.

in their moral convictions."[20] Singer is sceptical of moral theorizing that relies on common-sense intuitions and more impressed by the trustworthiness of abstract, philosophical intuitions.[21] His argument in "Famine, Affluence, and Morality" is actually driven hardly at all by reflection on *Shallow Pond*. Instead, it relies primarily on the supposed self-evidence of the following principle: *If it is in our power to prevent something bad from happening, without thereby sacrificing anything of comparable moral importance, we ought, morally, to do it.*

There are big methodological questions in play here, to which I can't do justice in this chapter. I am sceptical of the top-down approach to moral theorizing favoured by Singer. I agree with McMahan that our intuitions about abstract principles should not be trusted unless we also know what they commit us to in particular cases.[22] While I agree that certain common-sense intuitions can be undermined by debunking explanations, I don't think this phenomenon is so pervasive that such intuitions fail to constitute a fit starting point for moral theorizing. Because of these methodological commitments, I believe the most powerful argument for a demanding conception of beneficence will be one that leverages our intuitions about *Shallow Pond* and its variants.

Obviously, these are just assertions. But if I am permitted an *ad hominem* of my own, I would note that Singer's presentation of his argument has tended over the years to place greater emphasis on the drowning child analogy. In Singer's "Famine, Affluence, and Morality" the analogy plays a minor role.[23] In *Practical Ethics* and *The Life You Can Save*, it is much more prominent and serves to initiate the discussion.[24] In Singer's 2013 TED talk on effective altruism, the analogy with walking past a dying child is the only consideration mentioned as support for a demanding conception of beneficence. This is unsurprising. In my own thinking, and in my discussion with other philosophers and with students, I have found that reflecting on our intuitions about *Shallow Pond* and its variants is by far the more compelling mode of argument.[25]

Setting aside these points, there is a second important respect in which proponents of the *Equivalence Principle* rely on intuitions about *Shallow Pond* and its variants: namely, in objecting to philosophers who reject the *Equivalence Principle*.

Consider a *Fair Share View* of the kind favoured by Appiah, Cohen, and Murphy.[26] Very roughly, this says that when there are many people in a position to provide help that comes with some total cost attached, we are to imagine a fair distribution of this cost, with each individual obligated to do her fair share, but not any more than this. When there is only one person in a position to help, as in *Shallow*

[20] Singer (2007, p. 480).
[21] See Singer (1974, 2005); de Lazari-Radek, and Singer (2014, pp. 66–114). Compare Huemer (2008).
[22] McMahan (2013). [23] Singer (1972). [24] Singer (1993, 2009).
[25] Of course, Singer may grant that such arguments are *psychologically compelling*. He may be taking a strategic approach: arguing in a way he thinks is epistemically suboptimal, but more likely to rouse people to action.
[26] Appiah (2006, pp. 164–5); Cohen (1981); Murphy (1993, 2000).

Pond, the entire burden falls on that person, and so aid may be very costly. However, when there are many people in a position to help, as in *Donation*, we are each required to do only our fair share, which may be modest.

There is a well-known objection to the *Fair Share View*, pressed by a number of philosophers, including Singer.[27] Consider:

Two-Person Pond: There are two children drowning in the pond and two people available to save them. Since making the effort to save an additional child would slightly increase the damage to your clothes and shoes, a fair distribution of costs requires you each to save only one child.

Supposing the other person walks away without saving any of the children, it would intuitively be wrong of you to just allow the second child to drown once you have saved the first, because the cost of saving the additional child is insignificant in comparison with the value of that child's life. Since this contradicts the implication of the *Fair Share View*, we should reject this view.

This is a powerful objection, but it would cease to function as such if we were to conclude in the face of the *Callousness Objection* that our intuitions about *Shallow Pond* and its variants aren't to be trusted. In defending his view against the objection, Murphy highlights that a view like Singer's also does not give the right response when we consider apparently minor variations on the original *Shallow Pond* case, since if saving the child involves ruining your suit, then Singer's view requires you to let the child drown "if the cost of a suit would allow OXFAM to save more than one life."[28] If we respond to this point by suggesting that these intuitions should not carry very much weight in adjudicating between moral theories, we cannot appeal to our intuitions about *Two-Person Pond* as a cogent objection to the *Fair Share View*.

This covers my two primary reasons for thinking that a dismissive, bullet-biting response to the *Callousness Objection* is harder to defend than it initially seems. As a less significant consideration, I add the following. It just seems that something *is* added by the *Callousness Objection* over and above the initial counterintuitiveness of the *Equivalence Principle*. It seems to me that it is not as difficult to believe that our obligation to save a life through donations is at least as strong as our obligation to save a life by pulling a child from a shallow pond when these obligations are presented as non-competing duties arising in distinct cases, as when they are placed in competition with one another within one and the same scenario. Ideally, I think, a response to the *Callousness Objection* should say something to account for that. The dismissive, bullet-biting response does not.

[27] See Arneson (2004); Barry and Øverland (2016, pp. 57–8); Cullity (2004, pp. 75–6); Rachels (1979); Schmidtz (2000). See also Singer (1972, pp. 232–3) Singer (2009, pp. 144–6); and Unger (1996, pp. 39–40). For replies, see Cohen (1981, pp. 76–8) and Murphy (2000, pp. 127–33).

[28] Murphy (2000, p. 129).

By contrast, the view I discuss in Section 4 performs very well in this respect. Before we consider that view, I want to discuss a different response to the *Callousness Objection*.

3.

The response I want to consider in this section may be described as bullet-biting, but not dismissive. It seeks to capture, rather than brush off, the intuitive discomfort highlighted by the *Callousness Objection*, but without giving up on the implication that allowing the child to drown is the right thing to do. To capture our intuitive discomfort, this response highlights the difference between evaluating a person's actions and evaluating their character. It turns on the possibility that there are cases in which doing the right thing may nonetheless be indicative of a morally flawed character. The intuitive discomfort highlighted by the *Callousness Objection* can then be accommodated by the suggestion that although allowing the child to drown is right, a person who can bring themselves to do this must be deficient in at least one core moral virtue.

Let's begin with the idea that a person who does the right thing may thereby betray a morally deficient character. Consider:

Avert Catastrophe: Terrorists will horrifically torture and kill some number of people unless someone horrifically tortures and kills a small child in order to avert this outcome.

Assume that absolutism is false and that the number of people threatened by the terrorists is *just* great enough that someone torturing and killing a child to save these people would be right. Nonetheless, we might have misgivings about the moral character of someone who goes through with the act. The suggestion, then, is that we might say something similar in response to the *Callousness Objection*: letting the child drown is the right thing to do, but would evince a character flaw. This seems to be Singer's own view. Gomberg writes that "Singer (in correspondence)... says that while we would shudder at the sort of person who would walk past the child, she does the right thing."[29] Woollard suggests a similar response: "it could be that such behaviour is morally troubling without being morally impermissible. The behaviour may trouble us because it seems cold, calculating, and inhuman."[30]

My key concern regarding this proposal is as follows. Assuming the *Equivalence Principle*, it is not clear why allowing the one to drown and saving the greater number should be indicative of a lack of virtue. Virtue is a matter of being correctly

[29] Gomberg (2002, p. 45). [30] Woollard (2015, p. 156).

attuned to moral reasons in one's actions, thoughts, and feelings. If there is greater moral reason to save the greater number, why should doing so contra-indicate a virtuous character?

Obviously, a person who does this might not satisfy our ordinary conception of what it is to be virtuous. Even so, they could be thought to manifest virtues that are insufficiently recognized in ordinary ethical thought—or that should be thought of as such by those who endorse the *Equivalence Principle*. Bertrand Russell notes that although sympathy in many people goes only "so far as sympathy with suffering which is portrayed vividly and touchingly," in others it goes so far "as to enable a man to be moved emotionally by statistics".[31] Russell describes this kind of sensitivity as a "capacity for abstract sympathy", noting that it is "as rare as it is important". Abstract sympathy is exactly the sort of virtue that philosophers like Singer are likely to believe in and regard as undervalued. They should presumably say that whoever lets one drown to save a greater number through donations manifests exactly this virtue.[32] Furthermore, Russell's emphasis on being *moved emotionally* by statistics indicates that this sort of person need not be conceived as cold and robotic. They might simply manifest an unusual capacity to be moved by abstract considerations.

It might be said that the objection I have raised here could equally well be put against our intuitive verdict regarding *Avert Catastrophe*, *mutatis mutandis*. If we agree that virtue is a matter of being correctly attuned to moral reasons and that in *Avert Catastrophe* harming the child is the right thing to do, why should we not be equally willing to say that going through with this action is entirely compatible with a virtuous character?

In my view, it is harder to imagine that the agent in *Avert Catastrophe* could be virtuous because it is harder to imagine a good person actively and intentionally inflicting some terrible and degrading harm on a child, as opposed to allowing the death of an unknown person as a foreseen side-effect. In Nagel's evocative description, a person who intends suffering for another is aiming at something that by its very nature should repel us, and thereby "swimming head-on against the normative current".[33] You need not believe in a deontological constraint on doing and intending harm in order to go along with this line of thought, though it no doubt helps. Even if there is no intrinsic significance to the doing/allowing distinction or the intending/foreseeing distinction, it may be that doing and intending harm are contingently associated in most cases with certain additional wrong-making features,[34] such that the relatively coarse-grained dispositions that make up the psychological profile of the virtuous agent would set her especially against acting in these ways.[35]

[31] Russell (1926, p. 401). [32] See Chappell (Chapter 14, this volume).
[33] Nagel (1986, p. 182). [34] Compare Rachels (1975); Bennett (1995, pp. 74–7).
[35] Should we worry that this line of argument at best supports a mere difference in degree between *Avert Catastrophe* and *Shallow Pond* in respect of their ability to contra-indicate a virtuous character,

Here is an additional but less significant problem for the suggestion that we can answer the *Callousness Objection* by appeal to the distinction between character-evaluation and act-evaluation. This suggestion also suffers from the problem of weakening our ability to object to at least one key competitor to the *Equivalence Principle*.

I mentioned earlier that *Two-Person Pond* seems to represent a powerful objection to the *Fair Share View* endorsed by Murphy. I have already said something about Murphy's response to this objection, but I didn't give the full picture. Murphy's view is that allowing the other child to drown in *Two-Person Pond* is a case of "blameworthy right-doing".[36] In other words, what the agent does is permissible but betrays a deplorable character. Any minimally decent person would save the additional child, although doing so is technically supererogatory.

Murphy's reply here parallels Singer and Woollard's reply to the *Callousness Objection*. Singer, for one, is unimpressed by Murphy's response, insisting that "it isn't just the person's character that is a problem . . . What he has done is appalling".[37] But many would be tempted to say the same against Singer's view when considering the *Callousness Objection*. It is not clear why we should be entitled to dismiss Murphy's position on *Two-Person Pond* if our own response to the *Callousness Objection* so nearly mirrors it.

4.

If we hope to do better, I think we should consider appealing to an important distinction noted by Parfit between two different senses in which we can compare the strength of different obligations: a *cost-requiring sense* and a *conflict-of-duty sense*. One obligation is stronger than another in the cost-requiring sense iff a person is morally obligated to take on greater costs when such costs need to be borne in order to fulfil the obligation. One obligation is stronger than another in the conflict-of-duty sense iff one ought to comply with this obligation and not the other in cases where one cannot do both. In Parfit's view, it is a mistake to suppose that an obligation that is stronger in the one sense must be stronger in the other. He argues that obligations not to harm are stronger than obligations to aid in the cost-requiring sense, but not in the conflict-of-duty sense.[38]

Consider, then, the following reply to the *Callousness Objection*. When the *Equivalence Principle* states that your obligation in *Donation* is at least as strong as your obligation in *Shallow Pond*, this should be understood in the cost-requiring

and not a difference in kind? I don't believe so. For those of us who believe in such things, we may insist that infringement of a deontological constraint expressing the inviolability of persons *does* mark a difference in kind.

[36] Murphy (2000). [37] Singer (2009, p. 145). [38] See Parfit (2017, pp. 369–94).

sense. The *Callousness Objection* asks us to focus on a case involving a conflict of obligations. Equal strength in the cost-requiring sense is compatible with unequal strength in the conflict-of-duty sense. Thus, the *Equivalence Principle* is compatible with the view that you ought to save the child in the pond rather than saving a greater number through donations.

Call this the *Ecumenical Solution*. Considered in the abstract, it seems to give us everything we want. The challenge is to make good on the proposal. Apart from offering a "happy face" solution to the *Callousness Objection*, is there any reason to believe in the *Ecumenical Solution*? The next section explores this question in greater depth.

5.

In *Shallow Pond*, saving a life means saving an *identified life*: there is an identifiable person whom you know will live or die depending on whether you implement some rescue action. By contrast, in *Donation*, saving a life means saving a *statistical life*: it is known that someone or other in some suitably large population will be saved if you act, but there is no identifiable individual whom you know will live or die depending on your decision, which instead provides each individual in the population with a slightly improved chance of survival. Thus, there is no Malawian child to whom we can point and say that *this* child will die unless you donate to the Against Malaria Foundation. Instead, by funding the distribution of bed nets, your donation will serve to decrease the risk of lethal malarial infection by some degree for a relatively large group of children, in light of which we expect a life to be saved. Nor, presumably, is this a special feature of saving lives through donations to the Against Malaria Foundation: it is generally true that saving a life through donations involves saving a statistical life.[39]

Suppose, then, that we had a plausible theory on which the obligation to save an identified life is stronger in the conflict-of-duty sense, but not in the cost-requiring sense. This would vindicate the *Ecumenical Solution*. The remainder of this paper will consider the possibility that a recent theory of the moral significance of the distinction between identified and statistical lives due to Frick fits the bill.[40] This discussion will end inconclusively.[41] Even so, it demonstrates that the *Ecumenical Solution* deserves to be taken seriously and need not be a mere figment of wishful thinking.

Frick's approach relies on a *competing claims model*, inspired by Nagel and Scanlon.[42] When we cannot help everyone, we are to consider the different

[39] See Singer (2009, pp. 46–50); Unger (1996, pp. 48–9, 51–2). Compare Hare (2012, p. 383).
[40] Frick (2015a, 2105b).
[41] Sadly, I also don't have space to address recent criticisms of Frick due to Horton (2017).
[42] Nagel (1991); Scanlon (1998).

individuals whom we can aid as each having a claim on our assistance. In deciding what to do, we are not to adopt a procedure of aggregating these claims without restriction. This would allow that a sufficiently large number of trivial claims could in aggregate outweigh a very urgent claim to assistance held by a single person. Within standard competing claims models, it is only when competing claims are equal or roughly similar in moral seriousness that the numbers count, such that we may have a stronger obligation to help the many as opposed to the few.[43] We must otherwise act so as to satisfy the strongest individual claim.

Frick defends the view that when the effects of our actions are not known with certainty, we should apply the competing claims model in such a way that each individual's claim for or against some action or policy is proportional to the *ex ante* probability that she will be benefited or harmed.[44] Thus, if it is very likely that someone or other in a large group of people will be benefited significantly if some action is undertaken, but each individual bears only a very slight *ex ante* probability of being the one who is benefited, each individual has only a relatively weak claim on the performance of this action.

Given this framework, Frick shows that it is relatively straightforward to derive the conclusion that we should prioritize saving identified over statistical lives. Saving an identified life means saving someone who is *ex ante* very likely to die unless we intervene and very likely to survive if we do. By contrast, saving a statistical life means performing some action such that each individual whom we could benefit by this action has only a very limited *ex ante* probability of being the one whose life is saved as a result. Each person in the latter group therefore has only a very weak claim on our assistance, in comparison to the identified person who is virtually certain to live or die depending on our decision. Since the competing claims model entails that we ought to satisfy the strongest individual claim unless there exist sufficiently many competing claims of equal or roughly comparable moral significance, it follows that we ought to save the identified life rather than the statistical life.[45]

Note that Frick's derivation of priority for identified lives assumes a context in which we must choose between saving either an identified or a statistical life. Since we must act to satisfy the strongest individual claim, Frick argues that we ought to save the identified individual. Insofar as this supports the view that the obligation to save an identified life is stronger, it would seem to do so only in the conflict-of-duty sense. The question being addressed is that of which obligation we should satisfy when we cannot satisfy both. We are given no reason to suppose that the obligation to save an identified life is greater in the cost-requiring sense.

Is there any reason to suppose that the two obligations should in fact be viewed as equivalent in cost-requiring strength? I believe so. Standard developments of

[43] Scanlon (1998, pp. 238–41). [44] Frick (2015a); compare James (2012); and Kumar (2015).
[45] Compare Daniels (2012); Hare (2012).

the competing claims model do not insist that the numbers never count. As a matter of fairness, a view of this kind may posit that we should be willing to shoulder greater burdens in order to help the members of some group insofar as their numbers are greater. If we are unwilling to bear greater costs in order to save $n + 1$ as opposed to n lives, we treat at least one of the $n + 1$ people as if they had no moral weight at all, and thereby wrong them by repudiating their moral status.[46] Of course, all this comes with the proviso that each of these claims is not "silenced" by a (significantly) stronger competing claim held by someone else. If such a claim exists, it should be satisfied instead, numbers be damned.

If Frick is right, then in choosing between saving either an identified or a statistical life, the claims of the people in the group from which the statistical life can be saved are "silenced" by the competing claim of the identified victim. But suppose there is no competing claim: there is no identifiable individual whom we might save instead. Then the numbers should count in just the way described in the previous paragraph. The obligation to aid will be stronger, in the sense of requiring greater costs to be borne, insofar as the number of claimants is greater. If the number of people in the group from which the statistical life can be saved is great enough, the obligation to save a statistical life can therefore be as strong, in principle, as the obligation to save an identified life.

One might object that this argument ignores the claims of the agent herself. Suppose that some rescue action would be very costly for the agent, where this cost is certain. Then, we might suppose, she has a claim against being required to perform that action, proportional in strength to the size of the cost. Suppose, also, that her rescue action is one that would save a statistical life. Each individual who could be saved by the rescue action has only a very small *ex ante* probability of being the one who is benefited. In that case, even assuming there are no other identifiable beneficiaries whom the agent could help instead, shouldn't the agent's own significantly stronger claim "silence" the claim held by each potential beneficiary in the group in which the statistical life can be saved? If so, it would seem that there is no obligation to save a statistical life at all.

My response to this objection will take a while to get going, as it starts out by addressing a different objection to the view under discussion, which I have so far omitted.

Consider again the case in which you must choose between saving either an identified life or a statistical life. (Assume each action is costless to you.) We've seen how Frick's view justifies priority for identified lives. For all that has been said so far, it looks as if this priority is entirely independent of the numbers. If some rescue action will save n statistical lives and each individual in a much, much larger group of m people has an equal chance of being one of the n who are

[46] Compare Kamm (1993, pp. 114–15); Scanlon (1998, p. 32).

saved by the action, then each individual in this group has only a very weak claim on our assistance. The significantly stronger claim to be rescued that would be held by a single identified victim will "silence" each of these claims and should apparently be satisfied in preference, regardless of the value of n (so long as $n << m$). This is clearly absurd.

In response, Frick suggests that the *ex ante* competing claims model should be thought of as specifying only one significant class of right-making properties, concerned with fairness or equity.[47] Reasons of fairness must generally be traded off against considerations related to the value of the consequences of our actions. When the difference in the value of the consequences is not so great, fairness may take precedence. Therefore, it may be that we ought to save a single identified life rather than a slightly greater number of statistical lives. However, if the difference in the value of the consequences is much greater because the number of statistical lives that could be saved is very great in comparison, then we ought to let the identified individual die.

Frick's proposal is in line with Lenman's suggestion that the best way of applying the competing claims model to cases involving uncertainty will involve drawing on both *ex ante* and *ex post* perspectives.[48] From an *ex post* perspective, if there is someone or other who will be benefited significantly by some action, then we are to consider there as being a person who has a claim on the performance of the action that is not discounted at all in light of any *ex ante* improbability that she in particular would have been benefited.[49] We could arguably restate Frick's view so that it appeals to a balancing of *pro tanto* obligations specified within the *ex post* and *ex ante* perspectives, rather than a balance between fairness and consequences.

Let us now get back to what really interests us. Suppose we agree that the best way of applying the competing claims model to cases involving uncertainty will involve drawing on both *ex ante* and *ex post* perspectives. Then even if we suppose that a person who has the ability to save a statistical life in a suitably large group of potential beneficiaries at some modest cost has an *ex ante* claim that "silences" the *ex ante* claims of the potential beneficiaries, it need not follow that she has no obligation to provide rescue, since the corresponding *ex post* claims must also be taken into account.

More importantly, we may be led to question the supposition of "silencing" among the relevant *ex ante* claims. When one *ex ante* claim is significantly stronger than another, should the former be allowed to "silence" the latter if the *ex post* claim corresponding to the former is significantly weaker than that corresponding to the latter? Suppose not. Call this the *Feedback Principle*. If the *Feedback Principle*

[47] Frick (2015a, 2015b). [48] Lenman (2000).

[49] See Reibetanz (1998); Otsuka (2015) for a view emphasizing the moral significance of *ex post* claims.

is correct, then the person who is able to save the statistical life will *not* have an *ex ante* claim against being required to perform the life-saving action that "silences" the *ex ante* claim of each individual in the group in which the life can be saved.

Is the *Feedback Principle* correct? I am not sure, but it strikes me as a reasonable enough constraint on "silencing", and certainly as no less reasonable than its negation. It captures the idea that the *ex post* and *ex ante* perspectives should not be considered as separate and non-overlapping sources of obligations, but as reciprocally informing each other.[50] There should be some back and forth between the two, and not merely a final weighing of the moral reasons they each separately output. The *Feedback Principle* captures one element of this to and fro, insisting that a claim cannot "silence" another within one perspective if the corresponding claim would be "silenced" by the other within the other perspective. Because they should reciprocally inform each other, the two perspectives should not be allowed to pull in such radically opposed directions.

Even if we grant the *Feedback Principle*, there are other difficult questions to consider. If the one claim does not "silence" the other within the *ex ante* perspective, how exactly do we weigh them up? Will the correct weighing procedure still support the *Equivalence Principle*? There is a lot more to be said about all this. Sadly, there is not space within this already overwrought paper to pursue the matter any further.

6.

In this chapter, I have tried to show that the *Callousness Objection* is more powerful than it might initially seem. Biting the bullet carries significant costs, regardless of whether we adopt a dismissive approach in dealing with our intuitions or attempt to accommodate them by emphasizing the distinction between act-evaluation and character-evaluation. These costs are additional to the initial counter-intuitiveness that already attaches to the *Equivalence Principle.*

Arguably the most promising reply to the *Callousness Objection* is the *Ecumenical Solution*. I've explored one attempt to develop this response, drawing on Frick.[51] As I've made clear, a lot more needs to be said if we are to be convinced by this account. But even if we reject it, there may be other theories out there that support the *Ecumenical Solution.* If nothing else, I hope to have convinced you that the possibility of a disassociation between comparative strength in the cost-requiring sense and the conflict-of-duty sense should be taken more seriously by both opponents and proponents of the *Equivalence Principle* in thinking about the *Callousness Objection.*[52]

[50] See Lenman (2008, pp. 115–17).

[51] Frick (2015a, 2015b).

[52] I'm very grateful to Theron Pummer, Hilary Greaves, and Richard Chappell for their helpful and incisive comments on previous drafts of this paper.

References

Appiah, Kwame Anthony. 2006. *Cosmopolitanism: Ethics in a World of Strangers.* London: Allen Lane.

Arneson, Richard. 2004. "Moral Limits on the Demands of Beneficence?" In Chatterjee, ed. *The Ethics of Assistance: Morality and the Distant Needy*. Cambridge: Cambridge University Press, pp. 33–58.

Arneson, Richard. 2009. "What Do We Owe to Distant Needy Strangers?" In Jeffrey Schaler, ed. *Peter Singer Under Fire: The Moral Iconoclast Faces His Critics*". Chicago and La Salle, IL: Open Court, pp. 267–93.

Ashford, Elizabeth. 2000. "Utilitarianism, Integrity, and Partiality". *Journal of Philosophy* 97: 421–39.

Ashford, Elizabeth. 2003. "The Demandingness of Scanlon's Contractualism". *Ethics* 113: 273–302.

Barry, Christian, and Gerhard Øverland. 2016. *Responding to Global Poverty: Harm, Responsibility, and Agency*. Cambridge: Cambridge University Press.

Bennett, Jonathan. 1995. *The Act Itself*. Oxford: Oxford University Press.

Chappell, Richard. 06 February 2016. "Opposite Day: 'Charity begins at home' edition". *Philosophy, et cetera*. Accessed 25 July 2018. Available at http://www.philosophyetc.net/2016/02/opposite-day-charity-begins-at-home.html.

Chappell, Richard. "Overriding Virtue". Chapter 14, this volume.

Cohen, Jonathan L. 1981. "Who is Starving Whom?" *Theoria* 47: 65–81.

Conee, Earl, and Richard Feldman. 1998. "The Generality Problem for Reliabilism". *Philosophical Studies* 89: 1–29.

Cullity, Garrett. 2004. *The Moral Demands of Affluence*. Oxford: Oxford University Press.

Daniels, Norman. 2012. "Reasonable Disagreement about Identified vs. Statistical Victims". *The Hastings Center Report* 42 (1): 35–45.

Lazari-Radek, de Katarzyna, and Peter Singer. 2014. *The Point of View of the Universe: Sidgwick and Contemporary Ethics*. Oxford: Oxford University Press.

Frick, Johann. 2015a. "Contractualism and Social Risk". *Philosophy & Public Affairs* 43: 175–223.

Frick, Johann. 2015b. "Treatment versus prevention in the fight against HIV/AIDS and the problem of identified versus statistical lives". In *Identified versus statistical lives: an interdisciplinary perspective*, Norman Daniels, ed. Oxford: Oxford University Press, pp. 182–202.

Fried, Charles. 1969. "The value of life". *Harvard Law Review* 82 (7): 1,415–37.

Gomberg, Paul. 2002. "The Fallacy of Philanthropy". *Canadian Journal of Philosophy* 32 (1): 29–65.

GiveWell. 2018. "Cost Effectiveness Analysis Version 3". Accessed 25 July 2018. Available at https://docs.google.com/spreadsheets/d/1IhtZJcWWUQRndEHFHgty5OLdLL4FkNbFMTsKcwGz03g/edit#gid=1537947274.

Hare, Caspar. 2012. "Obligations to Merely Statistical People". *Journal of Philosophy* 109: 378–90.

Horton, Joe. 2017. "Aggregation, Complaints, and Risk". *Philosophy and Public Affairs* 45: 54–81.

Huemer, Michael. 2008. "Revisionary intuitionism". *Social Philosophy and Policy* 25 (1): 368–92.

James, Aaron. 2012. "Contractualism's (not so) slippery slope". *Legal Theory* 18: 263–92.

Kamm, Frances. 1993. *Morality, Mortality, Volume 1: Death and Whom to Save From It.* Oxford: Oxford University Press.

Kamm, Frances. 2000. "Does Distance Matter Morally to the Duty to Rescue?" *Law and Philosophy* 19 (6): 655–81.

Kumar, Rahul. 2015. "Risking and Wronging". *Philosophy and Public Affairs* 43: 27–51.

Lenman, James. 2008. "Contractualism and Risk Imposition". *Politics, Philosophy & Economics* 7: 99–122.

McMahan, Jeff. 2013. "Moral intuition". In *The Blackwell Guide to Ethical Theory, 2nd ed*, LaFollette and Persson, eds. Oxford: Wiley-Blackwell.

Miller, Richard. 2004. "Beneficence, Duty, and Distance". *Philosophy and Public Affairs* 32: 357–83.

Murphy, Liam. 1993. "The Demands of Beneficence". *Philosophy and Public Affairs* 22: 267–92.

Murphy, Liam. 2000. *Moral Demands in Nonideal Theory*. Oxford: Oxford University Press.

Nagel, Thomas 1986. *The View from Nowhere*. Oxford: Oxford University Press.

Nagel, Thomas. 1991. *Equality and Partiality*. Oxford: Oxford University Press.

Otsuka, Michael. 2015. "Risking Life and in Limb: How to Discount Harms by Their Improbability". In *Identified Versus Statistical Lives: An Interdisciplinary Perspective*, Norman Daniels et al., eds. Oxford: Oxford University Press.

Parfit, Derek. 2017. *On what matters, volume three*. Oxford: Oxford University Press.

Rachels, James. 1975. "Active and Passive Euthanasia". *New England Journal of Medicine* 292: 78–80.

Rachels, James. 1979. "Killing and Starving to Death". *Philosophy* 54: 159–71.

Reibetanz, Sophia. 1998. "Contractualism and Aggregation". *Ethics* 108: 296–311.

Russell, Bertrand. 1926. "The Aims of Education". In *The Basic Writings of Bertrand Russell* edited by Robert Egner and Lester E. Denonn. London: Routledge, pp. 391–407.

Scanlon, T. M. 1998. *What We Owe to Each Other*. Cambridge, MA: Harvard University Press.

Schmidtz, David. 2000. "Islands in a Sea of Obligation: Limits of the Duty to Rescue". *Law and Philosophy* 19: 683–705.

Singer, Peter. 1972. "Famine, Affluence, and Morality". *Philosophy and Public Affairs* 1: 229–43.

Singer, Peter. 1974. "Sidgwick and Reflective Equilibrium". *The Monist* 58: 490–517.

Singer, Peter. 1993. *Practical Ethics, 2nd ed.* Cambridge: Cambridge University Press.

Singer, Peter. 2007. "Review Essay on *The Moral Demands of Affluence*". *Philosophy and Phenomenological Research* 75: 475–83.

Singer, Peter. 2009. *The Life You Can Save: How to Play Your Part in Ending World Poverty*. London: Picador.

Smith, Patricia. 1990. "The Duty to Rescue and the Slippery Slope Problem". *Social Theory and Practice* 16: 19–41.

Unger, Peter. 1996. *Living High and Letting Die: Our Illusion of Innocence.* Oxford: Oxford University Press.

Woollard, Fiona. 2015. *Doing and Allowing Harm*. Oxford: Oxford University Press.

Index